Vigasana

THE

HEALING

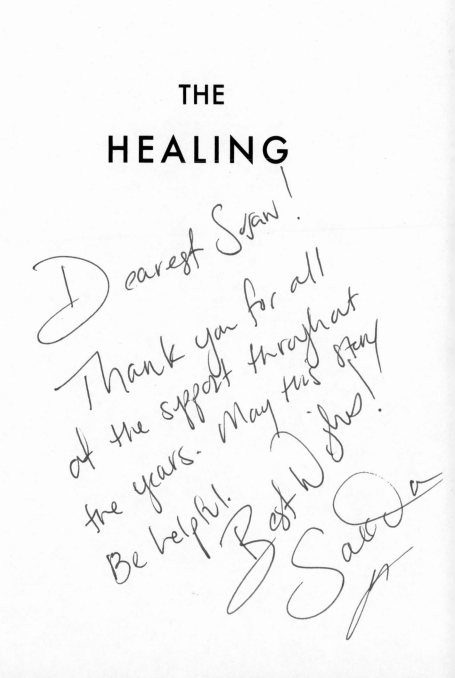

Dearest Susan!

Thank you for all
of the support throughout
the years. May this story
Be helpful.

Best Wishes!

Sara

THE
HEALING

SAEEDA HAFIZ

SAN FRANCISCO, CALIFORNIA

The Bed's Too Big, Music and Lyrics by Sting. © 1979 G.M. Sumner. All rights administered by Sony/ATV Music Publishing LLC, 424 Church Street, Suite 1200, Nashville, TN 37219. All rights reserved. Used by permission.

saeedahafiz.com
For more information contact: saeedahafiz@icloud.com
Design and Illustration by Josh Michels
Author Photo by Susan Beallor – susanbeallorsnyder.com
Yoga Photography by Frances VonWong – francesvonwong.com

Library of Congress Cataloging-in-Publication Data will be available upon request.

ISBN 978-0-9903829-0-4

Printed in Canada

2 3 4 5 / 20 19 18 17 16 15

This book is dedicated to my nieces and nephews and their offspring who might want to understand some of the details behind our family story. I dedicate this book to family as an inspiration and an acknowledgment of our struggles and how important it is to heal.

CONTENTS

TO THE READER

This memoir features recipes and yoga postures that have helped to keep me grounded and from falling into a life of abuses such as drugs, alcohol, or domestic violence. I know my remedies might not be for everyone.

Even though I've kept a journal since September 1981, recalling all of the exact information regarding dates, places, people, and conversations was a challenge. That being said, I still render each story as truthfully and compassionately as I've remembered it. I've changed the names and identities in order to respect the privacy of those involved. I apologize in advance to anyone I might misrepresent, offend, or hurt.

This memoir is told in a way that captures the essence and meaning of my life. It wasn't an easy story to tell, but in my mother's words, "Well, it all happened." I, like her, see this book helping other women who find themselves in similar situations and are finding their way to their own healing.

Recipes and yoga posture instructions are provided for you in the appendices. If a particular recipe or posture that interests you isn't there, you will most likely find it at saeedahafiz.com.

This book is not meant to treat, diagnose, or prescribe any healing remedies for any specific ailments. It only outlines my journey toward health and healing and how I chose to use food and yoga as guideposts to help me listen to my own internal wisdom. It details how I became more aware of my mind, body, and spirit and is meant to inspire you to be wholly involved in your own life and well-being. Please consult your medical professionals for any conditions or symptoms that need attention. My medical team included, but was not limited to, a medical doctor, a holistic health practitioner, a homeopathic doctor, a massage therapist, and a licensed psychologist. It felt good to have a team of people to help me understand the process of healing. Different people provided different things but they all empowered me to become an active ingredient in creating my own good health from the inside out.

Note: Neither the author nor the publisher accepts any responsibility or credit for your health and how you choose to use or interpret the memoir, recipes, or yoga postures in this book.

TO BUILD A SWING

You carry
All the ingredients
To turn your life into a nightmare —
Don't mix them!

You have all the genius
To build a swing in your backyard
For God.

That sounds
Like a hell of a lot more fun.
Let's start laughing, drawing blueprints,
Gathering our talented friends.

I will help you
With my divine lyre and drum.

Hafiz
Will sing a thousand words
You can take into your hands,
Like golden saws,
Silver hammers,

Polished teakwood,
Strong silk rope.

You carry all the ingredients
To turn your existence into joy,
Mix them, mix
Them!

From The Gift, by Hafiz
Translated by Daniel Ladinsky

WORD SPREADS
ABOUT GOOD COOKING

The movements of our hands help build the
Unseen.

We add to the universe by our efforts.
Whatever we do, we should never think it is
irrelevant;

whatever we do, we should not conclude it
is so important either. Between those two

poles find your balance; between those two
regions your talents will bloom.

Word spreads about good cooking. Become
that, an exquisite meal for us.

The alchemy stone is waiting to retire and
confess...*something in us is its power.*

By Hafiz
From *A Year With Hafiz,* by Daniel Ladinsky

Khwāja Shams-ud-Dīn Muhammad Hāfiz-e Shīrāzī
(no relation to the author) known by his pen name Hāfiz
(also *Hāfiz;* 1325/26–1389/90) was a Persian poet.

INTRODUCTION

I SAT IN NANCY'S KITCHEN LOOKING at the "before" pictures of her newly renovated house. When I asked Nancy, a private yoga client, what made her think that she could buy and renovate a dilapidated house on a yearly salary of only $15,000, her reply was: "One paycheck at a time, and I can do most of the work myself."

Nancy was the first person to really show me, in a concrete way, the successful outcome of setting one big goal, breaking that goal down into weekly goals based on what her paycheck could afford, and then breaking those weekly goals down into daily goals. Those tasks that she could do each day would ultimately lead to the main goal, her vision of a fully renovated home.

This concept helped me with my yoga instruction, because once every few days, a student would ask me something like: "What can I do to improve my yoga practice?" or "How can I decrease my anxiety?" or "I noticed you talked about how this posture works on the lungs; how can I strengthen my lungs using yoga?"

I found myself giving yoga homework that fit with Nancy's one-at-a-time approach and the traditional Chinese medicine concept.

But the overarching challenge for me was to apply Nancy's structure to renovating my own dilapidated life.

Nancy's vision and commitment inspired me to write this book. This story is my offering to you. It's an illustration of how food and yoga, two very fundamental tools, became the guideposts for a journey that I call *The Healing*.

CHAPTER I

ON THE BUS

PITTSBURGH SEEMED LIKE 20 DEGREES as I waited for the bus, 71A Negley. It was late winter 1990, and I just wanted to be at home in my new apartment. Warm, comfortable, and safe. When it arrived, I quickly got on. Tucking my long, black, wool coat around me, I nestled myself between two other passengers. I removed my burgundy leather gloves, placed them inside my matching Coach purse and looked down at my wet mahogany boots. In this outfit, I felt like an African-American career girl from *Essence* magazine. As a 23-year-old corporate marketing database manager, I was *That Girl,* from the 1970s TV show, which portrays a woman who chooses to have a career first instead of getting married and starting a family. So between *That Girl* and *Essence* magazine, I had grown up to be—That Black Girl.

As the bus drove to the next stop, I wiped the steam from my glasses, and suddenly tears crowded into my eyes. The "ding" from the stop-requested bell transported me back to a scene from my past.

I am five years old. My father comes home from being out late. The door slams shut, and just like the "ding" that started the Ali-Frazier fight that I'd watched on TV, I'd hear a ding inside my head, signaling that the fight in my house was about to begin. All night I listen to my father beating my mother. The next day I see her black eye peeking out from behind her dark sunglasses.

Even though I was looking down, I knew that we were passing the Kaufmann department store building with its spring fashion collection in the window, an image I'd see twice daily, month after month, as I rode the bus back and forth to work. Again, I heard a "ding."

I am eleven and sitting beside my paternal grandmother. She pulls bright shiny brass knuckles from a brown paper bag. Drunk, she whispers, "Your grandfather uses these on me. Don't ev-ver let a man hit you."

I looked toward the bus driver, then out of his partially defogged window. The round dormitory buildings belong to the University of Pittsburgh. "Ding."

I am thirteen and my mother has just thrown a sewing box filled with sharp needles, scissors, thimbles, and thread at my younger brother. It misses him.

Head hung low, teeth grinding, hands shaking, I pulled the cord, hard. "Ding!" Inside my head, I yell *"Stop! I want to get off."*

At Negley and Ellsworth, I staggered off the bus, wondering why I was suddenly having these horrifying memories for the first time.

My legs shook as I walked across the street toward my apartment. Blinded by my tear-speckled eyeglasses, I fumbled for my keys.

Emotionally exhausted, the small flight of stairs left me winded. I opened the door to my apartment, took off my coat, and sank to the floor, back against the wall. I looked around at the empty rooms, bare walls, and curtain-less windows, seeing only a futon mattress for sleeping, an expensive All-Clad cooking pot, a professional chef's knife, and a secondhand four-piece Mikasa fine china dish set.

It wasn't that I couldn't afford to begin furnishing my place. The truth was that I wasn't sure I wanted to. I didn't want to fill it up with the should-haves from the latest TV commercials. It was my first place, and I wanted to decide what furnishings best represented me. Part of me liked not having furniture. It gave me the feeling of building a new life from the ground up.

I started to cry again, and my salty tears came down like a monsoon with snot hanging from my nose. I sat on the floor like a four-year-old, hugging my knees. Then I heard the voice of my mother inside my head.

"What are you crying for? I was the one who suffered all those beatings. Girl, you'd better go on and be happy. You got a 'good' job. You make almost three times more than I do. You have a college degree, and your own apartment. You are not one of those single, black mothers raising babies. Just go on and be happy. You made it."

I cried even harder.

Had I made it? Did I want for me what society, black America, and my mother, wanted for me?

I continued to sit on the floor, and more violent images appeared in my mind's eye. My body flinched each time I remembered a scream or loud thump from my childhood. But it was the memories of the long periods of silence from childhood that were the scariest. I never knew if the fight for the night was over. So my eyes would shift back and forth in the darkness of my bedroom, waiting.

Even though Pittsburgh seemed like 20 degrees that day, the memories of my past were just beginning to thaw out.

CHAPTER 2

FOR THE FIRST TIME

I DIDN'T REALIZE IT THEN, but the day I sat in my empty apartment on the floor crying something significant was starting to happen.

Although the memories seemed like they came out of the blue, certain pivotal events had led up to that day. For three days in late winter 1990, I had made all of my meals from scratch. I didn't consume any processed food or eat anything with refined sugar. I was only eating whole foods—grains, beans, tofu, seeds, and fresh fruits and vegetables—as instructed by my cooking teacher.

Three months after my first cooking class, I decided to do this three-day test. Taking cooking classes was a symbol of my entering the middle class. As a member of the middle class, I reasoned, I would need to know how to make complete meals.

Growing up, I remember my mother telling me, "Eat as much of the school lunch as you can, so I can save money on the food bill." Each week, my mom would clip coupons—kids-eat-free, two-for-one, or half-off at the local Ponderosa—because she was too tired to prepare dinner. She would set up the freezer with boxes of discounted steaks and french fries. "Fend for yourselves," she often told my little brother and me. It never felt like a home. Instead, it felt more like a refugee camp with each person trying to survive after a 25-year, bloody civil war.

It was different at my friend Barb's house, in her middle-class neighborhood. Her mom waited for us to get off the school bus. "You girls must be hungry. Take your things off and sit down at the table." She poured us hot bowls of homemade turkey soup with chunks of fresh carrots and celery. She served us oven-fresh, warm Italian bread. She made us a green salad with fresh tomatoes. That experience had etched itself in my mind, making me think that cooking classes and preparing homemade dishes, daily, was how middle class people lived. Now, it had become an aspiration.

❁ ❁ ❁

The morning of my first cooking class was a crisp and clear Saturday. I decided to ride my new $500 Fuji mountain bike to class. The bike was yet another symbol of being a young urban professional (known then as "yuppies") who was not interested in buying a car. And I was killing two birds with one stone by riding my bike to get me where I needed to go while getting exercise at the same time. Efficient. I would just be commuting as I challenged myself to ride the hills of Pittsburgh, from Shadyside to Squirrel Hill. It was a steady two-mile climb. One mile flat, and then one mile downhill. For someone who had never really moved her body much, this was a new way of being.

I got to class 10 minutes late, and sweatier than I had anticipated. I removed my helmet and biking gloves and quietly took a seat in the back row.

There were only about 10 students in the class. The room was fairly small, but the metal in that kitchen shone brightly, making it seem bigger. I knew nothing about kitchens, but it seemed state-of-the-art.

"This course is called Food as Medicine," said Gia, the instructor. "We'll learn how simple and common foods can help heal and prevent illness." Gia stood in front of the class, a thin yet fit woman with dark, wavy hair, brownish eyes, wearing a loose cotton shirt. I expected a plump instructor wearing chef whites. She wore an apron. She talked about the healing powers of a vegetable soup she was about to make. Holding up a root vegetable, she explained, "Daikon is a white radish often used in Japanese cooking." Gia told us that this white root helps to dissolve fats inside the body, especially the liver. She went down the list, telling us the main properties of each ingredient, and told us that she owned her own business, Holistic Wellness.

I soon realized that the cooking class I thought I'd signed up for was not at all what I was about to get. Obviously, I hadn't read the flyer carefully, if at all. My assumption, since it was in a middle class neighborhood, was that it would be a course in how to cook lamb in wine, and other bourgeois standards. I'd imagined a mock Julia Child cooking show. Instead, I learned how to use soft barley porridge to reduce a fever. I learned that an umeboshi plum could help reverse a hangover, and how a broth made from sweet vegetables, carrots, butternut squash, cabbage, and onions could help you manage your pancreas and sugar cravings. Gia's teachings were about how specific foods can resonate with specific body parts such as organs, glands, and bones, to promote or impair good health. As the class progressed, it became an idea that thrilled me.

Even though this was not what I had expected, I was in the right place. I had nothing to lose. My family suffered from all kinds of sicknesses such as heart disease, diabetes, high cholesterol, asthma, eczema, and hypertension, not to mention addictions to drugs, alcohol, and food.

Excited, I left the class with the power to choose how to contribute positively toward my health. My family history no longer held me captive; it was only one factor, not the whole story.

Eating more whole grains and exercising could lower my high cholesterol. Consuming less refined sugars could hold off diabetes. I could actually strengthen my pancreas by eating foods that are naturally whole and sweet. Choosing not to drink or overindulge in alcohol could block an alcohol addiction. Even if I couldn't choose my gene pool, I could choose my habits.

I jumped on my bike, tackling that first hill with more enthusiasm than I had when I left that morning to go to class. Joyfully, I peddled harder and faster. Reaching the top of the hill, I coasted along the flat road, a cool breeze sweeping across my face. I knew that I had more say about how my life was going to turn out.

✺   ✺   ✺

Six months after graduating college and three months after my first cooking class, I had put most of my middle class living activities into practice. It was February 1990 and I thought I was home free, just like my mom said I would be. I'd escaped the life pattern that promotes addiction and violence. I was all set to do what my college friends and peers did: go on vacation, eat good food, read books and magazines, and only date successful young men.

Instead, I continued to be plagued by memories of my past.

"Yeah, you know he'll have to stop cold turkey," my mom said to her mother about her younger brother, Paul, who suffered from heroin addiction. "He'll have to go down into someone's basement and sweat it out."

"I know. But that's the easy part. The hard part is facin' those demons that made him use the heroin in the first place," my grandmother explained.

"Yeaaaah. When those drugs wear off, the pain is still there. And I can't figure out why people use drugs in the first place," my mom said.

I wasn't using heroin, but not having refined sugar in my system for three days had me sitting on the floor, with my back against the wall, hugging my knees. It felt like a drug withdrawal, primarily because it illuminated my demons and my history.

It was hard for me to believe that eliminating sugar could make me feel this way. I didn't know it then, but research is proving that sugar destroys the liver in the same way alcohol does, causing it to be fatty and scarred, not to mention the extreme emotional highs and lows.

My new world was very different from my family's. I wondered: *Can I have a middle class life and climb upwards socially while my siblings are drowning in drugs and alcohol? Can I dodge the statistic that clearly states kids like me can't transcend their environment?* I yearned to vanish from that world. But it felt inevitable that the boogieman would get me.

On that day, when I was crying on the bus, my struggle began. Later that day, on the carpet, I stretched out flat, and stared at the white stucco ceiling, exhausted.

I trudged to the kitchen and leaned on the sink. Then I went into the bathroom, dampening my face with warm water and looking in the mirror. "I know what they want from me," I thought. "But what do I want from me? How can I create the life I want from the inside-out?"

I went into the kitchen and started cleaning the dirty pot used to cook the morning's steel-cut oats. I pulled out the food I had prepared for cooking that evening's dinner and thought, for the first time, "Maybe food can heal and maybe it starts with a bowl of steel-cut oats for breakfast and ends with a dinner plate of black bean stew over short grain brown rice, baked sweet potatoes, steamed kale, and a small side of hijiki caviar.

After that thought, I trembled. If eating basic whole foods for only three days could unearth such a complicated past, what else would be revealed on this path to holistic health?

CHAPTER 3

IN THE CLASS

THE YEAR WAS 1990, JANUARY. I was periodically adding whole food dishes to my diet and ready to incorporate something called yoga to my routine. I had always wanted to try yoga in college. I didn't really know what it was, but I was curious; it seemed peaceful.

The yoga class I signed up for started at 9:00 A.M. on a Sunday. The very first position was a resting pose called Savasana. I lay on my back, legs apart, breathing. We did leg lifts to warm up, followed by a series of standing poses. Quickly, I noticed that I was the only one who could not hold the yoga poses for the instructed length of time.

I stared at my crestfallen face in the large aerobic studio mirror and watched myself struggle, lose my balance, and have to release a pose before everyone else. I heard the instructor, Abela, say, "And remember, go at your own pace. Do what you can for today, and most importantly, listen to your body."

Her words soothed me. Then she instructed the next posture. "Inhale, while lifting your right arm up toward the ceiling. Slowly lean over to the left. Breathe deeply and hold the posture. This is a basic side bend."

My lungs contracted and I coughed. Once again, I had to come out of the pose. I felt weak, while everyone else seemed fine.

I don't know why I hadn't noticed it earlier but, looking around the room, I realized I was the only African-American student in class, and everyone was either double or triple my age. I was pretty sure I didn't belong.

At that point, I was ready to quit. My mind wandered. Maybe yoga was not for me. I should stick to walking and learn how to use the treadmill and StairMaster. Corporate middle class people do that, right?

"Watch me first," the instructor said, interrupting my daydream. She held both arms straight out in front of her, and began to lower, bending her knees. She looked like a human chair. "We will use the Chair Pose to transition into our next asana." We all followed her lead, listening to our knees crack on the way down. With our arms out in front, balancing on our tippy toes, we all looked like a row of chairs. The ball of my foot and my toes started to hurt from the pressure. I was happy when she said, "Place your hands on the floor and extend your legs, one at a time, and sit L-shaped." Again, we followed her lead. I felt my toes tingling.

"Inhale, lifting your arms out to the side and then up. Next, exhale. Extend your arms toward your toes and hold your hands anywhere along your legs. Go to a point of a stretch, not strain. This is the Forward Bend pose."

Wow. I was touching my toes. This stretch felt good. I felt good. Abela continued to instruct us to breathe and relax, to just let go. I did just that. Finally, a pose I could rest in. I wasn't coughing or struggling. I kept on breathing and holding. For the first time since I was a kid, I was enjoying myself as my body and breath opened up. But, most of all, folding forward released something that allowed me to relax, and to surrender.

"You'll be teaching this one day," I heard a voice say. I lifted my head slightly and looked around. No one was speaking to me. In fact, no one was talking at all. Then I heard it again. "You'll be teaching this one day, and get closer to your grandfather."

I stayed in the pose. My head was down and I didn't dare move. My breathing was slow, but many thoughts raced across my mind. "Am I going crazy? Do I have schizophrenia? Mental illness might run in my family, too. What's happening to me?"

My attention snapped back to Abela. "Now, exhale all the air from your lungs and inhale, stretching your arms up toward the ceiling." I lifted up from my core. From the center of my bellybutton, waves rippled throughout my abdomen. I felt as if a heavy rain drop splashed onto my navel, causing concentric circles to vibrate and encompass my entire body.

I looked around suspiciously, now talking to myself under my breath: "Should I be scared? Am I having a freaky mind-body-spirit experience?" But I didn't feel afraid. I simply felt open and curious.

I kept observing my body and mind until class was over. Abela kept teaching, and I kept holding the poses, again only half the allotted time.

At the very end of class, we did a longer Savasana, for 20 minutes. I wasn't accustomed to lying down, doing nothing. At first I gazed up at the ceiling, wondering what would happen to me if I closed my eyes. There I lay, flat on my back, legs apart, and arms down by my side with palms facing up. I felt vulnerable, but I finally closed my eyes. With each breath, I surrendered. I drifted off while the soothing music played; I floated to a place that was still and quiet. I wasn't asleep, and I wasn't awake. I was suspended in a peaceful place. It was dark and black. It was a place I had never been before. In this place, I didn't have to be anything or anyone.

I felt safe while my body experienced a myriad of sensations. At times, my body felt heavy, then light, then warm, tingly, and then complete stillness. Some part of me observed a separation between my physical body and, for lack of a better word, my soul. My soul lifted out of my physical self, expanding to the size of the room. It felt like it was being nourished, the opposite of my usual feeling of being chronically depleted.

When class finished, I was overcome with the desire to sustain that nourished feeling. I knew that I couldn't yet hold the poses, but it didn't matter because whatever I could do brought me an incredible experience. I wanted to learn more. When the teacher brought us back from that place, I sat up and wondered, "Where did I just go? Was it real? How do I get there again? Is yoga really for me?"

CHAPTER 4

THE FLAVORS
OF MY LIFE

TASTING THE SWEETNESS OF SAVASANA, hearing that voice during the Forward Bend pose, and revisiting my childhood trauma were just the start of my holistic journey.

When I signed up for my first cooking class, I was simply doing something that I perceived would move me more into the middle class. I didn't realize that I would be challenged to integrate all of my different flavors into a healthier and more self-caring version of myself.

I wanted to learn more about this holistic health lifestyle and how I could participate in creating my own good health. Holistic Wellness regularly sent newsletters to my home. But it was the personalized letter that Gia sent to me that encouraged me to schedule an in-home consultation. The letter seemed to speak directly to my need to rebuild my shaky foundation.

After getting the letter, I immediately called Gia to schedule an appointment. She came to my house in the way I imagined doctors made house calls in the 1950s. But she didn't look like a physician; she wore loose-fitted natural fabrics, a kind of middle-aged Eileen Fisher chic. The way she moved in her clothes showed an easy flow with nature. I admired that about her.

After our initial greetings, she examined my whole life and my surroundings. I had never received this kind of attention from anyone. She made me feel like everything in my life mattered, and that it has contributed to who I am. I felt like I mattered. I must admit, that was a new feeling.

Gia pulled out her client notebook and glanced at the intake form. I fixated on her fingernails. They were short and manicured, but not polished. They were not like the nails I saw on the professional women in the corporate world, which were lengthened with gel, silk, or acrylic and polished flawlessly. Gia's hands looked strong, natural, and yet beautiful.

As she talked, I listened raptly. "Saeeda, the basis of holistic health is to have our internal world be at peace with our external world." She went on to ask me about my sleep, menstrual cycle, a significant other, family, and friends.

Gia was like a doctor who made house calls. But she also went a little deeper, like a psychologist, a clergyman, and a friend. Nothing was off limits. I got the impression that my health mattered to her.

She explained that outside things affect how we express peace and harmony, or dis-ease and dis-harmony, and vice versa. Holistic health looks at the whole picture, physically, mentally, emotionally, and spiritually—not to mention financially. She talked about being at peace with it all.

After Gia took inventory regarding how I viewed my life, we visited my kitchen. Opening up a small beige metal cupboard door revealed two boxes of Cracklin' Oat Bran and tomato sauce (the other four boxes and jars were in the freezer, since I stockpiled two-for-one coupons just like my mother.) I had bowtie pasta noodles, herbal teas, orange juice, milk, bread, ketchup and very few fresh fruits and vegetables—one onion, several stalks of celery, a carrot, and a few apples. I also had the remains of my bulk cooking ingredients from the class—brown rice, lentils, steel cut oats, barley, and shiitake mushrooms.

I handed the Cracklin' Oat Bran box to Gia and she showed me how the cereal contained multiple forms of sugar products, all of them refined. We examined most of the food items in my cabinets, refrigerator, and freezer. I was amazed that so many items were loaded with sugar: my dry cereal, tomato sauce, ketchup, and even my bread. Not only did sugar appear in everything, I learned it was listed under different aliases such as cane sugar, brown sugar, corn syrup, sucrose, maltodextrose, and high fructose corn syrup.

Gia departed, leaving me with lots of information and food recipes to make. I thought long and hard about what she suggested. I could slowly phase out these items or give it all away and start fresh with better quality foods. She encouraged me to cook more and share meals with others. I was committed to following her instructions, even if I didn't like to cook that much. I didn't realize it at the time, but what I did was a radical detox, no processed food, no sugar, and only whole food meals.

I learned later that my regular consumption of refined sugar (both the known and unknown) affected my pancreas (insulin levels) and my liver (a place to store sugar as fat). Sugar made me feel tired and grumpy, especially during pre-menstrual time. But mostly, I felt spaced out and numb.

When I stopped consuming sugar, I experienced a chemical withdrawal from it similar to my Uncle Paul's heroin withdrawal.

I became depressed, yet I was no longer fuzzy. I was less irritable and fatigued. I was in the process of sobering up. Even though it was challenging, I knew it was the right thing for my body and my mind.

The detox reminded me of the time when I went through the entire fourth grade without knowing something was wrong with my eyesight. By fifth grade, I'd had my eyes tested and, lo and behold, I needed glasses! With glasses, I could see much better. I didn't like everything I saw at school or in my neighborhood or at home, but at least everything was clearer.

The three-day detox had a similar effect to wearing glasses. I didn't like what I saw, but the picture was clear.

At Gia's advising, I made a broth called Sweet Veggie Drink. It nourishes the pancreas and helps eliminate processed sugar cravings. I wanted to add a kind of sweetness to my body that was not experienced in a quick or refined way, but rather in a way that lingered. This was how I was starting to feel about life. Since I was no longer numbed by the wrong kind of sweetness, and I sensed that I wanted to taste a richer and fuller life. I didn't want instant gratification anymore; I wanted to experience life's flavors in a healthy way. I wanted a delicious life, where my inside environment was at peace with my outside environment.

So I took inventory of my life, from what was in my cupboards to what was in my heart, and I found flavors that were sour, pungent, and bitter.

CHAPTER 5

THE
CONVERSATION

I STOOD IN THE KITCHEN, chopping vegetables for the next day's soup while my dinner for the night was heating up.

Dinners at my house felt more elaborate than I had been used to. This was ironic since I didn't really like cooking that much, but I wanted the effects of good eating and couldn't get this quality and quantity in restaurants.

During the week, I used at least 15 different kinds of vegetables, three to four different kinds of whole grains, two to three different kinds of beans, fruits, and seeds. I am allergic to most nuts and fish; otherwise, I would have used them, too.

I often started dinner with a raw veggie press salad, and then moved on to a soup. The main entrée was a combination of whole grain, bean, tofu or tempeh, and steamed greens like collards, kale, or chard. Desserts were wholesome, too: gourmet baked apples, pear tart, or carob cake with a raspberry jam sauce.

Compared to what I used to eat, dinners were packed with lots of nutrients and lower in calories, even though I was eating more in quantity and variety. After a meal, I often felt lighter, calmer, and clearer—like I was ready to take flight somewhere.

One day, months after my public bus meltdown, I was enjoying my dinner, reading my *Yoga Journal* magazine, and relaxing into the evening while a new soup was cooking. When the soup was done, I started to clean up the kitchen. Without warning, another memory surfaced.

I'm 12 and babysitting a neighborhood girl named Kelly. She is seven and sleeping over at my house. We are eating popcorn and watching TV movies. She and I lie across the living room sofa bed, laughing and joking around. I'm proud of myself, earning my own money and doing a good job at it. Money—one less thing I have to ask my parents for.

Kelly and I become sleepy and decide to go to bed. I tuck her in first and then I slip under the covers, too. We talk softly for a while and start to doze off. Suddenly, a thunderous rumble shakes the ceiling. My dad is beating my mom up, again. I feel Kelly wince, and I start to sweat, not knowing what damage would appear: broken lamps, dislodged furniture, or bruises and broken spirits.

Unable to do anything, my babysitting confidence crumbles. I think, "I'm the sitter. I'm supposed to protect her from danger. I studied for two summers to get my childcare certificates. I passed all the drills. I've proven that I'm responsible, and now, in my care, I expose her to violence.

We lay there frozen and, just like a bad thunderstorm, the rumbling, screaming and crying magically stops. I feel insecure. I shake with anger. I'm furious at my parents, particularly my dad.

I'm embarrassed, ashamed, and tired, so tired. This happens all too often and I don't understand why my parents fight. Why can't they just grow up and act like adults?

I was totally blindsided by yet another memory resurfacing. I had tried so hard to move on. I believed my mom and mentors, who said that once I earned my college degree, got a "good" job, and started making more money, I would only go forward and never look back. I foolishly believed there was a pot of gold waiting for me at the end of the rainbow.

Instead, I found myself in the kitchen, feeling suppressed anger surfacing. It literally made my skin itch. I was itching to talk with my mom about my new insight into experiencing what she might have felt all these years and how she saw her way through this awful situation.

I needed to call my mom and tell her what was happening to me. Surely *she* would understand, having been the victim. Besides, I wasn't necessarily angry with her and I felt that having a frank conversation would bring us closer to each other. Perhaps we could become allies because now, as an adult, I understood so much better the brutality my mother lived through. And now I could help her see how the past was starting to affect me, too.

I didn't know this at the time, but my flashbacks—being right back in a situation without warning all over again, feeling every sensation, hearing every sound, remembering every odor—must be what people today experience as PTSD. Surely my mom would guide me through it with her healing words of wisdom.

I exhaled and dialed the number, thinking, "Whew, I don't have to hold onto this anymore. I don't have to keep these shameful secrets."

She picked up on the third ring.

"Ma, I called to talk to you about a few things going on with me. I started to remember some of the fights that happened in our family."

"Why are you tryin' to drive a wedge between us?"

I looked at the phone, confused.

"Ma, I'm only bringing this up because I thought it would bring us closer together."

"Why can't we just continue with the way things are? Girl, leave well enough alone."

"I can't just continue." I tell her. "I feel too much pain and anger. I want to heal…from all the fighting."

"Nothing is wrong with us. You're the one that needs help."

"Fine. Let's go to therapy together."

"I'm not goin'. *You* need the help."

We exchanged a few closing remarks and then hung up. With steely eyes looking at the phone, my heart hardened. I felt unseen, and then I felt an invisible protective shield go up around me, like Wonder Woman getting into her invisible jet. Like a powerless kid, I told myself, I need superpowers to protect myself from rejection and vulnerability.

The soup, now slightly warm, was ready to go into the fridge. I opened the refrigerator door, and the cool air refreshed me and the blink of the light snapped me back into my newer self.

It was clear. I wasn't going to pretend or hide from my past anymore. This new me didn't want to numb myself again, just so I could pretend that my old life didn't happen while trying to live in this new one.

Besides, I had been there all those years for my mother, playing the role of the one-dimensional "good" girl. I knew that if I continued to play this role for her I would be rejecting dimensions of myself. My new holistic health lifestyle demanded that I become more of who I really am: not just good, but *authentic.*

In my new way of being, I wanted my mom to acknowledge my newfound ways, ways that were putting me on the path to healing my past and creating my future wellness. As corny as it sounds, eating a whole foods, plant-based diet in a holistic health fashion made me feel more whole. It gave me fortitude to confront my past and the people in it. I didn't really know how or why it was working, but it was. So I set out to discover more, a life beyond just aspiring to be middle class. Instead, I looked toward a way of living that asked me to trust myself and to trust life.

CHAPTER 6

THE ENERGETICS
OF TRUST

I HAD BEEN PRACTICING YOGA for about eight months, and there was only one place where I could fully trust life. It was the last 20 minutes of a 90-minute Hatha yoga class, where we practiced the relaxation pose lying on our backs. In Savasana, I didn't have to be anything to anyone. I just was.

At the same time, I was both everything and nothing at all. I expanded outside of myself while simultaneously disappearing altogether. I was free.

As I lie in Savasana each week, I felt like I was going through intense pre-soak, a washing machine cycle, and then a commercial dryer. My mind and body were the badly stained garments. My whole foods plant-based diet was a powerful eco-friendly detergent. My active Hatha yoga poses were a state-of-the-art washer, and Savasana was the dryer. Each of these worked in partnership to lift the past, which had left long-lasting stains on my soul.

The garments felt too valuable to throw away, yet, too damaged to be worn in public. But perhaps with the right care and effort these articles of clothing could be fully functional again.

In the same way, eating wholesome foods during the week felt like a pre-soak to my internal organs. For instance, using whole grains daily to naturally cleanse my colon, the fibers helped to dislodge old meat products stuck in my large intestines. I was literally getting rid of old shit. Then on Sundays yoga started the washing machine cycle, lifting a few encrusted stains, physically and emotionally.

The beginning physical movement of the class scrubbed a little deeper into the fabrics of my life experience. The nutrient-enriched diet lathered up my internal organs and muscles. Within the first 15 minutes of class, I could feel the cleaning agents working. My clenched jaws would relax and my eyebrows would unfurrow.

Savasana centered my mind. The single-leg raises lengthened my muscles and perspective. The knee-to-chest poses and gentle spinal twists stretched my hamstrings and back, opened my hips and massaged my small and large intestines, stomach, pancreas, liver, and spleen.

All of this is important because I was being stretched, pulled, twisted, and compressed from the inside out. These movements were mining into crevices that were otherwise hard to reach.

For about 53 minutes, I did postures that looked easy and static, but in fact were challenging and dynamic. Internally, I experienced the equivalent of a final rinse with an extra spin cycle. I was wet and wrung out.

Last, I had to hold onto my center for fear of spinning out of control. For the remaining 20 minutes, I had to lock myself in. The guided relaxation began the dryer cycle. While I lay there in Savasana, also called Corpse Pose, I was holistically tossed around. My daily troubles evaporated, and life's wrinkles straightened themselves out.

This happened every week. I entered class drenched from life, past and present. Then I left class feeling less stained, less damaged.

With each washing, my clothing was becoming more and more functional. I had a feeling it would never be a Cinderella Ball gown, but it could become a sturdy pair of jeans, classic fit, worn any day of the week at home and in public.

Savasana was a space I could trust—a place where the truth of who I was could live without the shame of having been stained.

CHAPTER 7

WHEN AM I YIN AND WHEN AM I YANG?

SOON I STARTED TO SEE THE SUBTLE WAYS that I was choosing to live my new lifestyle increasingly each day. Holistic Wellness, Gia's company, was always offering cooking classes, macrobiotic food education courses, holistic lifestyle workshops, and study materials to support the clients who wanted to deepen their practice and knowledge of holistic health living. I was one of those eager clients.

Having had such powerful experiences with whole-foods nutrition and Hatha yoga so far, I was hungry for healing. So I signed up for more study.

It was fall 1990—about eight months after my first cooking class—and I was taking Gia's eight-week workshop, called "Creating Holistic Well-Being," and soaking up the basic teachings of traditional Chinese medicine (TCM) and macrobiotic philosophy.

I felt the evening breeze as I walked to the class from my house along Squirrel Hill's tree-lined streets and gazed at the big houses. The sun was setting. The leaves were turning yellow, orange, rust, and brown. My gait lengthened with excitement; I was about to learn something new, something important. I felt like my life was just about to begin anew. In the class, I was experiencing the true meaning of commencement, not like with the speeches I had heard at Temple University and East Allegheny High School. The truth is that I didn't even listen to those speeches. Instead, I sat in the crowd, exhausted, only thinking about what the occasions meant to my mother.

When I got to class, there were about eight chairs set up in a semicircle with handouts on them. The instructor's chair and an easel were in the middle, facing the students. Sitting in this room, listening to the words of the instructor and chatting with my new classmates, who were older and all white, I was learning things that confirmed my suspicions that my life would be different from my friends' and siblings'. Gia said, "Everything in the universe is a vibration." I leaned in closer and thought, "I have always believed that." It felt thrilling to hear someone validate my intuition.

As Gia taught, I became mesmerized by her philosophy.

Here are a few of the many core principles that resonated with me:

- Eat in harmony with nature as much as you can.

- Our bodies and environment [always] seek balance.

- Everything in the universe is constantly changing.

- One of the main tenets of macrobiotics is that when you understand the changes that govern our lives…you are in a better position to achieve harmony in your body and mind.

The idea seemed simple. Don't go against nature. In my mind, I started to hear myself say, "Everything you eat has the potential to nourish every single cell in your body." That whispered idea held power over me, and it still does.

One of the most powerful concepts I learned in this course was that of yin and yang, the idea of expansive and contractive energies. Yin is considered to be expansive energy associated with woman, the moon, softness, and passivity. Yang is considered to be a contractive energy associated with man, the sun, hardness, and activity. They are opposites, but they need each other to exist.

Everything in the universe can be described as having a dominant characteristic of either yin energy or yang energy. The explanation that resonated with me the most was that a headache could either be a yin headache or a yang headache. A yin headache, say from drinking too much alcohol, is a headache where the cells and tissues expand too much, causing a headache. A yang headache, say from overworking, is one where the cells and tissues contract too much in the other direction. We know a yin headache as a hangover and a yang headache as tension headache.

As Gia continued going through the course material, I began thinking about where yin and yang appeared in my family life.

We kids grew up with one big, contractive yang headache. My parents' relationship made us all feel uptight, tense, and defensive. We cringed each time my dad walked through the door. We recoiled as their voices increased in volume. Over the years, I watched our parents' random acts of violence wind the four of us up so tight that we were always looking for release from the pain. Applying this yin/yang principle, I understood my family and myself better.

We were all reacting to the yang environment we were immersed in. Right then, I knew that one way to get ourselves back to center was to find an excessive yin element.

My concentration again turned to Gia, who was explaining how yin and yang related to food and other activities. She shared a lot of fascinating information, like this food chart:

GENERAL YIN & YANG
FOOD CHART

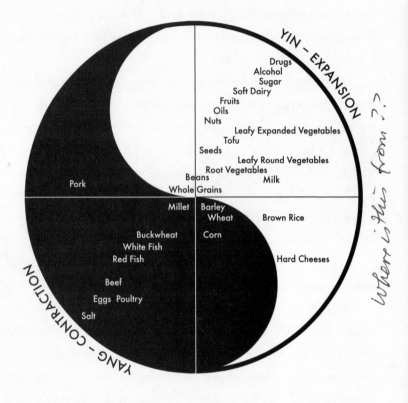

YIN - EXPANSION

Where is this from ??

Drugs
Alcohol
Sugar
Soft Dairy
Fruits
Oils
Nuts
Leafy Expanded Vegetables
Tofu
Seeds
Leafy Round Vegetables
Root Vegetables
Beans
Milk
Whole Grains

Pork

Millet
Barley
Wheat
Brown Rice
Buckwheat
Corn
White Fish
Red Fish
Hard Cheeses
Beef
Eggs Poultry
Salt

YANG - CONTRACTION

This chart helped me put my past experiences in a digestible context. I could look at the events more objectively and without shame. I could see that my siblings and I were only reacting normally to our trauma. I learned that most drugs and alcohol are yin-based energy. Logically and energetically speaking, drugs and alcohol are the perfect things to choose when you are scared or anxious or want to be pulled out of a tight situation. Drugs, alcohol, and sugar will help you feel centered for a little while, but then they pull you to the other side, where you feel spaced out, or even numb.

food choices as therapy

I, on the other hand, was learning to choose healthy foods, not drugs that increased yin. The chart was showing me how practicing yoga and eating whole foods could boost much-needed yin energy. My new life-style was working for me just like my siblings' drug/alcohol experience was working for them, except my approach had healthier side effects than those from smoking crack and drinking 40-ouncers. I started to see how changing my diet could also move me to a more harmonizing center, es-pecially because I was not burying my past. Instead I was integrating it. I was eating foods mostly made up from the center of the chart. It pulled me away from my tight experiences, but not too far up or out.

In fall 1990, about 10 months into living this new lifestyle, I remembered being mildly worried about not fitting in with my friends, who socialized in clubs and bars. We always had a good time when we went out. I still wanted to be part of that group, but I didn't want to drink.

One day my friend Sage picked me up from my house to go to a local bar, Chiefs. It was a good watering hole for recent college gradu-ates and the neighborhood blue-collar workers. We parked the car, went inside, and found a couple of stools. I put money in the jukebox. I played the Thompson Twins' "Into the Gap," Terence Trent D'Arby's "Sign Your Name," and Marvin Gaye's "I Want You." I was in a groove. For the next few hours, we laughed, joked, and debated with other customers. Then a female friend of Sage's came in and started talking to him. They moved toward the back of the bar near the bathrooms while I kept on talking to others around me. Unbeknownst to me, Sage's friend was saying:

"Oh my God, that girl you're with is so drunk. She can barely stay on the stool."

"Who? Her?" Sage pointed toward me.

"Yeah, she's tore up."

"Hmmm." He chuckled, "She doesn't drink. She's been having water and lemon all night."

"Hahahahha. She's crazier than I thought."

When Sage later told me what his friend had said, it validated my intuition about myself: I could be more fun without alcohol. I could choose a healthy lifestyle and still be in bars, listen to good music, meet friends, and drink the water with lemon served in a martini glass. This revelation was equally intoxicating to me.

This giddiness was good news for me because I wanted to keep some of my old social ways of unwinding. I worked hard at my corporate job, which was another very yang experience that I wanted to balance with a healthier yin. I didn't want to use drugs or alcohol, like some of my relatives.

The trial and error of integrating these choices from the yin and yang food chart into my daily life seemed intuitive, but how it would work concretely was still a mystery to me. The more I learned about traditional Chinese Medicine, or TCM, the more I understood that it was not exactly the same as macrobiotics. Macrobiotics share some of basic holistic health philosophies, but TCM is much more intricate. Macrobiotics is simpler. It helped me focus on how a food or an activity was pulling me away from my true center. It was the perfect place to begin.

By the end of the eight-week course, I learned that holistic health encourages each person to work within her environment as best she can. I wanted this technique to be easy, but it wasn't. It was simple to understand, but not easy to do. I was living in a world where there was a pill for anything that ailed. I was in a middle-class community where self-help meant: "Just live this way and you will be rich." Alternatively, traditional Chinese medicine—the macrobiotic holistic health model—said: "There is no right or wrong, just an opportunity for you to improve upon your current situation."

So I finished the eight-week course mumbling my own made-up ditty:

"There is no right.

There is no wrong.

When am I yin?

When am I yang?

Hmmm. So much to discover."

✳   ✳   ✳

I was always in the offices of Holistic Wellness. I started taking more and more classes, getting Shiatsu massages regularly, and having private one-on-one sessions. I felt like Gia was taking me under her wing, especially when I assisted with other classes or helped out at events. I took advantage of this time to nourish my mind, body, and soul.

Then Gia introduced me to her macrobiotic and spiritual teachers. One spiritual teacher in particular was Emanuel, who often spoke to a group in Pittsburgh called the Rising Institute. This dynamic group was committed to learning about themselves through Emanuel's teachings, and to making spirituality practical. I loved this group, even though it felt extremely new-agey. But I didn't care because the message was always a positive, loving one (yin), with advice about specific ways to live love in the world (yang).

CHAPTER 8

SIGNS OF ACCEPTANCE

ON GIA'S RECOMMENDATION, I reached out to another student of hers who was just beginning her holistic health journey. Her name was Red. Gia emphasized that forming a community or having a friend during this lifestyle change can help an individual achieve his/her personal goals, and Gia thought that Red and I should cook and share meals with one another.

So one evening, I invited Red and my friend Buddy over for dinner. Buddy was my best friend. I was nervous about including him because when I first told him that I was cooking and eating macrobiotically, he said, "Urrrgghh...Why are you eating this way? You'll never be able to go out to restaurants. You'll be in the kitchen all the time. Why go through all that? You can afford to eat out."

Buddy's comments meant a lot because he was my best friend.

I met Buddy in college at Temple University through a game I made up. My dorm was on the way to the dining hall, so in the morning when random coeds would pass by my window, I would yell out from the second floor, "Hey! You!" And someone would inevitably look up, and I'd continue, "If you were on a game show and had to guess the correct temperature for $10,000, what degrees would you say it was?" I did this silly thing almost every day as a way to find out what kind of coat I should wear, if any at all. Buddy was one of those Co-eds who engaged me, a few times.

Then one day, I was in the dining hall eating with members of the men's tennis team and rowing club when Buddy sat down. He turned to me and said, "Hey, you're the girl from the window asking about the weather."

"Yep, that's me."

The college year passed along and Buddy and I found ourselves becoming friends, talking, and exchanging ideas. Mostly, he really listened to me. He listened to me so much that I thought, *This guy is truly a friend, my best friend.* I don't necessarily think that I was his best friend, but the way he made me feel, he became the closest person to me. So, his comments about my new eating habits confirmed a fear I had: that this lifestyle would separate me from the others. I wondered if someday I would need to make a choice.

The evening meal started with a basic Mushroom Barley Soup. I watched carefully as their spoons reached their mouths. "Mmmm. Good." Buddy said. And when they both raved about it, I felt perhaps this kind of cooking could actually appeal to my friends, instead of alienating them. Many other shared meals after that confirmed my suspicions that this kind of eating could be a way of connecting.

One such meal took place on a business trip when I sat down for lunch with a group of colleagues at the Philadelphia hotel where we were staying. The maître d' showed us to our seats at a traditional round banquet table with a plastic flower centerpiece, standard place settings, and burgundy cloth napkins.

Looking at the menu, I saw a pasture of beef dishes, a slop of pork entrées, and an ocean of seafood plates. If I were not allergic to seafood,

I would have ordered one of those dishes. There weren't any whole grain dishes, very little in the way of vegetables, salad made with iceberg lettuce, steamed broccoli, and a baked potato. I thoroughly scanned the menu and couldn't find a suitable entrée.

I sat up straight in my blue corporate dress suit, tapping my French-manicured nails on the table. When my fingers stopped, my foot started thumping on the floor. My mind was chanting as I clenched my teeth, "What to eat? What to eat?"

Deciding what to eat should not be a big deal. But for me, at this time in my life, it was huge. The reason I was sitting at that corporate table in the first place was because of an organization called INROADS. The organization's mission was to prepare talented minority youth for positions of leadership in corporate America and in the community. I had never belonged to an organization that was really invested in my worth and cared about my success. It was important that I didn't embarrass them or myself.

My INROADS training taught me how to navigate a sticky work situation, but this one was a bit out of my element. How could I predict that I was going to be eating a whole-foods-plant-based diet, and that people might react strangely to it? "What to do?" I didn't want to seem weird or difficult.

My INROADS training taught me to not make too many waves, especially on a business trip. For young corporate minority youth, INROADS was like Motown. Motown taught its young black musicians and singers how to walk, talk, and sit properly in white America. INROADS did the same for minority youth in the business world. This organization taught us to blend in with corporate culture as much as possible, down to what fork to use when. I was taught to be a positive example, a productive, professional African-American career woman. I was given insight on how to tiptoe my way up the corporate ladder without too much fanfare and unfavorable attention, so that upward mobility could happen for me and other talented minority youth.

INROADS put us through a rigorous training course covering all professional situations from how to run a corporate meeting to which eating utensil to use when dining out. INROADS wanted to make sure that the 30 students who were selected from the 150 minority students interviewing were prepared for this new corporate world. But it didn't cover how to make holistic lifestyle food choices when a menu had none.

My face began to feel hot, for fear that I might order the wrong way. The waiter came to me, and I cleared my throat and scratched out the question, "Sir, I know this is not on the menu, but is it possible to order pasta with sautéed mixed vegetables in olive oil and crushed garlic, with a wedge of lemon on the side?"

He sighed, "Ummm, I'll go ask the chef." I was sure that I had annoyed him. In a few minutes, he returned and said, "No problem." He turned next to my colleague. "And you, ma'am?"

I heard a voice come from the other side of the table. "What she ordered sounds good." My eyes widened. "I'll have that, too." The waiter wrote it down.

"Sir," another one of my co-workers called out, "Can I change my order to that veggie pasta dish?"

"Me, too," someone else said.

I was amazed at what had just happened. Five out of the six of us ordered the same customized and healthy dish. When the waiter brought out our covered dishes of bowtie pasta, we did not know what to expect. He lifted the silver cover and visible steam carried the pungent aroma of garlic.

"Ooooh," a few of us said. The sight of fresh julienne carrots, round yellow squash, and bright green broccoli was a rainbow of color. Some of us sprinkled freshly grated Parmesan cheese on top and others followed my action of squeezing the juice from the wedge of lemon. My mouth watered.

The first bite was a hit of sour from the lemon, then a sharp, pungent spike from the garlic. Chewing the carrot was a sensation of warmth, crunch, and sweetness. The smoothness of the olive-oiled bowtie pasta coated my tongue, and I was pleased. That day proved to me that a plant-based diet was indeed available in the corporate world. Not only that, but others had followed my lead. I felt like I could be an inspiration to others. I was also pleased that perhaps this experience was one that INROADS could endorse. I was the minority, in more ways than one, on a business trip with all whites. But this time my being different did not isolate me. Instead, it gave everyone a new option to try.

However, I was soon to learn the hard way that this sign of acceptance did not prove to be the norm.

CHAPTER 9

I AM BETTER
THAN YOU ARE

THE PHONE RANG WHILE I WAS LYING ACROSS MY BED reading the Sivananda Yoga Ashram pamphlet. I answered it. It was my friend George, asking about my plans for Memorial Day weekend.

George smoked and drank more when he was either out clubbing late at night or when he was under lots of stress from his financial banking job. I could tell he needed a break by the tone of his scratchy deep voice. George was another African-American graduate of INROADS who worked for Mellon Bank. He looked the part—thick, tall, and wearing rimmed glasses and a Brooks Brothers suit.

"I am going to California for a yoga vacation. This place sounds awesome." I read him the brochure. While he listened, I explained the schedule to him. At the ashram, we're expected to wake up at 5:30 A.M. to the sound of a gong. Then meditation starts at 6:00 A.M., followed by a two-hour morning yoga class. After the class we are offered a full-service buffet vegetarian brunch. Then we're assigned a community service project. When our chores are done, we have four hours of free time. One could choose such activities as swimming in the pond or hiking a trail. At the end of the day, there's another two-hour yoga class, buffet dinner, and, last, a two-hour session of meditation and chanting. Then, lights out by 10:00 P.M."

"Eeewww," he groaned. "You're fuckin' weird. Who would go on vacation to get up earlier than they do for work? That doesn't sound like vacation; that sounds like prison."

I was disappointed by George's reaction. I wanted to be supported by my friend, not criticized. I forgot to protect myself. I hadn't processed that he might not understand. And because this was new for me, I shouldn't have been so open, especially since I wanted some kind of encouragement or excitement. This schedule stimulated me so much that I didn't stop to think about how he might react. It was a different kind of vacation. There wasn't a beach, an alcoholic drink, or club scene in sight. My family didn't vacation much growing up, but I always thought vacation was doing what you wanted to do when you had the money and time to do it. I didn't think I had to conform to a vacation stereotype.

But because of George's reaction I was too shy to fully share with others what I was planning to do for Memorial Day. Instead, I was vague and told people that I was going to California to just chill and see what trouble I could get into. Friends seemed to nod affirmatively at that explanation, and then we would easily move on to the next topic. I did my own thing, but I didn't like that I couldn't be fully myself with my friends for fear of their criticism.

In college, my peers spent lots of money and time going to spring break parties, but I was never interested in that. I decided that if I ever got enough money to go on a trip, I would make it a life-changing experience and do something exotic for myself. So while my peers were going on spring break during sophomore year, I saved money to do a summer trip. I booked a ticket to Taiwan to live with a Chinese family for two weeks. My *pulling away fr. family + friends* (handwritten annotation)

language teacher had arranged for me to visit her family. Getting on the plane to California for my ashram weekend brought up the same feeling I had when I went on that trip to Taiwan. I went halfway around the world to see how other people lived. The same was true with my yoga vacation, except this time I wanted to explore deeper parts of myself and meet others who were doing the same. I was 24 years old and realized that I was once again making very different choices than my peers.

Four days before Memorial Day, using frequent flyer miles from my business travel, I flew from Pittsburgh to San Francisco on a nonstop flight. When I arrived, I got off the plane and walked through a crowded terminal to retrieve my bag from the carousel. I was told to wait in a specific area for the Sivananda station wagon. I stood in the designated spot, waiting. The San Francisco air had a unique smell to it; maybe it was the salt water from the bay, but I didn't recognize sea air or ocean spray then. Still, my nose knew that I was not in Pittsburgh anymore, maybe in the same way Dorothy knew she was not Kansas anymore.

I spotted the ashram station wagon and got in.

West Coast spiritual types had an unfamiliar way of talking about things. They reminded me of the people from Gia's classes, reinforcing that everything is energy, but the West Coast discourse sounded informal, almost like a different language.

"This your first time to the Bay Area?" The driver asked.

"Yes," I said.

"Where you coming in from?" he asked.

"Pittsburgh, Pennsylvania," I replied.

"What's the vibe like in Pittsburgh?"

"Vibe," I repeated in my head. What does he mean? Not knowing, I said, "It's an old steel mill city, U.S. Steel Corporation is now called USX. The X has to do with the company now developing more chemical products, or something like that, than steel. It used to be the third

43

leading corporate city in the U.S. Pittsburgh is also known for its hospitals and colleges." That was about as much as I could say with any authority. People didn't often ask me what the vibe was like in Pittsburgh.

"Far out," he answered, slightly dragging out "far" and raising then lowering in pitch when he said "out." It was almost as if he were singing it.

I was taken aback. Wasn't "far out" a 1960s expression? I looked around the station wagon. There were photos of two brown men, one bald and one graying, a tiny elephant statue on the dashboard, chanting music coming out of the speakers, and the driver smelled like incense. I felt relaxed, yet nervous. After a 90-minute drive, we arrived in the dark to an open plot of land. The stars were bright. The place was quiet and had a strange kind of peacefulness to it. I arrived close to bedtime, so I was led to my room, which I was to share with five other women who were already tucked in. The night was very cold—not what I expected California to be, although I had been told to bring warm clothes for sleeping. I bundled up, got into bed, and fell asleep.

The next day I experienced the schedule that I had described to George. The gong woke me up at 5:30 A.M., and by 6:00 A.M. I was wrapped in a blanket, meditating, or, more accurately, just sitting there cross-legged with my eyes closed. At 6:30 A.M. I poorly chanted strange Sanskrit words from a songbook. At 7:30 A.M. I was listening to a spiritual lecture on Hindu mythology. And by 8:00 A.M. I was practicing Hatha yoga on a beautiful hardwood floor. This place felt weird, but also like an honest place for me to be. I could live like this.

The smell of incense swirled through the air, the color saffron radiated through the ashram like the sun, and the *vibe*, my new word, was that of everyone actively practicing to become their spiritual best. I felt like I was doing something good for myself, even though it seemed much like a cult—at least according to the pop cultural definition of one. There were guru pictures on the walls, we chanted words like "Hare Krishna," and at

10:00 A.M. we ate vegetarian food communal style. More than a few times I thought, if George could see me now, he would definitely think, "You're fuckin' weird."

From 11:00 A.M. to noon I was doing assigned chores in the kitchen, chopping vegetables and washing dishes. We all did whatever needed to be done.

From noon to 4:00 P.M. I had free time in the sun by the pond and talked to my fellow yogis and spiritual enthusiasts.

From 4:00 to 6:00 P.M. I was in my second Hatha yoga class of the day. To my amazement, I had actually, for the first time, done a headstand. I felt terrific. In truth, I felt better than those around me struggling to get it right. Holding my headstand, I felt like saying, "Hey, look at me. Watch me hold the posture that is considered the king of postures."

In this upside down pose, I thought, "George probably can't do this." Then I started to wobble and had to come down to rest in child's pose. In child's pose, my mind drifted into thinking that I had come a long way from my childhood. I was in sunny Grass Valley, California on a yoga vacation, and not in my old neighborhood with only a partial college degree, agonizing over which boy from Project Tower A should love me.

As I transitioned from headstand to child's pose and back into headstand several times, a whole host of memories were triggered. I constantly compared my present day life to the collection of past experiences.

During the summer of 1985, one day in particular stood out. I had received a phone call from one of my friends from the old neighborhood. Paula and I were catching up, talking about our college experiences and summer plans. As we were talking, her brother Paul, also my friend, entered the room she was in. He asked who she was talking to, and when she answered, I heard him yell out to her, "Sy thinks she's better than us!" When I heard him say that, part of me was trying to decide did I actually think that. The word better meant quite a few things to me. Was who I was inherently better than my neighborhood friends? Or did I just want to do better and not be troubled by the chaos of lower-income life?

Since going away to college at Carnegie Mellon University (CMU), I was spending less and less time with the old gang and more and more time with my new friends from INROADS and CMU.

I was home from college, and about to start my second summer internship at The Bank. I found cheap summer housing through a friend at CMU—the Spirit House. This house was primarily filled with African-American students.

However, I met new people from all over the world, in fact my summer posse was made up of four Chinese guys, one from Malaysia, Hong Kong, Indonesia, and Singapore. They were also CMU students. But this was my first time being introduced to all different kinds of African Americans.

David was an electrical engineering major linked to ROTC. Donald was a chemical engineering major who had an independent way of achieving his goals, while Gail, in mechanical engineering, had a tutor in every subject and she carried a 4.0 GPA. My friends from my high school life were not like these people and neither was I, but I wanted to be like those CMU students. They had a confidence about living life. No one seemed to conform. In fact, they seemed to encourage each other's uniqueness. No one said, "You think you're better than us." My old friends didn't seem as focused. Some went to local colleges, but their hearts weren't in it. My new friends were doing better. I knew that both groups were intelligent, but my new friends were making smarter choices.

I fell out of the headstand and started resting in child's pose again. My mind and body were fully back in the ashram, in the yoga room.

I felt stronger, so I went into another headstand and while holding it, I drifted into another space and time.

I am eight years old, in our off-white Ford Mustang with my parents, and they are yelling at each other while my dad is driving. Their voices become louder and louder. The bass in my father's voice increases, and the treble in my mother's voice vibrates, but it is not music that I am hearing. It is a cacophony of chaotic sounds making the air in the car suffocating. The atmosphere in the car is so smothering. My father pulls over to the side of the road and the two of them get out of the car and continue screaming.

Looking out of the car window, watching arms wave and mouths move, I have had it with these two. I open the car door and scream, "Get back in the car! Stop fighting!" They stop. They look at me. My face is wet. I'm panting, an exhausted eight-year old. They get back into the car and we all drive off in silence.

That was my very first time consciously feeling a sense of being better than someone else. I was better than my parents. At eight years old, I knew that domestic violence was not the way, and I felt like my parents were not smart enough to figure that out. It was in that Ford Mustang, riding in silence, that I knew I was better, and maybe the deeper truth was that I had to do better, but I probably didn't know exactly what that meant then.

Upside down in that headstand, I was gaining a new perspective. I had to do better. Maybe the practice of standing on my head periodically could help me walk firmly on the ground and in the world.

Over that summer, the more I talked to the old gang the more it seemed that no one was progressing, and some were regressing. I was determined to be better and do better, even if that meant leaving my friends and family behind.

I realized that having an attitude of superiority was how I survived many pitfalls because there were lots of opportunities tempting me to crawl way down into a seductive hole of escape, drugs, alcohol, and sex.

I came out of the last headstand, feeling exhausted and invigorated at the same time. I rested in child's pose one more time, and then I sat up, resting on my heels. I remembered the times that I refused to drink alcohol at a friend's sleepover. I was in the ninth grade. My explanation to my friends for not drinking was that my grandmother was an alcoholic and she had died from cancer of the larynx. I explained that every day for years my grandmother drank straight whiskey from bottles covered in brown paper bags that she kept hidden in her bedroom. She drank so much it seemed to burn a hole in her throat.

My friends didn't care; they still tried to pressure me, but I stood my ground. I told them I grew up in a bar and had tasted plenty of alcohol and had even smoked cigarettes from age five to eight. My smoking buddy, Tee, who was two years older than I was, had even singed her ponytails one day when the wind was blowing and the matches we were using set her locks on fire. I explained to my friends that I had explored all that I wanted to explore with drinking and smoking. I realized two things. One, not drinking made me feel superior. And two, not drinking kept me from perhaps becoming a high school drunk.

I continued to move through this yoga class one posture at a time, new memories surfacing with each posture. While this was happening, the teacher-training students were busy preparing the evening meal. It surprised me that the sound of running water and clanging pots seemed like music to me. Sounds from another room usually caused me to jump, but in this case the commotion and aromas from the kitchen adjacent to the yoga studio settled and focused my mind.

The unknown bodies around me were colorful silhouettes, balls of energy moving right, left, up, and down. We all responded to the melodious accent of the teacher, who was South African. He was the first big-bellied yoga teacher I ever had. I thought all yogis were skinny, especially those living on an ashram. He challenged me. His big body stood in front of the class between the pictures of Swami Sivananda and Swami Vishnu Devananda, the men I had seen in the car from the airport, demonstrating so many graceful yet strong yoga postures. It was nice that

I could be with these yoga experiences and my memories more and more and not be re-traumatized like I was when I was detoxing from sugar. I could easily watch the memories float by.

❋   ❋   ❋

I peed in a cup for my friend Maggie, who was 17 years old. She had gotten herself pregnant, again, by her boyfriend Jerry, who was 25. Jerry already had a son and a wife. This was Maggie's third or fourth abortion. She had been dating Jerry for three years.

Maggie's relationship to Jerry needed to be a secret for two obvious reasons, his wife and her mother. Maggie's mom didn't really know about Jerry, but suspected some kind of trouble. So her mom started keeping track of her daughter's period cycles. Maggie was pregnant and had already made an appointment for another abortion. She didn't want her mother to find out that she was already pregnant. Her mother, on the other hand, made a different kind of appointment. Her mother was taking Maggie in for a pregnancy test. Here's where I came in. Maggie asked me to pee in a cup for her because everyone knew that I had never had sex before. In fact, she used to tease me about being a virgin.

Maggie teased me relentlessly about being a virgin, but I never teased her about the abortions.

❋   ❋   ❋

I watched my 14-year-old cousin with a 4.0 GPA have one abortion after another, even though she was taking the pill. But the pill didn't really work for her. This was also a very sad situation, and one that I didn't really understand. My cousin, now 18 years old and pregnant again, decided to keep the baby. I will never forget her words when she told me that she was going to have a baby. She said, "Well, I just got tired of killing them." She sighed and then we locked eyes, both filled with tears.

❋   ❋   ❋

At 16, there was a boy I really did desire. He was one of the smartest boys I knew, and he seemed to like me, too. We tried to have protected sex, but he couldn't get hard.

"Whew. Lucky me," I thought. For some peculiar reason, I felt protected, powerful, beautiful, and relieved. I felt maybe someone out there or up there was trying to protect me. After that, I decided to wait to have sex, maybe in college, or maybe after college.

❋　❋　❋

At the end of yoga class, we all set ourselves up for the 20-minute relaxation pose—Savasana. During this time, the alchemy of my intimate relationships with each person who had appeared as memories during the class no longer seemed to scare me, unlike my very first yoga class. In contrast, it seemed to bring up questions of: *What were we all trying to accomplish in middle school and then in high school? We were all sent to school for an education, but no one really taught us how to socially interact with one another, how to give and get love safely and honestly.* I lay there in Savasana feeling as vulnerable as I was in high school, but Savasana was safer than high school. I sank further down into that mysterious space of relaxation and realized that we all struggled for love and acceptance. No one was exempt; the pretty ones, the unattractive ones, the rich ones, the poor ones, the smart ones, the slow ones, the skinny ones and the fat ones—all casualties at one point or another—but we all tried to get what was essential for our own individual growth, basic affection, and affirmation. Strangely enough, it usually ended up in one big mess. We all deserved better.

❋　❋　❋

During my four-day yoga vacation, I had lots of time to think about the events of my life.

The first day, I followed the schedule and kept to myself. I was surprised that I didn't really talk too much to the other guests or teacher-training students, which was odd because I can yap on with the best of them.

During brunch time on my second day, I became acquainted with one guy that I thought was an anomaly. He was 21 years old and had just graduated from college with a degree in engineering—electrical, I think. He was dressed in traditional swami orange. I was a bit confused because the teacher-training students wore loose white pants and yellow shirts with a young Swami Vishnu Devananda in crescent moon pose silk screened on it.

"Let me get this straight. You're going to be a swami, not a yoga teacher?" I asked.

"That's right," he responded.

I tilted my head, like a dog that just heard a high-pitched sound, and before I could ask another question he continued with, "I went to the Sivananda center in Chicago and realized that I was being called to live this life. My family, basic Midwesterners, thought that I was being possessed by the devil."

I laughed.

"Now they see that I am okay, but they still think this is weird," he added.

As we talked some more, I wondered but didn't ask him if he'd also heard a voice like I had in my first yoga class.

Later that afternoon, during the last hour of a four-hour break, I asked him to teach me what some of the chants and prayers meant. I also wanted to learn how to break down the pronunciations so I could sing them better. The chants soothed me. The young swami's conversation comforted me.

That night, I went to bed bundled up and glad that I came to this incense burning Hare Krishna-like place.

On the third day I sat by the pond, feeling the heat on my face and arms, and remembering the most joyous day of my life. It was when my parents finally separated. I was 10 years old. When the news came to me that the separation was true, the song "Out of the Woods" from the *Wizard of Oz* played in my head:

> You're out of the woods
> You're out of the dark
> You're out of the night
> Step into the sun
> Step into the light

No more unpredictable fighting would happen in the middle of the night.

> Hold onto your breath
> Hold onto your heart
> Hold onto your hope

When my parents separated, there weren't any set rules of engagement or struggles over how often my dad could or could not see us. However, I do remember always waiting for him to show up. Most of the time he never came. When he did finally come to spend time with us, I always hoped to get fatherly affection, knowledge, and maybe even some cash. I wanted to love him, and my psyche needed his love even more. But I loathed him because I knew he had the potential to be an amazing dad and man, yet chose his hedonistic lifestyle, which didn't include me, every time.

It was a warm summer day and I hadn't seen my dad in a while —two, three, or four months. I got out of my mother's car in front of the bar, which used to be our home, a smile on my face, and happily gave my dad a hug. I must have been 12 at the most. He and I started to have a conversation, probably about school, and after a few exchanges he said, "You sound like a little white girl." I exhaled as my face was crestfallen. I'm not sure what the rest of the visit was like, I just remember not being acceptable to my dad.

After the visit, my mom picked my brother and me up from my dad's house.

Later I told my mother and my aunt Clair about this incident. They both saw red. "Don't ever feel bad about speaking English properly." Then the two of them launched into an ex-husband rant.

"He tried to pull that kind of shit with me, too," my mom said.

"Casey tried some mind control bullshit, too," Aunt Clair added, referring to her own ex.

"Those motherfuckers are crazy," my mom said somewhere in the middle of the rant to Aunt Clair. I started to tune them out.

Caught in the tug-of-war between my new world and my father's world, I decided that I was better than his world, where folks talk slick, drink lots of alcohol, and abuse women. I was mad; I needed and wanted a father. If my dad wanted me to sound more like him, why didn't he spend more time with me? Why didn't he have more conversations with me?...I was available.

❈ ❈ ❈

This yoga vacation was proving to be insightful. On my last day at the ash-ram, there was a yoga teacher-training graduation. The yoga vacationers were invited to watch the students graduate. Each student was marked with some kind of paint on his or her forehead, and then they bowed down to the various teachers and the photos of the Indian men I saw in the station wagon: one bald man called Sivananda and one graying man called Vishnu Devananda. There were a lot of *nandas* around this place. It did seem like some kind of cult. Each teacher-training student was called to the front. They, too, had been given some Hindu god's name. I stared at the only black girl there getting her certificate. The name she was given by the swami was "Kali."

Kali was a dark-skinned Hindu god. I guess that was fitting, since she was the only black girl in the teachers' training class. I watched her go up to get her certificate. Her Afro was short like mine, and I said to myself, "That's going to be me in a few years."

The next morning, I boarded the plane back to Pittsburgh, not sure how I was going to continue my life at the bank after experiencing this alternative way of living. I felt like a different kind of life was calling for me, but I wasn't sure what that really was.

Wednesday morning came and I went to work. I finished out the week as normal, but thought about my ashram experience often.

On Saturday night I got another call from George, asking me to go out to a bar. I said no.

On Sunday I got up early to go to yoga and was very excited to show my teacher my headstand achievements. Arriving very early to practice, I was the only one in the room. I moved slowly into the headstand. I stood on my head upside down, staring in the mirror. No one could see me. No one was watching. I closed my eyes and started to see my headstand differently.

The headstand is known as the king of the yoga poses. Accomplishing this posture can make you feel superior to others, and the longer you hold it, the bigger the opportunity there is for the ego to grow. But there is a deeper meaning to being able to hold a headstand: the posture will ask you to look at the world from an upside down point of view. I learned that day that the headstand was not asking the world to look at me, and it was not asking others to see me as better, but it was asking that I see the world around me from different angles. The headstand is still known as the king of poses, and on that day at the ashram, I learned that it was a humble and fragile king.

In yoga class that Sunday, I practiced with the intention of seeing life from a kaleidoscopic lens. Yoga was starting to shine more light on my strengths as well as my weaknesses. I left class feeling that I still had so much to learn. I needed to learn more about my friends, my family, my life, and who it was that I wanted to be in the midst of it all. Mostly, I learned that I deserved better. We all did. But how to achieve that was _ing to be the challenge.

CHAPTER 10

I DESERVE BETTER, BUT CAN I REALLY DO BETTER?

WHEN DRIVING, A BLIND SPOT IS WHEN I CAN'T SEE what is around me in the rear view mirror or the side mirrors. It is that spot, when I am changing lanes, where I must turn my head 90 degrees and look out of the corner of my eye to see if there is someone or something there that I might crash into.

A metaphysical blind spot follows the same principle. One such blind spot was revealed to me about 18 months after I started heavily incorporating my new lifestyle into my daily life, during a one-on-one session with Gia.

"Look up," she told me while examining my eyes. "There is a little spot on your right eye ball. Not your birthmark, which is black, but a gray one, to the right of your birthmark. It looks like a gray pencil mark on the white of your eye. This mark might indicate a cyst on your ovary."

I pursed my lips, not quite sure what she was telling me. She noticed my concerned gaze, and continued explaining that cysts can come from too much animal food. She told me that eating more plant-based whole foods and less animal food in the prescribed way can reverse it naturally, and that I should check with my OB/GYN to confirm whether or not a cyst was there. She spoke with confidence.

She continued: "Metaphysically, sometimes, these things can mean to check into your sexuality and what you believe about relationships," Gia said.

"Are you saying that what I believe about my body and men can affect my sexual health?"

She nodded. She went on to say that "in holistic health, we believe that diseases…" Gia pronounced the word "diseases" as dis [pause] eases. "…can be expressed in the body for numerous reasons, not just according to what you eat or don't eat. Everything in our environment can affect us, even our thoughts and belief systems."

"Wow. This stuff gets to be more and more tricky," I observed. "It's fascinating, but tricky. What else can I do besides go to the OB/GYN?"

Gia gave me homework. She asked me to journal about my relationship beliefs. Did I believe that I deserved a relationship? She indicated that the more we understand who we are and want to be, the more we can improve upon our health.

I left Gia's office feeling that true sickness and healing are mysterious. This caused me to think deeply about my one major relationship.

I met Ben on the porch of the ATO fraternity house at Carnegie Mellon University in Pittsburgh in the summer of 1985. I was sitting on a brick wall with some friends from high school. My friends and I thought there was going to be a big party, but instead there were only a few guys at home and not many living in the house that summer. They were taking summer classes to either catch up on work or get work done in advance. I loved this about Carnegie Mellon. I could be around people who didn't mind putting in the extra effort in their classes and could still find a good party. I liked that these students knew how to have a good time and still make the grade. I wanted what they had.

Ben walked out of the frat house through the glass double doors and approached us. He stood six feet tall, with his wavy brown hair parted on the side to make it swoop down across his forehead. He wore taped eyeglasses, which at first glance seemed a bit dorky, but he had a swaggered walk that made me think he owned the place. I really hadn't seen confidence like that anywhere, not even in the movies. He sat down next to me. I stared at his face, and behind those taped glasses was a lazy eye. That eye looked at me as if I were the prettiest girl ever. He looked weird to me, but I liked his conversation and his confidence. We talked for a long time. It was getting late, and my friends offered me a ride home. But he jumped in with his offer to take me and, just as fast, I agreed to let him.

We got into an old silvery blue Subaru. I didn't know what a Subaru was, but I remember him saying something like, "My cousin owns a Subaru dealership and I can get cars cheap there." I lived a few miles away, but the drive seemed slow, comfortable, and well-paced.

He parked the car, and then he walked me to my front door. He leaned in slow, and then barely brushed his lips against mine. He leaned back and softly said, "Good night."

After that kiss, I knew that I could spend the rest of my life with him.

❊   ❊   ❊

On my way home from Gia's office, my pace quickened, thinking about Ben. I thought about how he and I were inseparable that summer. I was 18 and he was 20. He took me to dinner dates three to five times a week, and I made him dinner sometimes. We went to foreign films, walked in the park, and took long city drives. He helped me discover architecture and a different point of view on history. He took me grocery shopping, picked me up from work, and introduced me to unfamiliar foods.

He took me to restaurants that I considered fancy. I remember ordering duck for the very first time at Jimmy Chang's, one of Pittsburgh's popular Chinese restaurants. I had never had duck before. Duck meat was rich and succulent, and the skin was crunchy and sweet. Ben felt like that to me—rich, succulent, and sweet. He also added a strange kind of crunch to my life.

This was the first time I felt cared for by a man. Along with all of his kindness, I never felt pressured into having sex with him, and I didn't. It was hard to not be with him because every time I was near him I felt intoxicated. My skin felt hot and I would lose all track of time.

One summer night, while I was living at the Spirit House on CMU's campus, the central house phone rang.

I was already asleep. I went to bed early, since I had to get up early for my Pittsburgh Bank internship. I liked getting my eight hours—even nine, or sometimes ten.

"Knock. Knock." I rolled over, and then someone whispered through the cracked door, "Saeeda, someone is on the phone for you. He said his name is Ben." I jumped up and went to the central house phone.

"Sy, meet me downstairs. Let's go for a walk," he said.

I got dressed, washed my face, and went outside the front door. It was a hot, humid summer night, and he was there waiting for me with an Italian ice treat.

"I brought you this," he said proudly, as if I had ordered it from him. He held up the lemon Italian ice and a small wooden spoon. He peeled back the top cover. I could see the sticky layer stretch between the paper and the cold ice. He dragged the small wooden spoon across the top and spooned some into my mouth.

"You are so hot. You better eat this before you melt it." He paused. "Let's walk to Flagstaff Hill and kiss underneath the stars and the midnight sky."

All I could do was grin.

Romantic moments like that happened all the time. I could never tell him no, and I made myself always available to him. This made me think that I was right; I could spend the rest of my life with this man. And because he was so giving to me it made me think he wanted to be with me, too.

Before our summer break ended Ben, who was taking summer college course, sat me down in his dorm room and told me that he wanted to stay in contact during the regular school year. "You've been a great girl, and we've had a lot of fun. I value our connection."

I could not believe my ears. He was securing a long-distance romance. We kissed passionately.

A few days later, I went to another ATO fraternity party, and as I approached that same brick wall where I met Ben, I saw him again. Only this time he was engaged in intimate conversation with another girl. I stood there feeling like I had run into that brick wall.

He noticed me standing there. He came over and whispered, "I explained last week that I wanted us to stay friends." Then it hit me. He was breaking up with me—not setting up our relationship for a long-distance romance.

I ran away from him, called to my college roommate, Felicia, and cried my eyes out, mumbling, "What a fool I am!"

I had never really cried over anyone before. I didn't understand how I didn't realize what was happening.

❋   ❋   ❋

My walk home from my session with Gia started to slow down as I could feel the synapses in my brain jump back and forth trying to figure out what happened that summer. I wondered if an event like that could possibly contribute to my having a cyst on my ovary.

I was not 100% sure that this was true, but I decided to be more conscientious about how all of life's situations—as in, my relationships with men, friends, and family—could affect me.

Later that night I read more of *The Self Healing Cookbook*, by Kristina Turner, and listened to Louise Hay's *You Can Heal Your Life* on tape. This was my first introduction to something called "toxic relationships." I went back to old college journals and perused what happened after Ben broke up with me. I thought, maybe my reproductive health could be linked to my relationship health. Reviewing my journals, I remembered the next Ben vignette.

❋ ❋ ❋

It was three months after he dumped me and I was back at Temple University in Philadelphia. I was watching Late Night with David Letterman. The phone rang.

"Sy? It's Ben. You don't know what I had to do to find you."

"Ben?" Just the sound of his voice sucked me back in. We talked for an hour or so. I was re-intoxicated. Just like an alcoholic who had been sober for four months and mistakenly drinks a spiked lemonade, only to find herself hooked again.

The next day, still high, I got on the elevator at the 10th floor on my way to class. A classmate got on at the 9th floor and greeted me by name, and a girl who was already on the elevator said, "You're Saeeda? Some guy was looking for you last night. He called the entire floor, waking people up asking for you." I was new to this dorm building and no one knew me yet.

I didn't know how Ben got my number, and I didn't care because when I heard his voice I melted once again, just like I did that summer. I missed him.

Ben had stolen my phone number from my friend Chuck. Chuck knew how hurt I was after what happened with Ben and was protective of me. But one day Ben went into Chuck's dorm room when Chuck wasn't there and found his phone book.

Ben had come looking for me. I could be with this guy for the rest of my life.

❋ ❋ ❋

A few weeks had passed since my appointment with Gia. I wrote in my journal what I believed about relationships and got in touch with an ideal version of what I thought about romance.

I also went to my OB/GYN, and I did indeed have a cyst on my ovary, as Gia predicted. I was not scared for some reason. The doctor suggested that we keep an eye on it before he would recommend surgery, but I also followed Gia's holistic suggestions for dissolving fatty cysts:

- Eating less or no animal foods, especially eggs.

- Eating more foods that dissolve fats, like daikon radish. I started making a daikon drink with lemon two to three times a week. I would grate some daikon, squeeze the juice into a mug, then put the pulp in, then pour hot water over it, with a wedge of lemon.

- I did yoga hip openers to send more energy to my reproductive area, as well as a basic healing meditation.

- I reread *The Self Healing Cook Book*.

- I took sitz baths, and made ginger compresses to put on my reproductive area to help dissolve the fats there that are often caused by too many animal food products.

I actively followed the prescription, and the cyst dissolved naturally in just a few weeks. My cyst was dissolving, but how was I dealing with the metaphysical aspect of relationships? Ben came looking for me during the winter of 1985, and I was convinced that he loved me, too.

I was also convinced that some kind of block was keeping him from having me as his proper girlfriend. Was it because he was white and I was black? Was it because he was a trust fund baby, and I was an impoverished one? Was it because I had a family background of addiction and domestic violence, and he had a sophisticated, worldly family background?

I was confused. Then Ben introduced me to the movie, *Same Time Next Year*, where a couple meets for an extramarital affair in the same hotel one weekend each year. Ben said maybe we were like that. I wasn't convinced that was the case. He and I weren't married to anyone, and I wasn't sure why we couldn't be together and get married. I followed this false hope for quite a few years on and off, and came to a haunting conclusion. Ben may have been better educated and richer than my dad, but he jerked me around just the same. I wasn't sure why Ben couldn't commit to me, and I wasn't sure why my dad couldn't spend time with me. Another eerie fact was that they shared the same birthday.

I deserved better. The real question was, could I figure out how to do better?

During my time of healing, I had an important realization: I let Ben drag me down emotionally. He was my drug. Whenever I would have contact with him, whether by phone, visit, or letter, I always lost a few days of myself, just like a dope fiend. I was trying to do better, but this was going to take lots of work.

Ben confused me, sending me loving letters from time to time that expressed his faith in me and our future. For instance, late in my junior year of college, he sent me a letter that started out like this:

Dear Saeeda,   *3/30/88*

Why have I not been as nice as you? You have always been there when I needed to talk or "whatever." You have got a confidence about yourself that is very attractive. I felt that when I saw you last especially. Whether it was the relationship that you had just ended on your terms or maybe your moving out from the dormitory; whichever you were your own woman. I felt really privileged to have spent that night with you. You are a great friend Saeeda.

I have been traveling since Philadelphia. I spent a few days in Chicago, then New York, and then Palm Beach. I dealt with a lot of shrewd investors and accountants. Yet, in your independence and confidence you will outshine them. I really believe that you have great potential.

withholding

Now, I don't want to push your ego too much. So let me bring down my oration a few notches. It's too bad about Temple losing to Duke. Keep your fingers crossed for next year. I hope the school year finishes well for you. I will call you soon. Keep in touch.

Love, Ben

Ben was putting me into a shadow-side romance, a romance that said *you are only good enough to be with when I say so, and here are the terms: one weekend a year.* Even though Ben was supportive and encouraging, I felt cheapened. *Same Time Next Year* wasn't the kind of proposal I wanted. My dad did the same thing. I was living in a shadow existence for both Ben and my dad. Didn't they know that I should have been celebrated in public as well as in private?

My passion for Ben was a major blind spot. I was trying to change lanes, but I could not see clearly. *what in S, made this an acceptable state of affairs?*

❋ ❋ ❋

Over the years, my cyst would naturally dissolve, periodically reappear, and then dissolve again. I don't know for sure if my relationship with Ben directly contributed to my reproductive health, but I did know that having a toxic romantic-love addiction was not adding to my healing.

One day, I realized where Ben and my dad were on the energy chart of yin-yang (see page 64).

In the same way that my siblings took drugs to make themselves feel better, being with Ben made me feel better. He was a great antidote to the shame I had tightly bottled up inside myself. He temporarily released the constriction I felt from years of domestic violence. He was temporarily filling the void of the absent dad.

constant feeling of angst — I'm not ok

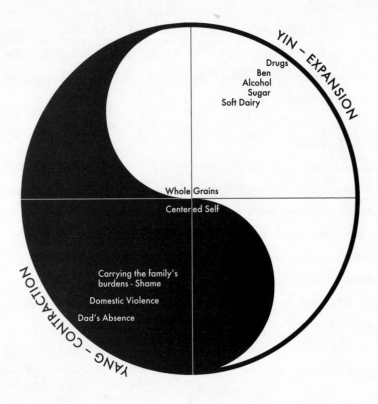

I wanted a proper and healthy relationship with Ben. The intoxication wasn't enough. Because he didn't want the same, our relationship was toxic, but that didn't stop Ben and I from riding the highs and lows of our connection. *me*

Often, I was able to re-center myself with my own home cooking and yoga practice. I had to do things that would move me to the center of health. I found myself spontaneously doing two sun salutes, eating brown rice, steaming veggies, simmering sea vegetables, and stewing beans, all with light seasonings. This helped to make my life simple and hearty. It was becoming my comfort food.

I noticed that most of my life experiences could be placed on the yin-yang energy chart. I learned that when I over-committed myself I felt irritated and craved sugar. This knowledge didn't always prevent me from bad choices, but it did help me deal with them.

Sometimes I was able to see what was in my blind spot and avoid a crash. But oftentimes it would be the crash that would let me know something in my life needed changing.

And it was usually during Savasana when the crash topic would be integrated into my life. I'd go to that space where I trusted life, the space where I could begin to solve my issues with an open heart.

I didn't trust Ben or my dad, but I did trust life. Ever since my experience at the ashram, trust was reaffirmed every time I was in Savasana. It amazed me that doing something so simple, so inactive gave me such a profound sense of peace. Life seemed to always give me a new opportunity to persevere, so I chose to stay the course. I didn't want to contribute to the growth of a toxic relationship or a cyst. One thing I understood from my holistic health class: I might not be able to combat everything, but I could also practice healthier habits that could keep serious illnesses dormant. Not everything within my body needed to be expressed.

But the question remained, could I do better when it came to life and love?

* * *

Ben and I were never in the same city. For example, when I was living in Philadelphia, he was living Pittsburgh. When I was in Pittsburgh, he was in D.C. and then California. Mentally, I moved on by entertaining other romantic interests.

One of them was Frederick, with whom I became friends in 1991. Frederick had graduated from an international MBA program and also worked for The Bank. He was multilingual, speaking French, Spanish, Portuguese, and English. He did everything possible to make sure that the people on the other end of his friendships knew that he cared a great deal. He didn't think my holistic health lifestyle was weird; he admired me for it and supported my efforts.

Most of the men I had gone out with since my holistic lifestyle change gave me the impression that they thought I was one big pain in the ass when it came to food. But here was someone who cleared the way for me to enjoy my dining experience even more.

For example, when we went to dinner he would call ahead and ask the maître d' if the restaurant had brown rice, tofu, or vegetarian options. And he made sure they could accommodate my allergies to nuts.

When Frederick and I were becoming just friends, it still felt romantic. We worked for the same bank and went out to lunch regularly. He'd call me on the phone to meet him in the lobby. Then we'd leave the building and he'd always walk next to me on the street side of the sidewalk, as if he was protecting me from hazards like mud splashing on me from a pothole puddle on a rainy day.

"Ms. Hafiz," he would call me, "Your outfit is very becoming today," looking at me while he opened the door to the restaurant. It was just lunch, but he would pull out my chair, ask me what I wanted to order, and proceed to tell the server what I wanted to eat, what I couldn't have, and what I was allergic to. The way he took care made me feel like we were in a small bistro in Paris, even though I had never been to France.

I felt sophisticated with him, like we were a Harlem Renaissance couple living abroad.

Frederick wasn't a tall man, but when he walked it was upright and with authority. He walked around the world as if knew that he would reap the benefits from the hard work he had sown. His black olive skin glistened just like that of the men in my family, especially when the sun hit certain angles on his face.

Frederick knew about macrobiotics; he knew people who were following a macrobiotic diet to heal from cancer, and others who just wanted to have a better quality of life.

He told me he could live a macrobiotic life during the week, but on weekends he would have to eat some junk food. Then, out of nowhere, he said, "Yeah, if I married you, I could see the family eating this way." He paused and chuckled and then continued, "But I would have to sneak the kids out for their quarterly McDonald's hamburger and remind them, "Don't tell Mom we were here."

I laughed, thinking, "Did he just refer to us as having kids? And then I heard myself say, "You're not taking our kids to McDonald's," giving him a fake mad face.

I had never met anyone like Frederick, so I had never fantasized about having a partner like him. Who knew such a man existed, and that he could be black?

When my friends were all experiencing their first boyfriends, I felt a bit left out, marginalized. I was that girl at neighborhood teenage parties eagerly waiting for a boy to ask her to dance. In black culture, girls dancing together in a group or dancing alone on the dance floor was not acceptable. So I would just stand there, popping my fingers and swaying back and forth and staring, as if in a daydream, at the boys and girls dancing close, in a seductive way. Dance partners bounced, rocked, and bobbed and weaved harmoniously to the R&B sounds of Parliament Funkadelic, or Kurtis Blow!

Then, when the slow jams of Luther Vandross, Teena Marie, and Prince came on, each boy would grab a girl and they would grind on each other. I rarely had this kind of closeness. I wasn't ugly, but I was thin and not as pretty or confident as my other friends.

I remembered thinking black boys just don't like me. I'm not what they want. I'm awkward, and I don't make sense to them for some reason.

Then the day came when I opened myself up to dating boys outside my race.

I am 15 years old. I go out with friends to an under-21 dance club, mixed with black and white kids. Not a neighborhood party. Thomas Dolby's "Blinded Me with Science" comes on. I watch girls go to the dance floor. They dance in groups, with boys and alone. I dance near my friends, then I dance alone. Then this really good-looking white guy comes up to me and starts dancing very close to my body and in my face. He whispers soft things in my ear while the synthesized bridge of the song melodically snakes into the air like a cobra being coaxed out of a basket by a flute charmer, his voice coiling around my spine. "This must be what my black girlfriends are experiencing at the neighborhood dance parties," I thought. "Well, maybe it will be white boys that find me desirable?"

At 15 years old I thought that only white boys would be my option. But when Frederick came along, I saw that there was a wide variety of men out there for me.

One night Frederick asked me to come to his house for dinner. He was cooking. He learned how to cook Brazilian food while living in Rio during graduate school, and he wanted to make me some Brazilian dishes that would fit my dietary preferences.

When I arrived, he opened the door and said, "Stunning." We hugged. Frederick's eyes gave me a pleasing look as he told me that my multicolored turtleneck sweater dress accentuated my yoga shape, and that my fuchsia tights were a nice touch. I felt comfortably elegant. "Stunning," he repeated. I thanked him. I was flattered but also felt a bit embarrassed. I didn't consider myself to be someone who had fashion know-how. My fashion goal was to not embarrass myself. So I preferred the uniform approach. I'd essentially buy whatever the mannequins were wearing in the store window.

Frederick's apartment smelled delicious. "Tonight, Ms. Hafiz, we have Sesame Seed Brown Rice, Creamy Black Beans, and Braised Collard Greens. Don't expect southern-style greens. These are different. I made an apple crisp for dessert."

Samba music played low in the background while we talked and ate.

He asked me if I did the Samba. I laughed. It felt wonderful to be asked that question in a serious way because I was never before asked if I Sambaed.

Just before dessert, he turned up the music, grabbed my hand, and led me to his open-spaced living room area. He had a white carpet so our shoes were already off. His place was simple and elegant, and the rooms spoke softly of his travels.

"Hold here." I put my hand on his shoulder. I felt awkward. I had never danced like this before. He told me to move my hips. I tried, but I'm sure that I looked silly. He told me to relax, so I took some deep yogic breaths to calm me down.

"You got it!" He cheered.

I smiled but felt frustration. He told me the more I practiced the better I'd get. Then he asked if I wanted to go to some Carnaval events. The new year, 1992, was fast approaching.

I told him that I would be interested, especially if I could get the hang of the dancing. Then he asked me to come and sit down. I was happy to because I was tired of learning and it wasn't coming naturally to me. This kind of dancing felt like work.

Frederick went into the kitchen to bring out the homemade dessert without sugar. When I sat down on the couch, I curled and uncurled my toes. I hoped he didn't hear them cracking. He put the bowls on the table and we sat. Over dessert we covered many topics, being careful not to spill any dessert on his expensive cream-colored sofa.

"You probably want to know why I have never attempted to kiss you," he blurted out.

I wasn't in any rush to be physical with him. I assumed the pace was Frederick's dramatic way of showing me that he cared. He did everything with intention. But I said the safe thing, "No. Not really. I thought we were just friends…right?"

"Well, …we are friends, but…we do a lot of date-like things. In fact, every time we go out, it feels like a date."

"True. It does."

"Well, I'm bisexual, but I haven't been with a girl in a long time." He paused. "I guess." He paused again, and this was the first time I heard him not be so sure of himself. "I mean…that I'm gay."

We both exhaled, deeply. We stared at the floor.

"Well, I thought you were a bit more stylish than most men at the bank, but I just told myself that it was because you are well-traveled. I thought you might be gay, but I also told myself, we're just close friends, so being romantic isn't an option anyway."

"We are close friends," he said, holding my hand.

Soon after, the evening came to a close. He packed me a lunch for the next day. I left his apartment confused and relieved. I went home, which was directly across the street from him.

A few weeks later my colleague Francine stopped me in the hall.

"I have a question to ask you. There's a rumor floatin' around."

"A rumor? About me?"

"Yep. The black folks at the bank thought that Frederick was gay," she said, "but noticed that he does spend a lot of time with you that seems romantic."

"Well, Frederick and I are close friends and do 'date-like' things, even though we have never been sexual. We haven't even kissed," I told Francine.

Doors that seemed closed to Frederick were starting to open up. I could see that he was happy about being accepted socially, not just for his business acumen and textbook knowledge.

He and I started to frequent lots of couple-like functions together, such as events with higher-ups at the bank. I was cool with it, and Frederick was finally the cool kid in school, not just the smart, well-dressed one.

He started to see the advantages of living a visibly heterosexual lifestyle. It was exciting and sad to watch and participate in. It was clear that his aim was to be an upper-middle-class African American who might earn enough to start his own foundation. He wanted a prominent place in society, and in 1991 his being gay was not helping, especially in Pittsburgh, Pennsylvania.

One night, while he was at my house for dinner, he confessed, "I've never had these feelings for a woman. This is the first time that I am questioning my sexuality in reverse." There was moisture beading up on his forehead. His dark skin glowed. "I know that I had joked about taking our kids to McDonald's and us being married, but I didn't want to admit to myself that I cared for you in that way. The more and more I think about it, I think it could really work between us." He took another big breath, paused, and then continued, "The only thing I ask is that you let me, two times a year, go out and be with men."

I was shocked. And then he said, "I can give you a comfortable life. We could be really great partners together."

"Frederick, if all things were equal and you were straight and came to me with this same proposal of twice a year you had to go out and be with another woman, I'd refuse. I don't want to live like that."

My heart started to really ache. It ached because I wanted to live in a world where Frederick could be himself and not have to hide or pretend with those who just didn't understand or thought it was against God.

He was perfect for me in so many ways, but I didn't think I could live with a man who essentially was on the down-low to others and out to me. I must admit, I was glad that he gave me the option. I know some men who just lie and live a double life.

All of this triggered my daddy issues of being told that, "I can love you on my terms, or these terms only." Of course, Frederick was always kind to me and he really did show up in my life, but I wanted to give myself a chance to create my own kind of happily-ever-after story. I didn't want to live with a man who was gay and requested to be with a man two times a year.

My fear was that something like this would grow. First, it was twice a year, then four times a year, then six, then once a month, then and then and then…I would be living a life that I didn't recognize.

It was a sad night for us because, even though he was gay and I was straight, we had fallen in love and we were remarkably compatible.

After we sat in silence for a few minutes, I asked, "Frederick, what made you think you could ask me to live in the shadows of your gay life? I think I deserve a fully committed relationship, and I deserve someone who wants to at least try and live this way, wholeheartedly."

"Well, I have friends who do it. They get it all—the wife, the kids, the careers, and the woman gets it all, too. Some black women find that the trade-off is a good one. They get the status of not being single, having kids, and a high-income lifestyle."

I grew more forlorn. I didn't want a lifestyle where I had to live in the shadows of someone's life. This was similar to the *shadow life* proposal that Ben made me. And once again I knew for certain that I didn't want a *Same Time Next Year* kind of life.

CHAPTER II

MY SISTER AND THE DUMBEST ONE IN THE ROOM

I WORRIED ABOUT MY LIFE A LOT, and I worried even more when I saw what was happening to my eldest sister, Rahima. At 16, her life was twisting and turning out of control unpredictably and with great velocity.

Up to that point, my sister had survived my parents' domestic violence episodes. I needed her to be successful. I needed her to show me the way out of our trauma. When it started to look like she couldn't escape, I was afraid that I would somehow be trapped in a depressing life too.

When Rahima was 16, I was six. I thought she was the most beautiful person on earth. She stood lean, coffee-colored, and 5' 8", similar to the model Iman, and resembling Somali royalty. I had always thought that my sister was the prettiest one, not just in our family but also in her crowd, or any crowd for that matter. Boys used to call her Rahim-the-Dream.

I tried to tag along with her whenever I could. She was athletic and played intra-mural softball. Sometimes she would let me come along, but not every time.

I am six years old and chasing her up Harriet Street.

"Take me with you!" I am screaming and running my little legs as fast as they can go.

"Go back home, Sy. Go back." Her long, gliding brown legs get smaller and smaller, and then they vanish around the corner.

I plop down on the cement and cry and cry. I don't want to go back home and be all by myself.

As we grew older, we did less and less together. Throughout the years, she had boyfriends who came over to watch TV at our house. One guy in particular was different. His name was Jackson. Every time he arrived at our house, he brought juice and snacks for the family to eat. This is where I learned that it is polite to bring a gift with you each time you visit someone's home.

When Jackson came into my sister's life, things were better for her and, weirdly, for my family. You see, my sister had not always done what my mother wanted her to do. But she seemed to be getting this one right.

My mother wanted my sister to go to college, marry a nice man, have a career, and then have babies. But when my sister said she was going to community college, it soon became clear that she was only pretending to go each day. We discovered that, instead of being in class, she was in the neighborhood braiding boys' hair. My mother then tried to follow my sister's interest by encouraging her to go to cosmetology school, but to no avail.

It wasn't until my sister started dating Jackson more seriously that her life had order and purpose. He had a good job as a manager in the railroad business. She rented an apartment and worked a steady job. Then, after about a year or so, he bought a house and she moved in with him, got pregnant, and became a great stay-at-home mom. My mom felt at ease, especially because my sister could help my mother's financial situation.

I was 13 years old when my niece Amilah was born. I was excited.

They paid me to babysit each weekend to give Jackson and Rahima time for a date night and then after-midnight grocery shopping, when the stores were relatively empty and the checkout lines were short.

My niece was adorable and easy to care for. My babysitting skills came in handy, and I enjoyed being with her. When Amilah grew bigger, almost three years old, I took her for rides on the public bus to show her our city. I knew people on the bus, with their disapproving eyes, thought I was a young teenage mom. So sometimes I would say in a loud voice, "Your mom put a nice dress on you this morning, and now your aunty is showing you the city. You are such a smart and pretty girl. Who's a pretty girl?"

I loved those weekends away from my own home. Rahima and Jackson had the house well supplied with fun snacks and juice. They weren't properly married, but they soon turned into a good role model for me to observe. Their system seemed to work. The bonus was that each weekend I earned $20.00.

This went on for years, and then Rahima had a second baby, Ameer. I continued this niece-and-nephew weekend ritual until I went away to college in Philadelphia.

While I was in college, life for my sister started to shift. I heard grumblings. She was unhappy because Jackson was never going to propose to her. He was clear about never wanting to be married from the very beginning, and his last girlfriend broke up with him because he wouldn't marry her. Now my sister was in the same situation, but with two kids.

I was confused because he was a good provider and significant other, whether or not they were legally married. Besides, she had gone along with this for seven years. The grumblings that I had heard was that friends and friends of friends had opinions like: *You should make him marry you. You don't have any security. He can leave you at any time.* Even my dad got on a soapbox, saying: *If he cared for you, he would marry you.* This was funny coming from my dad, a man who did marry my mother but didn't provide much. A few people said to my sister: *He treats you well; don't listen to them.* My mom even said: *You got a good thing here, don't mess it up.*

But, the you're-not-married comments really got to my sister. She gave Jackson an ultimatum. *Marry me by the time Ameer is five, or I am out of here.*

She kept her word. She left him. But, from that point on, Rahim-the-Dream's life started to become a nightmare.

Even though she had two kids, she kept her shapely figure and her striking good looks. In a flash, my sister found another man named Wendell who was nine years her junior. He and I had gone to high school together, and I didn't approve. But it was none of my business, so I stayed out of it.

When she got pregnant with her third child, Daoud, I wondered if it was planned.

I remember the first time I saw my sister's life unraveling. It was January 1988. I am home from college, visiting my sister at her new apartment, a newly built, low-income development behind Eastland Mall. It was stylish and clean, with new furniture and modern appliances. Rahima always could put together a look, whether it was an outfit or a room. Besides, Jackson was giving her more than fair child support. She never had to take him to court. He was generous that way.

Everything in my sister's life was different, but when she asked me to babysit her kids for a few hours early that Friday evening, I was happy to do so. She didn't even have to pay me.

My plan that night was to spend some quality time being an aunty, and then go out later to see my CMU friends in the city. She told me she would come back by 8:30 P.M.

Eight-thirty came and went. I had already put the kids to bed. Then 9:00, 9:30, and no Rahima. Later, 9:45, 10:00, 11:00. I tried calling around, mostly to vent my frustration. It was midnight, and I was vexed. Stretched out on the couch, I watched more mindless TV to sedate my raging thoughts.

"Why is she taking advantage of me? Why is she trying to trap me? Why does she not value my time and plans? Why does she think so little of me? She's doing what dad does." I drifted off to sleep.

Then I heard the keys fumbling in the door. I looked at the clock. Three A.M. Rahima opened the door and swayed back and forth with a chuckle. I sprung up.

"I will never again watch your kids," I growled.

It was clear that she was out drinking and having fun.

Early the next morning, I left my sister's house and got on the bus headed toward East Pittsburgh. I sat down and stared out the window. I watched Eastland Mall get smaller and smaller. I rode past the old neighborhood, and in my head I said goodbye to friends I'd had since elementary school. I gazed at Pittsburgh's George Washington Bridge, reflecting on the numerous times I stared out of the window from my house as a girl wondering what did the future hold for me. Now that bridge has come to symbolize my past as well as my future. Built in 1932, it is a stone structure with five parabolic arches whose construction was groundbreaking for its time. Its central arch had the longest span in the world then, but today bridge construction has progressed far beyond that. Just as my life was progressing far beyond my sister's. It was time to move on. I looked at everything from that bus window, hoping that the bus would take me far away from my family.

It was that very morning that I decided to surround myself with people who were doing better. At that moment, I adopted my new philosophy: "Always be the dumbest one in the room." My logic was that, if I were the dumbest one in the room, I would always have a better chance to improve myself. My ego could relax because I had nothing to prove. I was there to learn. Besides, I didn't want to get stuck in a quicksand environment where people could pull me under. My sister and other family members constantly battled that quicksand.

I went back to college determined to finish, even though classes were not easy for me. But Rahima's life kept spiraling down. My handsome sister went from living the life as a stay-at-home mom with two kids and a common-law husband, to the hard life of a single mom working as a medical assistant, to an even tougher hard life as the pregnant girlfriend of a short-term partner.

By this time, 1991, I had graduated from college in Philadelphia and started working full-time in banking there. I was creating my new life in the middle class. My sister's relationship with Wendell fell apart. Acquaintances from high school gossiped about the breakup and the fast hookup with another guy named Jerry, who married her right away. It was hard to stay focused on my dreams, since the new rumor about my sister was that her marriage was a violent one with lots of drug abuse. Jerry even tried to kill her. I'm not sure how and why she made the decision to move to Atlanta. But one day in 1992, with only her youngest child along, she packed up and left Pittsburgh.

Her downward spiral was halted. Rahima called my mother from Atlanta periodically, with good reports of having found a job as a hostess in a restaurant where famous people often dined. She would eventually send for her other two kids, who were now living with their father, when she got more settled. We were all thrilled by her efforts to make a fresh start.

At the same time, I kept practicing my plant-based diet and yoga. I didn't want to fall through the cracks. Yoga and eating whole foods were still giving me a deep sense of peace and the strength to keep on healing.

CHAPTER 12

YOU EAT
TOO LOW ON
THE FOOD CHAIN

TED WAS MY UNOFFICIAL MENTOR at The Bank in Pittsburgh. I'd often frequent his office for feedback. Ted stood 6'5" tall, with honey-colored skin and wavy black hair. His hair resembled that of mixed-race people, with loose curls that were neither tight nor kinky. He was medium build and had huge hands that were the color and structure of baseball mitts. Ted was in his mid-40s. He was in charge of the International Division, and he spoke fluent French. He might have been the only African-American man in an executive vice president position with the bank who ran an entire department. He looked Moroccan to me, but he said he was a black guy from Philly.

In January 1992 I was a quarter of a century old, and for two years I had been practicing an alternative lifestyle. But even though I worked in corporate America, I no longer wore dark business suits; instead, my wardrobe had evolved into nicely fitted, colorful dresses. I was hoping to communicate that I was an independent-thinking professional. I also didn't want to think too much about clothes or how to put them together.

I wanted to think more about my goals and who I could become.

The New Year was always a time for me to establish my goals, and I was excited to share my work plan with my mentor. I designed a strategy for how I was going to prove myself in the Corporate Marketing department. I showed Ted how I established an important morning goal and then an afternoon goal that fit into my department's long-term goals. I was applying all my *Seven Habits of Highly Effective People* strategies to my real-life corporate job. I also shared with him my new lifestyle of going to the gym and eating in a holistic way.

"What's holistic eating?" he asked.

"You know, eating grains, beans, greens, tofu, nuts, seeds and fresh fruit, and vegetables," I said.

"Grains, humph," he said. "What do you mean, grains?"

"You know things like brown rice, buckwheat, millet, and quinoa," I stated proudly, a bit perplexed that he did not know what I meant.

"Quin-What?"

"Quinoa." I said as he looked over his black-framed reading glasses. "It's a South American grain, high in protein."

"Girl, you want protein, eat steak. And millet, that's what poor Africans eat." He schooled me. "Your problem is that you're eating too low on the food chain." His voice was so matter-of-fact.

I, on the other hand, naively thought that I was doing what corporate bankers and other businessmen and women did in this world, working out and eating well.

I felt the corners of my brow furrow. I thought he would be proud of me. My old feelings of superiority rescued me. If he didn't understand that eating grains was a great way to get some protein, fiber, minerals, and vitamins (especially the B vitamins), then I was not the one to explain it to him. My face relaxed somewhat. Then I simply explained it all to him in terms that I thought he might relate to—African-American history. African Americans have a long history of high cholesterol, diabetes, and hypertension, and mostly because we eat foods that derive from the American slave table. But if we eat more foods from our rich African heritage, it can help us connect to our racial history, our biology, and ultimately our spiritual heritage. My teacher, Gia, emphasized that eating grains like millet and teff could better connect us to our African ancestry. This was my way of consciously choosing foods that promoted a sense of freedom, and besides, grain protein is absorbed and digested more easily than steak. I wanted Ted to understand this. So I held my ground.

"I lowered my cholesterol 100 points," I said, thinking about how spending so much time in the kitchen was paying off, especially since cooking was not my favorite thing to do.

"You had high cholesterol? But you are so skinny."

I explained to him that my high cholesterol came partly from heredity and partly from inheriting my family's same dietary habits. We ate plenty of fast food, burgers, french fries, milkshakes, donuts, and egg sandwiches.

As a new member of the Black Urban Professionals (Buppies), I had to show that I could hold my own and yet still be respectful to my mentor. This was another tactic that INROADS taught to us, how to get ahead in the corporate world, and Ted was pretty clear about how I was going to get ahead at the bank. He always painted a simple picture of what was suitable for me in banking, Pittsburgh, and the African American world, with statements like, "Save your money. Work your ass off. Find a good black man to marry, and he is not going to want to eat that kind of cooking you do." He implied that I better learn how to keep my black man happy.

I didn't always agree with Ted's point of view, but I did listen to him. He seemed to take a genuine interest in me.

"What'd ya do this weekend?' he would ask regularly.

"I saw *What's Love Got to Do with It.* The movie based on Tina Turner's life." I told him. "In fact, I saw it twice."

"Ugh." He said. "You went to see that negative portrayal of African Americans? Hollywood loves to demonize the black man." Pregnant pause "And don't get me started on *The Color Purple.*"

I paused and took inventory myself, and then said, "Well, a lot of the men in my own family have hit or beaten their wives or girlfriends." He gave me an even more disgusted look. He started shaking his head back and forth, slowly, alternating his looks between one of anger and one of disdain. He looked like he smelled rotten eggs.

I understood where he was coming from, but I still let him know why I liked the movie.

"I enjoyed the film. It illustrated how Tina mustered up the strength to deal with Ike's bullshit. She chanted her way to clarity. I loved that spirituality was the answer for her."

He sat in the chair, shaking his head. Then he told me a story about an abusive white woman.

"A French woman in Paris pulled a knife on me once. She disagreed with something I said about our relationship." He went into more details. I don't remember what they were, but I believed his story was his attempt at leveling the abuse between men and women. He wanted to let me know that each of us was capable of committing stupid acts of violence.

"That woman was crazy," he concluded.

I looked at him and said, "I still liked the movie. You should go see it."

I left Ted's office puzzled. Mostly because I thought that making money would alleviate my burdens, but it was in his office where I felt the heaviness resting on my shoulders the most. What is this new world? One thing was clear. I needed to represent so much for so many. I needed to be a credit to my race—meaning that when others looked at me, they needed to see that I was properly assimilated into the white world. People did not need to see that I came from poverty, domestic violence, a deadbeat dad, and substance abuse. Subliminally, the message I received was,

"Portray that you are not really that different from them, just black."

Throughout my life, I got lots of advice from authority figures on how to fit in: "Take up golf because that is where the deals are made." "Go on beach island vacations like Aruba. Learn to snorkel and take up hiking." "Take international trips to show your worldly sophistication." "Skiing in Tahoe or Aspen doesn't hurt either."

At The Bank, Ted was clear that I didn't need to eat so low on the food chain, especially when I could afford to buy meat and live a better life. Eating meat was the American way, and to prove it business dinners were often held at expensive steakhouses like Ruth's Chris. *had*

Ted and I didn't see eye-to-eye. I didn't eat steak but still continued to visit Ted's office. It was brightly lit, all in gray, with a big window facing the Point. The Point is the place in Pittsburgh where all three rivers meet, marking the success of the steel mills during America's Industrial Revolution. It connects the Allegheny, Monongahela, and Ohio rivers. Ted's office was like the Point, a place where everything came together for many of the blacks working at the bank.

It was in Ted's office where I was reminded of my duty to become an example for other young black college-bound girls. I was to be the role model for the ghetto girl to get herself out of poverty and assimilate into a respectable nine to five, or more like 8:00 A.M. to 8:00 P.M., career. I was expected to be a role model for the kind of bourgeois lifestyle a young black girl could see herself having.

❁　❁　❁

I saw my future as mysterious and unknown. Although I was approaching an almost 10-year career in banking, Pittsburgh never felt like my destiny. I constantly had a nagging feeling that—as that voice said to me during my very first yoga class—"You'll be teaching this one day." So over the summer months of 1993 I sketched a different plan for my life. I was ready to add the color of yoga teacher to my life's rainbow.

In August, I walked into Ted's office, where he sat with his feet propped up on the corner of his desk. With a nod, he looked over his bifocals to greet me. I felt confident, yet scared to tell him my new plan. I stood in the office doorway and blurted out that I was quitting my job. I told him that I'd be living for a month at a yoga ashram to pursue a yoga teaching certification. He looked stunned. I added that I planned to move to Atlanta to be a live-in chef for someone who wants to eat macrobiotically. Last, I explained that I still plan to work another corporate job, but I want to do all three somewhere away from Pittsburgh.

His glare penetrated my soul, and he said, "You're crazy. How long have you been with the bank?"

"Almost ten years, including my internship time." I stood tall, in my hot pink dress from Sacks Fifth Avenue with six gold military buttons on the chest. I looked down at him, scared yet confident in the knowledge that my life was my own.

"You've put in good time here, and you just gon' walk away from it." Pause. "You have received some nice raises and promotions here. You are one of the youngest banking officers, not to mention, not many African Americans get this title. He paused again. "Who's gon' eat that food? It's too low on the food chain. You're gonna find yourself livin' with some psycho. He'll murder you." He paused again. "And why would you want to do a domestic servant job anyway? You have a college degree. You're messin' up the plan and your life."

I sighed. My heart was ready to take the plunge into my new scheme. I had been involved with holistic living for almost five years now.

But I was torn. I didn't want to let my race down. I wanted to be a role model for the young girls who would come after me.

Maybe Ted was right. I was asking myself to do domestic work and teach yoga in a gym. What is the value in that? I wondered. It didn't really require a college degree.

Ted got up and walked to the window. His back was toward me. I was seated in the guest chair. He put his hands on his hips, or more like his lower back.

"Martin Luther King, Malcolm X, Rosa Parks, and Lena Horne didn't sacrifice so that you could do the same job as your grandmother." His head dropped, looking down toward the street. "W. E. B. Du Bois, Frederick Douglass, Fannie Lou Hamer, and Paul Robeson did not risk their lives so you could go to the black mecca (Atlanta) and do manual labor." He turned toward me while keeping his eyes on the city, as if to say "This could be yours." He continued his monologue, mentioning names like Jackie Robinson, Eartha Kitt, and Madame C. J. Walker. He addressed Pittsburgh, the nation, and me from that window view like Moses on the mountaintop. His speeches were always long, which was why it was hard to argue with him about what my role should be. It was like an unspoken code among the black intelligentsia. The post-slavery plight of African Americans was a marathon-relay race. It was a race where I was expected to pick up the baton from here, at The Bank, and carry it to the next rising African American stars. Ted emphasized that the track was already laid out for me, and all I had to do to win the race was save money, work my ass off, and fit in.

"You should get those crazy ideas out of your head," he said firmly.

I walked out of Ted's office that day feeling betrayed by him, but also feeling like I was betraying my entire race.

I too was familiar with Dr. King's words and actions. Except I understood them to mean that I could become anything I wanted to, and the only charge was to be the best person I could be, baton or no baton.

Even though I wavered, in my heart I knew that I was making the right choice. What I didn't know was the price I would pay for following my inner voice. At this time, I didn't want to represent my entire race, especially before actually becoming my most authentic self.

I left Ted's office reminded of the fact that I had a bigger duty: to find out who I really wanted to be, and then let *that* person be a role model to others.

nice

CHAPTER 13

YOU THINK
YOU'RE A BIRD

BEFORE PACKING UP MY LIFE IN PITTSBURGH, I thought back to my first yoga class and the voice telling me, "You'll be teaching this one day, and get closer to your grandfather." It was a bit confusing because I had every reason to want to keep a casual distance between my grandfather and myself.

I must admit, the directive never appeared harmful, so I guess that's why I decided to heed its call.

My first step in developing a relationship with my grandfather was to visit him every few weeks, if not every weekend. My habit was to bike there from my apartment. It was a 20-mile trek to his house. This was a huge success for me because I was never really physically active in my youth.

As I opened up the unlocked door to his house, shouting "Grand-dad!" he would sometimes respond with, "You on that bike."

"Yep. It was a sunny day, so I decided to ride."

"That's a far ride." Then he'd pause and say, "You think you're a bird anyway." He said that almost every time I visited, referring to the fact that I went on a skydiving trip one summer. His funny, nonjudgmental comments were always welcomed. He never said, *Don't do that!* or *Why would you do that?* He just called it like he saw it: *You must think you're a bird.* And I understood that to mean, keep on flying.

"Did you bring your own lunch?" he'd ask.

"I did," I'd say, showing him my stir-fry tofu and rice dish. "You can have some." I'd always offer.

Then he'd say, "I got some green beans and potatoes, if you want it. I know you don't want no oxtails to go with it." He smiled and laughed. Then I'd scoop some green beans and potatoes onto my plate. "No need to reach for the salt shaker. I'd seasoned d'ose beans purr-fekt-ly." He always said, implying that a good cook knows how to do the seasoning while cooking so the guest doesn't need to do anything but eat it.

He was right. His food was very delicious. Now and again he would reminiscence about the time he was a young man of 14, looking for a job at a sawmill. The manager told him he was too young, but then asked if he knew how to cook. "Our cook is sick and the men need to have lunch," the man said.

"I can cook," Granddad replied.

"Rose..." That was what they called my grandfather. It was short for Roosevelt. "You're the new cook." Then the manager just walked away, saying "See you tomorrow."

My grandfather cooked lunch, which was a huge success among the mill workers.

My grandfather never judged me for eating the way I ate. He'd always confirmed that my visits were the most important thing, not what we ate together. He'd always say, "I have food if you want it, but if you don't that's fine too. I'm just glad you're here."

During this time, I would catch myself thinking, *What am I supposed to learn by getting closer to my grandfather?* This is still the man who beat

Grandma. Isn't it? I was convinced that she was an alcoholic because of him. What could I learn here?

When visiting him, I couldn't help but think back to the day he evicted us from our home.

I am 13, and I hear this conversation over and over for months.

"Billie [my mother's nickname], you will get your money right off the top, once you sign the liquor license over to me, and we sell the bar," said my grandfather.

"I want my money at the same time I sign the paper," she responded.

For more than a year, my grandfather and my mother were fighting back and forth about the license. He wanted to sell the bar and make a profit, since my dad— his son—wasn't managing it properly. Secretly, I laughed at this situation. It all seemed silly to me. I felt, for as much hell as my dad had put us through over the years, I would have taken my chances with signing the paper early and seeing if my grandfather was going to be an asshole about it.

I listened to various conversations, disagreements, and fights between my grandfather and my mother. I also overheard various debriefs my mother had with Aunt Alice on the telephone. All I could think about was, "Just free yourself from these motherfuckers. It's not worth it. Fighting them only destroys you. No one wins."

Inside my adolescent mind, I kept thinking it's not only about five-thousand dollars, this is about power and seeing if one person can make the other person do it his or her way. Quite frankly, I didn't understand why my mother didn't just surrender and risk it. Maybe my grandfather would have screwed her out of the money or maybe not, but I knew on some intuitive level that it wasn't worth fighting my dad or my grandfather. Again, I felt wiser than my family members, and I was smart enough not to take sides. I decided to just watch the situation, and watching it was draining enough.

Whether I liked it or not, I was in the middle. Both sides were right and both sides were wrong. Even though I didn't blame my grandfather, I felt his final blow when he told us to get out of the house that he was renting us, a property that he bought for my dad. I didn't blame him, but I did question, "What kind of man evicts his grandkids?"

This was always on my mind when I visited Grandad, but it didn't stop me from creating a new relationship with him.

His house was like a time capsule. We sat in his 10' by 10' living room and listened to the Pirates playing the Dodgers on his transistor radio. Then he would tell me the story about why he supported the Dodgers over the Pirates. I never grew tired of my black history moments with him. The house still had a Dodgers' Jackie Robinson souvenir button hanging from a poster of Martin Luther King Jr., John F. Kennedy, and Bobby Kennedy.

Sometimes we'd just watch TV—the "The Price is Right" or "Family Feud." Other times we'd sit and talk, and when his black rotary telephone rang he'd pick it up and say, "Yell-low."

Without fail, I'd ask him about his day or his life and then update him about mine. On some visits he'd tell me about his summer crops while we walked down to see the bounty in his quarter-acre garden. There were collards, green beans, potatoes, carrots, peas, and squash. I was amazed that a man in his late eighties could still farm land that size all by himself. He said it kept him young. He always boasted that his collard greens kept his skin nice and smooth.

"Sy, I need to work the garden in the summer. It keeps me nice and slim. Over the winter I always gain 10 or 15 pounds, but I never mind because it comes right off in the summer months."

"That sounds good, Granddad." I said while looking at his smooth black olive skin. He aged well. He was trim and fit. These walks made it easy to talk with him.

One day I told him I was having trouble with my job.

"Do you have a union on your job?" he asked.

"No, I'm management. It's banking. We don't have unions," I told him.

"Hmmm."

"I just don't like it anymore," I explained.

"Like?" he paused, puzzled. "Like a job? ...Jobs aren't to be liked. What you like is that you have a job. What you like is not getting a pink slip. I've never been fired from a job," he stated with pride.

I thought long and hard about what he said, and realized that even that kind of statement was another slice of black history. I was living in a different time and place.

✻   ✻   ✻

One weekend, I asked him more questions about his childhood. He explained to me how he moved from McCormick, South Carolina, to Pittsburgh, Pennsylvania. He and his older brother George jumped on different boxcars to make their way north. But what he said next sounded as if it was out of a Mark Twain novel: *George was accused of murdering a white man, but he didn't do it, so we had to leave.* He explained how they were going to kill George if they didn't get out of town fast. His voice faded as he mumbled, We were only teenagers.

My grandfather was staring off in the distance. I wasn't sure if I should ask another question. I was so curious, yet I didn't want to cause him any unnecessary pain. Then I blurted out, "Tell me more about your brothers and sisters. Granddad started a story about his younger sister, then stopped. I saw that his eyes were beginning to well up. Then again in that mumbling voice he said, "My sister was killed by a horse."

The way he said it, it didn't sound like an accident. Sure, it was more common for people in the early 1920s to have accidents while riding a horse, but his voice was in pain. His face looked confused. Then he said, "Why you asking me all this?" He was on the verge of manly tears. "Why you bringing up the past like this?"

"I just want to get to know you better," I said.

"Well, my dad built houses. He was respected. They didn't call him *boy*. They called him *uncle*. That was the highest respect a black man could get. And your dad wanted to go and change his name from Quarles to Hafiz. Why?" Again, his eyes showed hurt. "If I would have treated your dad the way he has treated y'all. Oh, my. He just ducked from all of his responsibilities."

When I listened to my grandfather, I was part his granddaughter and part historian understanding the bigger plight of the African American in the United States. When we sat and just talked about his life, I was not mad, but understanding. I understood that we were all victims of victims.

❊ ❊ ❊

My grandfather watched my independent spirit move about the world, traveling, getting a college education, biking up and down hills, choosing vegetarianism. One day he blurted out, "Too bad you're not a boy."

I smiled. I should have been mad, but I think that was the highest compliment my grandfather could give me. Then he described the kind of life he imagined for us: "If you were a boy, we could have really done some things. Your dad didn't want to do the real estate plan I had in mind, so…" he paused and then continued, "you and I could have built a nice little business together." I just listened to him, smiling internally. Perhaps he was right, but we will never know because I am not a boy, and I am following my own path anyway.

❊ ❊ ❊

Later, my granddad must have known his end was nearing. He asked me to be the executor of his will. I wanted to help out, but being in the middle of a discussion between my dad and my aunts would feel like a person being in a head-on collision between two Mack trucks. I politely declined and I secretly realized that he didn't care that I wasn't a boy. I felt extraordinary because he saw all of me.

Each visit was a little more precious. He called me and said, "Come visit when you want. Remember, you don't need an invitation."

I could sense the words between the lines saying *I might not have that long to live.*

My grandfather died in spring 1993. Visiting him every few weeks was strangely reassuring. It allowed me to forgive him, understand my dad better, and connect even more to my cultural heritage.

At his funeral, I watched his body lay still and prideful. He was physically dead, but I was connected to him spiritually. I sat in the back pew, but I knew that I was the closest person to him. And in that moment I understood why the voice told me to get closer to my grandfather—it was so that we could fully see each other. I was a girl who was fully capable of jumping out of airplanes. He was a black man who wanted to farm his own land. He was a young man who left town when danger appeared, and I was a young woman who needed to leave town to explore my destiny.

Nineteen ninety-three was a significant year. With my grandfather gone and my siblings strung out on drugs, I was ready to leave Pittsburgh and end my nine-year banking career.

The voice and the path were clear: "You'll be teaching this one day." So I enrolled into Sivananda's month-long yoga teacher-training course.

CHAPTER 14

PETRI DISH

I LEFT PITTSBURGH, THE SMOKY CITY, only to arrive in a different cloud of smoke. The Sivananda Yoga Center in New York City was filled with S-swirls of incense smoke dancing from one end of the room to the other. Pittsburgh had a wide range of smoke, everything from my dad's small marijuana puffs to the large steel industry billows that made the city look gothic. But the smoke from those cylinders didn't open my nose quite like Nag Champa. This perfumed incense was a frangipani and sandalwood blend that seemed to cleanse the air I breathed, instead of triggering my asthma like the smoke I was accustomed to.

When all of us arrived at the New York City yoga center to participate in our orientation, an evening meal, and a Satsang—a two-hour session of chanting and meditation—we were told that not all of our luggage would fit on the bus headed to the ashram, and we should only take what was essential.

Groans and moans came from the crowd. I assumed it was because all of us had packed so carefully for our one-month rustic stay in the wilderness.

"When will our other bags arrive?" one student asked.

"Not sure," an attendant answered. "We're still trying to work out the details."

People looked around the room as if to communicate, "They don't have their shit together at all."

I heard whispers: "This place is so unorganized."

"I heard upstate New York gets cold at night. I need my flannel pajamas," a woman said.

"My hairdryer is expensive, I don't have to take it, but I also don't want it to arrive broken," another mumbled.

"I need my eye mask to fall asleep. I guess that's essential."

"I only brought one bag," I chimed in.

I'm not sure how it all worked out, but we managed to consolidate and cooperate.

The ashram followed a structured routine that was similar to what I had experienced in California, with less free time. The days and nights were intense. One day played into the next rhythmically, probably because we started and ended each night with Satsang, a meditation and chanting of songs. Five days had passed, and the swami asked, "How are you all managing without your stuff?"

"I'm actually wondering why I packed so much," someone blurted out.

"Yeah," the crowd responded in unison.

"You all seem to be doing quite well without your…" he paused and put up air quotes, "baggage." We all chuckled. Then the swami said with a smile, "I have good news, your bags have arrived."

I don't remember which arrived first, the physical baggage or the emotional baggage. But not long after being at the ashram I realized that whatever problem, conflict, or weakness I needed to work on, there was somebody or something giving me the opportunity to work it through. We were 50-odd people, 30 days, 20 shared rooms, two tents, and a lifetime of personal issues all living on one remote ashram.

When I told people that I was going to leave the corporate world to go live on an ashram for a month, they had one of two responses.

"Are you going to become a Hare Krishna, shave your head, and be part of a cult? You'll never be able to come back." Or: "Wow. You are going to be so blissed-out for 30 days. Must be nice to just stop life."

Neither one of those situations quite happened to me. Instead, every person I met, every spiritual book I read, and every lecture I attended brought up a present-day issue that I needed to work on.

On day one, I walked into my room and introduced myself to my roommate, who gave me the once-over. A round, pale girl with dirty blond hair, she seemed kind, but I wasn't quite sure what she was thinking. For some reason, I felt judged.

Later in the week she asked me, "How do you stay so long and lean?"

"I don't know. I eat vegetarian and do yoga, I guess." I responded.

"Hmmm." She responded.

After the first week, the temperatures dropped, and I pulled out my green cardigan sweater.

"Nice sweater," she said.

"I got it at a flea market in D.C. when visiting a college friend," I said. "It's really a man's sweater."

"I thought it was a bit big on you," she commented.

"Yeah, but it's warm."

"Let me try it on," she squeaked. "Perfect. It fits me perfect."

"It does look good," I said, but something in that moment made me feel that her energy was a lot like my mother's energy. She wanted something I already had. In my mother's case, she wanted something I had accomplished. It was eerie, because I didn't really know this girl.

Unpacking that green cardigan at the ashram was like unpacking my main issue with my mother.

On day four, I got seriously annoyed with my roommate. We were given instructions to not talk to anyone until after the morning meditation. This technique was to encourage us to listen to our own morning chatter. It also was to conserve our morning energy after a night's sleep. Ancient yogis felt this was a great time to deepen stillness within. I wanted this kind of peace and self-mastery, but my roommate insisted on thinking this rule was dumb and tried to talk to me every morning. I didn't want to snap at her, so I grunted a few "hmms" and "uh-huhs."

On day five, I said sternly, "Stop talking to me in the mornings. I paid my money and I want to get the full experience of this place. I will probably never get to do this again in my lifetime. I want to follow the rules. I want to see if something magical or spiritual can happen to me." I paused and took a deep breath. I realized that I just snapped. "Look, we can talk after meditation or at lunch." I felt weird afterwards because I wanted the boundary, but also didn't want her to think that I was not friendly.

The second week at the ashram, I encountered a good-looking African man. I thought he was Nigerian. He looked a lot like my dad and the men in my family. I noticed him the first week, but he was always talking with one particular brunette girl who had a kind, round face. Her eyes seemed to sparkle, as did her spirit, especially when she was sitting next to him. They looked cute together.

During the second week, he sat down next to me at brunch and I asked, "Where's your girlfriend?"

He said, "She is not my girlfriend, but we are friends."

"Hmmm," I said, not knowing whether to believe him. I wasn't really interested in finding romance during my ashram experience, but I also wasn't trying to block it either. Mainly, I wanted to immerse myself in the ashram life and, for lack of a better explanation, burn up negative karma even though I wasn't clear on what karma was.

"Do you want to go for a walk after dinner?" he asked me.

"Sure."

The evening air was crisp. The leaves were yellow, red, orange, and brown. The reflection from the sunset made the Catskill Mountains appear mythical.

We went on a long, slow walk while having a deep philosophical discussion about life and destiny. It was nice. We returned to the ashram, refreshed ourselves, and went to meditation. This happened for three days in a row.

On the fourth day, he asked me to go on another walk. The evening air was colder, the wind blew a little harder, and the leaves were in fact falling off the tree branches. It felt like autumn in the Catskills. I was moving deeper into my own soul and away from the world's outside physical stimuli. I could see why people end up living at the ashram. It's like diving into an ocean. The deeper you go down, the more you discover. I realized that if your life was always spent at several thousands of feet above sea level, you might not think the other direction has anything to offer. But, as I discovered, it does.

He reached out his hand to hold mine, and I pulled away as if touched by something surprisingly hot.

"Come here," he commanded softly.

"No. I am not ready to be touched by you," I said.

His nostrils flared and his eyes were beady.

"Fine," he said calmly.

On the fifth day, I agreed to go on another walk.

Again, he reached out his hand to hold mine, and again I pulled my hand away as if it had touched something hot.

"Don't," I said.

"Why do you keep pulling away from me? You're going to make me not desire you," he said.

"Look, I just don't want this here," I said. I was attracted to him, but I didn't want a fast and furious romance during my ashram days.

Day six, the same routine followed.

"I want to ask you a question," he paused.

I was prepared for the questions "Are you gay?" since I had the ashram as my priority, not him.

"Can you give me $50?" he asked me.

My teeth clenched tight.

"I'm in a bind," he said, starting to give an explanation that felt like a lie.

To avoid confrontation, I agreed to give it to him.

I quickly reviewed the past few days, and I felt like I had been set up for a heist. I let this happen, and I was too caught off guard to tell him to go to hell. Part of me didn't want to think this was happening to me at the ashram. I also thought if I gave him the money he would move on. This man, like my dad, moved through the world painting the picture that he is the ultimate victim and that the world owed him something. He didn't realize that he was causing a lot of pain, harm, and confusion to others or worse, he didn't care.

Day seven, he was sitting down next to someone new.

❀　❀　❀

Week three. I settled very well into my karma yoga job. Karma yoga, known as "selfless service," is a volunteer job; one does it without expecting anything in return. My task, computer database entry, was similar to my corporate persona. This job did help me get to know my swami better.

Swami Shankara had a rugged, medium build. He was a white South African at a time when that was not popular. He was so down to earth that the yoga students affectionately called him Swamji, a friendly, less formal term of endearment for our guru.

"Saeeda, you left your corporate job to come and learn how to teach yoga?" Swami Shankara asked me.

"Yes, Swamji."

"Big step, huh?" said Swamji.

"Yeah. I knew that I was headed this way when I started describing my corporate marketing work in yoga terms," I said. I wanted to tell him about hearing the voice in my first yoga class, but I did not want to sound too freakish, even at the ashram.

"Oh?"

"My boss promoted me, and I became one of the youngest corporate banking officers. My boss asked me what I thought about the promotion. I said, 'Well it's like yoga says, do the hard work that it takes to get yourself into the position, then once you are there, relax and let intuition take over.'" Then Swamji laughed at this story and walked away.

Swami Shankara didn't say a whole lot, and he was a gentle soul. He told us stories of how he had found love and respect for this brown man, Swami Vishnu Devananda. Swami Vishnu Devananda was known as *The Flying Swami* in the 1960s because he promoted peace by doing dangerous stunts such as traveling in a hot air balloon over troubled areas in the world like Belfast, the Suez Canal, and the Berlin Wall. He risked his life to spread the word that we should all live in peace. By watching Swami Vishnu Devananda, Swami Shankara was transformed from his racist white South African roots.

Swami Shankara was a true example of Martin Luther King Jr.'s dream. He knew how to challenge each of us without letting his ego or personal weaknesses or insecurities get in the way. He didn't even let his value system manipulate ours. Swami Shankara was one of the first people I trusted unconditionally. Most of the other people I met in my life seemed to have an agenda for me to follow.

"Swamji, I didn't expect to be so sore." I said.

"Doing two physical yoga classes a day can be tough. I found that using tiger balm soothed my achy muscles when I was going through my teacher's training course."

"I'll try it."

"It's tough, we know. Keep doing the yoga, use the tiger balm, and get to bed by 10:00 P.M. The aches will eventually go away."

Around day 17 or 18, situations continued to challenge me. Shiva Kami was a yogini (a female yogi) in her mid-20s who was on a power trip with her authority, real or imagined. In this sanctuary, where everyone was trying to grow, she seemed to always start some kind of fight. I usually just ignored her. But one day as I was helping out in the kitchen she barked at me, "That's not how you cut those carrots!"

I replied: "You don't have to talk to me like that. We're all just tryin' to get the work done. I paused. "Look, I'm not gonna take your crap." I wanted to say shit, but I stopped myself. I didn't expect to have so many confrontations at the ashram. I prefer to suppress my desires to avoid a fight.

Not sure why I did this, but I told the ashram leadership about Shiva Kami's behavior. " First, I tried to work with her diplomatically," I explained. "Next, I ignored her. But I refuse to take her abuse."

"Shiva Kami?"

"Yes, Swamji."

The swami and his assistant nodded, and I left the room.

The next day, Shiva Kami was assigned new duties, gardening alone. Within a short amount of time, I realized that the ashram, especially if you are not on vacation there, was a Petri dish where living organisms grew at a rapid clip. In 30 days, we were challenged to grow rapidly and organically. It was a controlled environment that gave us tools to stay somewhat intact while we went into our souls' untapped crevices. Shiva Kami was an example of how to confront a disagreeable force head on.

The ashram was a controlled environment, but that didn't mean the outside world never seeped in.

During the last week at the ashram, I called home. My mother told me that my nephew, Rahima's son Daoud, had been abandoned in an Atlanta apartment and was in foster care. It seemed that my sister was on drugs and that no one was there to care for Daoud.

When I got this news, I decided to go to Atlanta whether or not I had an immediate job there. Even though I had applied for jobs nationwide, I wanted to be in Atlanta with the hope that my sister might see me as a rung for her to grab on to. I wanted my sister to know that she had family nearby. I wanted her to see a familiar lighthouse while she was swirling in her own mysterious Bermuda Triangle.

The day I received the news about my sister and her little boy, participation in the evening Satsang was different. Turning the page to the directed chant in the booklet, the soft pages fell open, and that time my heart felt hollow as if the blood was pouring out of it. I had a new hole in my heart and I could feel it breaking.

News from my family, often bad, made me physically sick, but this time I felt that I had the tools to help me. Sivananda provided an atmosphere that fed me good food and two Hatha yoga classes daily, spiritual scriptures to read, meditations to ponder, and chants to sing. That night one particular chant gave me a glimmer of hope for my sister.

The chant was called "Hey Durga-Ma." It evokes the power of different Hindu goddesses, Durga, Kali, and Lakshmi, just to name a few.

My sister was a goddess in her own right. I was certain that she was looking for her way home, if only someone would evoke her personal power. The chant Ma Durga called out to each of the Hindu goddesses, beginning each name with the word "Ma" as an invocation of the divine mother. We sang, "Hey Ma Durga, Ma Durga!" I extended verses to include my sister's name, "Ma Rahima, Ma Rahima." I chanted this over and over each day. I didn't have a pretty voice, but I sang a throat sound directed toward her heart. I visualized her hearing my tone and feeling my embrace. I mentally pictured her in a safe place, while I was still brokenhearted.

❋ ❋ ❋

While at the ashram, a newly Atlanta-based company, Care International, responded to my résumé. The manager's secretary called me to set up a phone interview to manage their marketing database.

The interview went well. Then I thought, "I can actually move to Atlanta with a job and start my business as a live-in chef and yoga instructor, while being there for my sister."

❋ ❋ ❋

When I first started yoga, Savasana synthesized my practice at the end of class, and Satsang was harmonizing with my teacher's training. I was not blissed-out for 30 days, as some had predicted, but I did have an encounter with Bliss.

Bliss revealed itself slowly, like a woman trying to engage a man for a lifelong commitment. She gently said, if you want this "vibration," here are the guidelines: Show up for each date, singing a song or humming a tune. And like the good woman Bliss was, nothing happened at first. For lack of better phrasing, I did not get "laid." Instead, Bliss only made me smile and laugh in a way like no other. I was intrigued.

I'd show up for our dates, again and again. I'd sit down, cross my legs, hum tunes to Bliss and focus on my breathing—my life force, my prana. I'd tried to use my prana to blow in the eternal ear of Bliss. I whispered my commitment to her, but she was not impressed. Yet, I would feel my body tremble at the very thought of merging with her. Bliss had a stunning, quiet beauty that I just wanted to be near, even if she did not fully let me merge into her. She revealed herself slowly. Her pace helped me understand her power and value. At the end of each date, I did indeed feel high, but Bliss was not like any kind of drug that I knew. My Bliss made me feel a profound sense of satisfaction and salience. I was joyfully alive in this state.

I imagined that my Bliss was not the same kind of high my siblings experienced. My younger brother Omar once told me that my older brother Samir described getting high on crack as a hundred times better than an orgasm. "It's like busting a nut one thousand times." He said, "Man, crack is cheap and only lasts a few seconds. I was hooked rrright away. And all I wanna do now is get high. Nothin' else matters." Samir's high was a different kind of bliss. However, I'm sure that my lift off into Bliss matched his experience of being high. But how we both took off and landed started and ended in two very different places.

My meditating in Padmasana, sitting crossed-legged, was coming from the opposite direction. I couldn't shoot Bliss in my arm, snort her up my nose, or mix her in with fruit juice. She would not allow me to inhale her through cigarette paper or a pipe. She wouldn't let me place her on my tongue to be washed down with a fizzy beverage. I could breathe her in, but only straight from the earth's atmosphere.

My Bliss required that I merge with her through singing, chanting, gardening, Hatha yoga, cleaning, repeating Om, and reading scripture from holy books. She asked that I breathe fully, expanding my lungs, retaining my breath, and then exhaling deeply. This merged my outside world with my inside space. Finally, she would give me a breath full kiss of pure chi/prana. She'd straightened up my spine and lifted my conscious self above my body. I knew that I was still sitting on the ground, but it felt like I was floating, levitating. Then, Bliss softly suggested that I become one with everything around me—no separation. I felt the thing that lots of people have jokingly described, a merge with the cosmos—one with everything. I was sure this feeling lasted longer than my older brother's crack high, because when I returned to my body, *everything mattered.* Life was salient.

Bliss asked me to not drop out of life. She asked me to be more loving and serve others because everything in life mattered—my sister, her son, my ashram life, the green cardigan, the fifty dollars to the Nigerian, and my authentic path. But my challenge was to prioritize and discern all that mattered and not become overwhelmed by the weight of it all.

The last day at the ashram, my bags were packed with my new visible and invisible tools. Navigation tools for the world awaiting me. Then Swamji's words echoed in my mind, "It is easier to be peaceful at the ashram, but the real challenge is being peaceful in the secular world, a world that needs peace more than ever."

His words scared me.

CHAPTER 15

THAT TAO GIRL
AND HER SISTER

THE FLIGHT FROM NEW YORK CITY to Pittsburgh was late. Spontaneously, I went into shoulder stand to release that you-have-to-wait tension. There I was in an airport full of people, and I was upside down, feet in the air, standing on my shoulders for two minutes.

When I landed in Pittsburgh, I rented a car. I needed to gather up my belongings and say goodbye to my Steel City friends before going to Atlanta.

Leaving the sparkling side of downtown, I decelerated as I headed east, toward the abandoned steel mills of Braddock, Pennsylvania. As if the music was cued up from the soundtrack of my life, the cassette tape played the melody of "Hey Durga Ma" vibrated from the car's radio speakers. Bursting into my own rendition of "Rahima-Ma," I was determined to evoke the mother goddess that I knew lived inside my sister, the mother goddess that could save her.

I was often playing the song "Durga Ma" in the car as I went to say my goodbyes to family and friends. Each goodbye felt loving and sincere, except that my mom and I had a weird and confusing mother-daughter farewell. She seemed super sad and clingy, yet I couldn't wait to break free.

❋　　❋　　❋

Several days later, I arrived in Atlanta.

I thought about my sister, and how we had a similar upbringing but our paths had greatly diverged. I constantly sang the goddess chant using her name along with the name of other goddesses, while adding an affirmation, "I am here. I am your beacon. Find me."

I don't know how or if my chanting was working, but one night I had a lucid dream about her.

Rahima was living under a bridge like a troll. The bridge reminded me of the Duquesne Bridge that connected our old neighborhood, Rankin to Homestead. There were broken glass and needles everywhere. It was dark, with only one highway light working, and the stench of urine zipped into my nose. I was frightened, but felt like I needed to be there to watch over her. I wanted to run from it all as I saw her crawling on her belly through sewage and sludge.

I woke up chanting "Rahima-Ma," and I could still smell the pee from under that bridge. Next, I showered, meditated, and then visualized my sister becoming strong enough to worm her way out of that crack-high hole and live the meaning of her name—peace and safe. At this time, I felt like the only help I could offer her was invisible, because her experience was becoming worse and I didn't know where she was and she didn't know that I was in Atlanta.

Meanwhile, my Atlanta life was about firmly planting myself into fertile soil. I was now living in a place where Martin Luther King Jr. had a dream, where historical black colleges like Morehouse and Spelman were built, and where there were plenty of successful African-American men and women living in million dollar homes in black neighborhoods. They were successful doctors, lawyers, investment bankers, and entrepreneurs.

It was easy for me to be the dumbest in the crowd. Atlanta was the place for me to implement my new intentions and vision, which was living a dynamic, organic life. Perhaps it would land me in the middle class, but just being middle class was no longer the goal. I wanted to find my own way, even if it wasn't a popular one.

❃   ❃   ❃

In Atlanta, the Black Mecca, being That Black Girl was how every young African-American woman was living; it was the status quo. The young African-American career woman drove a nice new car, dated her socio-economic counterpart, and was usually from another city, where she was the most educated one in her group.

After she received her bachelor's or master's degree, she made her professional pilgrimage to the Black Mecca. I did the same. But, I was also looking for my sister and I didn't quite fit the image of That Black Girl anymore. My spiritual foundation had evolved, and just fitting into the black middle class wasn't my aim anymore. I wanted to fit into my true holistic, spiritual nature based on Asian philosophy called Taoism. I aspired toward becoming what I called That Tao Girl.

As That Tao Girl, I was spending more money on quality sea vegetables and organic produce, instead of on a leased BMW and McDonald's drive-thru food. Luxuries went *into* my body, as opposed to on my body. I knew that material things did not motivate me, and I was beginning to tap into my heart's true desire. I wanted to learn how to respond artistically to the life of yin and yang.

"I see myself as supporting others on their path," Stacey said when I asked her why she was letting me live at her place until I found a suitable living situation.

"That's cool. It's nice that you don't seem to have an agenda for me," I said, thinking back to when I first met Stacey. We were at an INROADS alumni conference at the San Francisco Hyatt Hotel. She and I were on the alumni board of directors, recent graduates from college. We weren't fast friends at the meetings, but that soon changed when she had noticed that I was reading *The Tao of Pooh*. In an instant, on the elevator, Stacey went from the president of our board to a hip girl I could talk to about my Taoist philosophy. We must have talked that night for a few hours. I was left with the impression that she was a person who might "get" me, even though she was a Wharton graduate from the University of Pennsylvania.

"People become successful in different ways, doing different things," Stacey said. "Besides, I've seen you teach. You transform into Saeeda-Sen. You could have a successful business teaching yoga."

I smiled humbly. I didn't know if I transformed when I taught, but part of me, the everyday Saeeda, seemed to leave the class. It felt like something else within or outside of me took over the class. Perhaps that was part of my destiny. Stacey's words calmed and encouraged me. She was the first person from the black intelligentsia who supported me as That Tao Girl.

But while I was becoming That Tao Girl, who was supporting my sister and what was *she* becoming?

CHAPTER 16

RAHIMA-MA

IT WAS WINTER 1993, AND I WAS 27 YEARS OLD. All at the same time, I had secured positions in Atlanta as a live-in macrobiotic chef, a corporate marketing database manager, and a yoga instructor.

I was the first yoga instructor Peachtree Center Athletic Club (PCAC) had ever hired, and this was my first professional yoga job.

Immediately, I noticed that some students projected images on to me. Some thought that I could heal their physical ailments. Others thought that I would cross-train their type-A training workouts by adding a deep stretch. Some thought that I would be a spiritual beacon who would guide them toward peace. Still others thought I would help them attain a body that would look like mine, long and lean.

At the end of each class, inevitably, someone would ask me a personal question about my life based on their own yoga practice. "Saeeda, what led you to yoga? Did you always have that kind of body? Are you vegan or vegetarian? Did you chose your spiritual name yourself? Do you only teach yoga? Are you naturally flexible and disciplined? Saeeda, did you always want to live this kind of lifestyle?"

Each question triggered my definition and redefinition of my life's path. One day I was in an intense spiritual conversation with a PCAC massage therapist.

"How did you make your way here to Atlanta from Pittsburgh?" he asked.

"I set my intentions, visualized, and meditated on it," I responded.

"Wow! And you got it just like that?" he said.

"No, not just like that. I did what my spiritual teacher taught me: First you set up your intention, the invisible energy, and then go out in the world and do the work," I explained.

He crinkled his brow. "You mean you are not one of those spiritual types who just says this is what I want, and if it is meant to be it will happen?"

"No. I'm the spiritual type that does the work in, three parts. First, I set my intentions, visualize, and meditate. Second, I make the calls, post the flyers, and do the work needed to make it happen. And last, I'm grateful and acknowledge whatever the outcome is," I said.

"You have a good spiritual teacher." He nodded. "And you are a good spiritual teacher, too."

"I understand that we are spirits living in human bodies, which means we have weaknesses to overcome. I feel my biggest weakness is that if I don't have to do it, I won't. So I have to set up my life in a way that gets me out of bed," I told him.

"Really, you seem so disciplined," he said.

"I'm not. I just look at things long-term, or thoroughly. If being a drug addict wasn't so much work, I would have loved to just escape from this life," I said.

He chuckled.

"I am the kind of spiritual person who finds it easier to use her effort, putting her sail in the direction of the wind instead of just letting the boat drift. And it's easier than rowing."

He laughed. "Rrr-ight."

I went on to tell him that living this holistic lifestyle is as much practical as it is spiritual. I teach what it is I need to learn. I create venues that require me to show up. This way, I can learn and earn at the same time. For example, if I want a healthier body, different from my family members', then I need to practice and teach yoga, and cook and eat whole foods mostly from plants. I reported to him how my family members managed their sicknesses, and it seemed much harder to me than living a healthier lifestyle.

He agreed. He sadly mentioned how his Mid-western family is overweight and thinks that massage therapy is not a "real" job.

Another time, one of my fitness colleagues said to me, "You are definitely not like the spiritual types I know. They are more the go-with-the-flow types, let-it-come-to-me folks," he said. "You seem to put in all the effort with a spiritual emphasis."

Then, to my surprise, he said, "and then what happened. Tell me about the live-in chef job."

I was winded, but I finished the story.

I explained that I took a scouting trip to Atlanta before going to the ashram, thinking that if I found a live-in position before a full-time job, I'd move to Atlanta without solid employment.

I placed flyers all over the city. I went to every natural foods store I could find. I went to places where people who might want my services shopped. I finished it with a for-the-highest-good-of-all-involved prayer.

A month after moving to Atlanta, I landed a live-in chef position. A man from New York City who was visiting his daughter in Atlanta randomly saw my advertisement and said to his daughter, "Susan, maybe that guy Craig who has non-Hodgkin's lymphoma might want a macrobiotic live-in chef to help him. At the potlucks, Craig mentioned that he was too weak to cook." Susan's father battled prostate cancer, and ate a macrobiotic healing diet himself. Susan called Craig and told him about my flyer. Craig interviewed me and offered me the job. Susan and I became friends.

When I moved into Craig's house as his live-in chef, I remembered what my bank mentor, Ted had said to me. "You'll move into someone's house and they will probably murder you. People don't want to eat that kind of cooking."

I told him that I only needed one person who wants to eat this way, not the majority of people. Ted's words fueled me. While posting flyers, I chanted and prayed over them to fulfill my vision.

"Damn girl, you worked it," my co-worker said.

"Yeah, so far it is working. I feel like I'm on my path," I said.

"Keep manifesting what you want" he said as he prepared to massage another client.

❋   ❋   ❋

The next day, I called the Crab House looking for my sister. When Rahima got settled in Atlanta a while back, she had told my mother that she was hired at a fancy seafood place where some of the Atlanta elite dine.

"I understand Rahima Hafiz works as a hostess in your restaurant," I said to the woman who answered the phone.

"Uh, you'll have to speak to a manager," she said.

"Okay. Can I speak to a manager?" I asked.

"You're going to have to call back. We're setting up for dinner hour," she explained.

The calls went like this for the better part of a week, until I finally got more news.

"Rahima used to work here, but we don't have any more information. Sorry."

That night, I cried myself to sleep…chanting Rahima-Ma.

CHAPTER 17

THAT TAO GIRL IN ACTION AND INACTION

IN ATLANTA, I HAD MANIFESTED three very important aspects of my life all at once. I was a corporate database manager for Care International, a yoga teacher at Peachtree Center Athletic Club, and a live-in macrobiotic chef.

Big tall trees surrounded Craig's house as I pulled my rental car into his semi-circular driveway. Craig was my new employer for the live-in chef job, and this was my first visit to his new home.

When I'd interviewed with him for the job, he lived in a cookie-cutter apartment in Buckhead, an uptown district of Atlanta. The new house was located right outside of Buckhead, off of Highway 75, on Moores Mill Road. The area was close to the center of the city, yet it had an antebellum, rural feeling.

Though it was 1993, looking at the trees surrounding the house, I felt my racial ancestors stir within me. Not having traveled at all to the south, but being educated about the black man's plight there, starting with slavery and Reconstruction stories, I had strange thoughts of black bodies being lynched or hiding out in these trees. Billie Holiday's song "Strange Fruit" was on my mind. It was a feeling I hadn't expected.

I got out of my rental car, softly treading along the paved walkway as if it were rice paper that I didn't want to tear. I wasn't sure how I was supposed to act or who I was supposed to be. I caught myself firmly gripping my Day-Timer, leaving fingerprints of perspiration on my leather binder, and thinking, *What will this new adventure hold? Could my banking mentor be right? Will I be in harm's way living with a stranger? Can I do this kind of job?*

I wasn't Jacques Pepin, the famous French-American chef, about to live in the house of the French president. I also wasn't hired help for a busy suburban housewife with three kids. My new duties felt unique. I felt unique. I was about to embark upon something that felt significant, which also made me anxious. I had never done anything like this before. Was I ready to be a pioneer and potentially discover new parts of myself?

Craig opened the door, standing about six feet tall, and greeted me in a friendly manner. He showed me around. I walked through his ranch-style house, which reminded me of the house on "The Brady Bunch" TV show. Especially because the kitchen had an island sink and stove that opened up into the eating area, just like on that show. The refrigerator and cabinets surrounding it were angular, and the colors were soft yellows—not dingy, not bright.

My bedroom was all mauve, including the window blinds and the shag carpet; even my bathroom had mauve-colored tiles. I didn't care. I just needed it to be a clean and safe place. Besides, Craig bought the house with the intention of remodeling it, and I was there with the intention of helping Craig remodel the internal workings of his body. Even though he was a financial guy for the federal government, Craig knew how to remodel a house. In the same way, I knew how to cook, even though I had come from banking.

We sat down in the family room. I noticed that he was quite skinny and fragile. Then he removed his baseball hat. His head was bald, due to the radiation treatments for his cancer. But when we discussed at length the cooking schedule and details, I could tell that his spirit was strong. He described what he liked and didn't like about the healing diet. I didn't expect to laugh much, but he was funny. He had the kind of laugh that said, "I might be sick, but I want to survive." When he smiled, it was bright.

I felt good about our agreement. Leaving, I knew two things: One, I could only be me and do what I knew. Two, doing something I had never done before, I was about to discover a me that I hadn't known existed.

✻　　✻　　✻

During my first week at Craig's house, it was comfortable. But at night I had some fearful thoughts. *Is his place really safe?* The adult in me understood that the child in me experienced the violent traumas at night, but it didn't stop me from being afraid to sleep in new places. I feared that an old memory would be triggered, or worse that I would relive it with someone else.

Then I thought about what Ted, my mentor at the bank, said about moving in with someone who would murder me. I knew that I was taking a risk, but I still wanted to live out my plan to be a live-in chef.

So I decided to just get down to business and be a live-in chef. I challenged myself to follow all of my training in developing seasonally balanced meals for healing. For an entire year, I experimented with not repeating the same dinner menu twice. Also, Craig and I discussed what foods would specifically help him heal based on his macrobiotic consultations for his cancer, and I happily researched new twists on healthy meal planning.

Cooking became increasingly fascinating, especially since I didn't particularly like to cook. What I did like were the results of healthy eating. Being fully present with food preparation and cooking simpler meals put me more in touch with the characteristics of each food and the relationship between foods. My main study with food came from macrobiotics, but the basic food concepts that I learned at Sivananda were also in accordance with what I was practicing. Sivananda emphasizes that a yogi's attitude toward food should be "eat to live, not live to eat," and also it emphasizes that a yogi should consider both her knowledge of food and her internal experiences so that she can create the most positive effect on the body and mind while minimizing harm to other beings. The best way to support the earth is to eat a diet that creates the best you in body, mind, and spirit. I loved that philosophy when I first learned it, and I still do.

When preparing a dinner menu, I wanted to emphasize local and seasonal ingredients. But it was also important to have all seasons or cooking styles represented, so the body and mind can have a holistic experience. In the winter a short grain brown rice can be made in a pressure cooker for warmth, but it might be coupled with steamed carrots, a known springtime cooking style and food item. The meal might start with a summer-style pressed-raw salad and end with a baked apple in a rich tahini raisin sauce representing autumn and winter.

I observed that I wasn't being led by taste alone, although my taste buds were constantly being reawakened. My new labor-intensive cooking adventure made me feel like an alchemist in a laboratory, changing lead into gold for the body and soul.

I had felt robbed when I fully understood that most of our food is masked in salt, sugar, MSG, fats, and the like. As a macrobiotic chef, my tongue was being liberated to taste the true flavor of each food. Food was no longer bland, or good, or bad. It was a gripping experience in simultaneous subtlety and intensity.

Case in point, I discovered that millet possesses a nutty flavor with a sandy richness. I didn't realize that my tongue longed for such texture. I savored the plump sweetness of baked yams minus the brown sugar, marshmallows, and butter. I learned to taste the natural sugar of a hot baked yam. Chickpeas were bites of soft pillows that calmed me down from a long day's work. Steamed kale with lemon juice was a curly crunch of spring. Each dish potentially stored healing characteristics that could assist in arresting or reversing some serious illnesses.

"Cooking," in the words of macrobiotic chef Cecil Tovah Levin, "is the highest art and the highest responsibility for human beings to take on. We have the power in our hands and in our kitchens to change our destiny." My first year's challenge as a live-in chef inspired me to create a basic seasonal recipe guide. It was also nice to hear Craig say each evening, "Wow, another great meal!" I was pleased because it really was basic, simple, fresh food. I realized that so many of us just don't eat or appreciate the taste and energy of basic, simple, and fresh food.

Because of all the cooking I did for Craig, I took my lunch to work regularly. Within my first month of working at CARE International as their marketing database consultant, I had a few conversations like this one.

"What are you eating?"

"Millet, chickpeas, yams, and parsnips," I said, failing to mention the sautéed collard greens and mixed vegetable soup still in my bag.

"What the hell is millet?"

"It's a grain. It's the same grain CARE feeds its recipients; you know, like sorghum or rice."

"Why are *you* eating it?" It sounded like a demand and not a question.

"It's good for us. B vitamins, fiber, and I think magnesium."

My colleague gave me a blank look before marching back to his desk.

❊ ❊ ❊

Four months into my CARE International job, I attended a day long seminar, which meant a series of slideshows, lectures, and group discussions. This also meant we were sitting down most of the day, so I packed my food for the occasion.

At home, I'd eaten short grain brown rice mixed with some buckwheat groats cooked with raisins for breakfast. These are good grains for the winter. On top of the warm cereal, I sprinkled some roasted sunflower seeds and drizzled a dollop of maple syrup. This sustained me quite nicely and kept me away from drinking coffee and eating pastries.

Mid-morning at the seminar, I ate an apple while others finished the pastries.

For lunch, I had creamy carrot ginger soup from my thermos, garlicky black bean stew, brown rice, steamed greens, and a sea vegetable salad. For dessert, I made a kabocha squash pie with an oatmeal crust. I watched my work-mates eat sandwiches, takeout, Lean Cuisine meals, frozen lasagna, or pizza.

Late afternoon, I snacked on my own mixture of almonds, dried cranberries, dried currants, nori sheets, peanuts, and plain popcorn.

It felt good to have my own tasty, nutrient-dense stash.

The next day, while strolling down the hallway, I heard someone call my name. I turned around. I saw a senior manager leaning out of her office doorway and gesturing for me to come into her office.

I walked back to her office, where she offered me a seat. I didn't know what she wanted so I was a little nervous. My anxiety lessened when I saw the vulnerable look on her face.

"Saeeda, I hope this is not too personal, but yesterday I watched you eat your way through the entire seminar and you still look great. I mean, you're nice and slim. What were you eating?"

I told her.

"Did you grow up eating that way?"

"No," I said, reflecting back to my childhood and choosing not to blurt out every detail about how I had actually come to this cooking-yoga life. "I just wanted to make healthier choices and started really applying myself. Now I have a few private food and yoga clients." I didn't

want to tell her that I was also doubling as a live-in chef. I wasn't sure h
that would go over in my corporate world.

"I want to start preparing better meals for my family. Can I hire you
to consult for us?"

I was honored that she asked me to consult, and agreed to take her on
as a client. I put together a comprehensive meal plan for her and her family
with meal suggestions and strategies to help them incorporate healthier
foods and eliminate not-so healthy ones. Though she actually paid me my
asking consulting fee, I wasn't thoroughly convinced that what I did added
any value to her family or humanity as a whole. I guess it just seemed so odd
that she didn't know how to do the very basics, cooking simple healthy food.
Still I was happy, especially since Ted my banking mentor had predicted
that no one would want my food services.

He was wrong. In addition to my consulting clients, my live-in client
was proving to be kind. We didn't spend lots of time together, but when
we did we had good conversations about religion, philosophy, and his latest stock investments.

Six months earlier, if you had told me that I could visualize something
into a reality, I would have been skeptical. But there I was, in Hot-Lanta,
the Black Mecca, cooking, teaching, managing a marketing database, and
making some cool new friends.

In Pittsburgh, when I pursued my own interests I was often the
youngest one and the only black one. But in Atlanta, it was not that way.
In fact, there was always someone like me in the group. In Hot-Lanta, I
felt like I could become anything, and anything, and anything.

※ ※ ※

In Atlanta, I had what I called a bike-pedaled life. It was a life in which I was
going places but all the energy was coming from my own legs in motion. I
was busy, and I was meeting socially fabulous people: Akshak Alexander,

a lawyer for the Atlanta Olympics; Joie Chen, a CNN anchor; Susan Snyder, artist and wife of a Turner Broadcasting executive; J. Quincy Jones, business consultant extraordinaire; Nan Haggerty of Haggerty Furniture; Kenny Leon, director and playwright; the Morehouse College men who started Delights of the Garden, a raw foods vegan restaurant; and Dr. William Richard, founder of the Atlanta Center of Preventive Medicine, just to name a few. I was always meeting, greeting or entertaining someone. And I pedaled faster on my bike than I ever had before.

In May 1994, I reached a fork in the road. I was torn, one foot in the corporate world and the other in the holistic health business world. I felt like I needed to give my full attention to one or the other.

I burned with curiosity, especially because I had heard if you want to see what you are made of spiritually, start a business. I had always wanted to be a business owner, but didn't know if I had the fortitude and faith to succeed.

One day, I decided to take the leap of faith, and I went into CARE International and quit. This was the perfect time to become a full-time entrepreneur. Though it was a surprise to my co-workers, friends, and family, it was even more astonishing to me—for all the same reasons. I had put all of my efforts into creating this new life, which included a corporate marketing database job. I had never been so consciously focused on my intentions and what I wanted to create. And I got most, if not all, of what I wanted. I was amazed that after seven short months I was willing to walk away from the corporate job. It had even paid me more than the bank, and I didn't mind the work—at times, I'd really liked it. But I was listening to my inner voice, which by then was a trusted companion.

I didn't know what my new life was going to be like, but it felt like the perfect time to take the leap. I was a live-in chef, so I did not have the typical rent worries. I had savings and I was only 27 years old, which meant that I could fail royally and still have the rest of my life to pick myself up and try again, or just get another job. Either way, I wouldn't live the rest of my life with the I-never-started-my-own-business regret. Also, I had no dependents; I just had uncharted Saeeda-territory to explore.

❋   ❋   ❋

As last, both my feet were in the holistic health world. In fact, my to-do list easily buried me up to my eyebrows. Doubtful thoughts stabbed into my brain like darts thrown at a dartboard, with conversations like this playing constantly in my head:

"Do what you love, the money will follow."

"Will it? Will it really follow me?"

"You're here to contribute your unique talents to the world."

"Am I really? Maybe I am just here to do nothing in particular."

And the Chinese proverb, "Be careful what you wish for, because you just might get it."

Well, I got it. In some kind of fashion, I got everything I wanted.

As a little girl of nine years old, I wanted to have my own business. When my friends were playing with dolls and playing house, I was playing office. I remember getting a calculator as a gift. This gift triggered infinite hours of play. I set up the calculator, an old unused Bell rotary telephone, and a notepad on a small wooden desk in our upstairs hallway. I would sit at the desk, pretend I was answering phone calls, and then give orders in a loud voice to the imaginary people who worked for me.

At 11, I wanted to be a teacher, at 15, a psychologist, and at 17 a computer programmer. But mostly I had always enjoyed sharing my knowledge, no matter what I imagined. I liked to teach.

Here's where it got confusing. Sometimes I felt called to do something purposeful in life, something that had a greater meaning for the greater good. At other times I felt like I had to create my own life, and I wasn't certain if anything mattered much at all. Spiritual living gave me the opportunity for my life to become a Petri dish. As a living organism, I was challenged daily to become more of my true self, but without truly knowing where my limitations or true potential lay.

So when the mysterious voice in my very first yoga class predicted that I would one day teach yoga, it felt right to quit my job and go to an ashram. When I followed those new-agey books and actually manifested the life I thought I wanted to live, I felt I must be on the right path. But the misconception was that it would be easy and joyous to do all that I wanted to do.

In reality, my calling, and my new life, was a different kind of hustle.

Most mornings I was up and out the door by 5:00 A.M. I'd teach my first yoga class at 6:30 A.M. Then I'd eat breakfast, food shop for the upcoming meals, and market my services to a prospective client, all before lunch. Next I'd teach a midday yoga class, have lunch, and prep the veggies for the few new dishes that I would make later. I'd take a short late-afternoon nap, and then I'd go and meet another client. After that client, I'd come home to eat dinner. Finally, I'd rest for a bit before heading out to my evening yoga class. I'd go to bed by 9:30 P.M. or 10:00 P.M. I liked what I was doing, but I felt that I was always doing it, and I didn't like that. Was this really my calling? Had my life become the famous Buddhist quote, "Before enlightenment, chop wood, carry water, and after enlightenment chop wood, carry water"?

During one particular night, I was slow in getting ready to teach my private clients.

I sat in my room, pondering whether or not to cancel the evening's yoga class. I must've looked just as worn out as the 1970s mauve window blinds hanging in my bedroom window. I sat on my futon bed and stared toward the window, peeking between the blinds at the grass and my black Nissan Sentra, a purchase I had to make since commuting by bike in Atlanta was not really feasible, and thought, "What do I do for my clients, anyway?" Then, I slid down onto the mauve shag carpet and touched my toes in a forward bend and thought, "Isn't it strange that people pay me to tell them to touch *their* toes? How can that be important?" Then, I rolled over into plough, and thought, "I know that I receive tremendous benefit from every single yoga class that I take, but that can't be happening to my clients, too. Can it? Does this work even matter?" I uncoiled like a worm, and then I was flat on my back staring at the 20-year-old ceiling lamp. Like a good yogi, I went into fish pose to counterbalance the plough. Upside-down, my eyes roamed my room of austerity. My desk—a small bed tray—adequately housed my tiny office. I had grown from that nine-year old girl playing office to a 27-seven year old yogini (female yogi) working in a Zen office space, partitioned by imaginary walls dividing my work and sleep space. "Maybe this is my destiny playing itself out," I thought, "even if it is a hard path to travel." With this thought, and lying flat in the relaxation pose, I drifted into a deep sleep.

※　　※　　※

After I awoke in the dark from my deep nap, I faced another lingering problem. I needed money. I got up from the floor and looked at myself in the mirror, long and hard. I said, "Who am I? What am I? What the hell am I doing? Was Ted right? Am I regressing my race and myself by just being a yoga teacher in a health club and a live-in chef? These things didn't necessarily require a four-year college degree. I no longer have the corporate title or status. Will people take me seriously? Can I take myself seriously? What value do I really bring to the table, anyway? I work hard, and I am always on the go? Shit! I need the money."

I dressed, left the house, and got into my car. I headed toward my client's house, where three women gathered once a week for their private yoga class. Driving there was a struggle for me, but I arrived on time. I taught the class, but at the end I felt the need to confess my state of mind. I am not sure why I needed to confess, but I just did. "It was really hard for me to keep tonight's appointment. I was going to cancel."

"Noooo," Ellen tearfully said. "This is my only hour of peace a week. I hadn't told you guys this before, but I'm in therapy. I told the therapist that I have been contemplating suicide but my private yoga class, once a week, is the one place where I can feel some peace. Life seems possible."

Another woman, Diane, chimed in: " I have been depressed for such a long time, but I find that this class helps me not feel as depressed."

My eyes swelled with tears. "I had no idea this class was so meaningful."

Nancy, the other student, said, "I am doing this class because a close friend of mine had serious cancer and she said yoga is helping her to recover. My friend and I talked about how yoga can be a pound of prevention. Coming to this class is also a great time to bond with my friends. I get tired of meeting people over coffee and cheesecake."

At that moment, I got it. Yoga affected us all. It also revealed one of my weaknesses. I have a habit of thinking that my experience could only happen to me. My students couldn't possibly feel the peace I felt. Could they also begin to heal from their traumas the way yoga was healing my trauma?

❋ ❋ ❋

In my struggle to redefine myself in Atlanta, I recalled a conversation I had with one of my spiritual teachers, Rosemary. I went to Rosemary in Pittsburgh, when I first started to combine my corporate work, yoga teaching, and holistic cooking. I told her how I questioned whether or not yoga was a genuine discipline.

My encounter with Rosemary really made me think. She said, "Saeeda, think about it, is banking really real? It is a system that has been made up by human beings about money and material goods. Money isn't even real. It is a made up symbol for energy, physical items, and time. Banking was *created.*" The longer I live, the more I see the truth in her statements. How else would we have had such creative banking scandals of 2008, the subprime mortgage brouhaha in 2010, the savings and loan debacle, ENRON, etc.?

Hatha yoga, on the other hand, is an innate human system. We have all observed babies doing yoga. No one taught them how to do it. They just do it naturally. It helps them grow from one stage to the next. We are preprogrammed to do child's pose, cobra, downward dog, etc .

I thought long and hard about this. Rosemary was right. How we move or do not move our bodies is more real than the abstract concepts of money, interest rates, and loans. Before humans invented money, there was yoga; before humans developed language, there was yoga. Movements and stretching are very real; they do have value. Why was I conflicted?

In fact, I could apply what I had learned in my computer class to describe how I viewed food, yoga, and myself in a holistic system. As this diagram shows, a computer is a processor that processes whatever information you put into it.

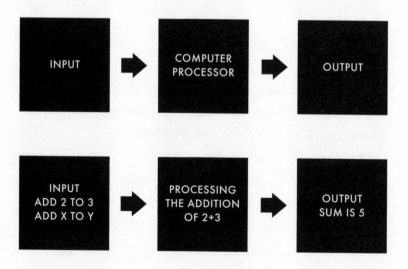

Our bodies function similar to computers, however, with both process known and unknown processing functions. Holistic systems can also fit into this diagram. Our bodies and minds are the great processors. Our outside world is one big, giant input. How we express and experience ourselves results in various outputs.

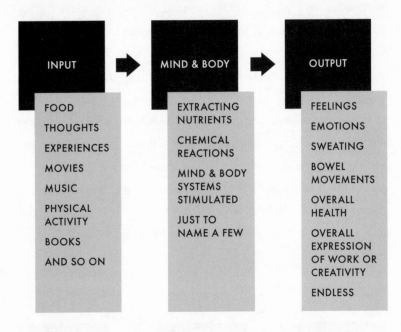

The outputs from the holistic life that I was leading felt tricky. I was thrilled that I was living out the vision of my deepest self. I ran my own business, providing two holistic health services that I believed I was meant to give to the world. I knew that I wanted to live in the world as someone who practiced a holistic lifestyle through food and yoga.

I was doing it, but resisting it too. I felt alone. The deeper I got into the work, the more I resisted providing the services. Every time it was time to go teach, an inner fight broke out. "Who are you to do this work, anyway? It's too much responsibility. You are not a guru. You're a fake. You don't really bring value. You don't even like cooking."

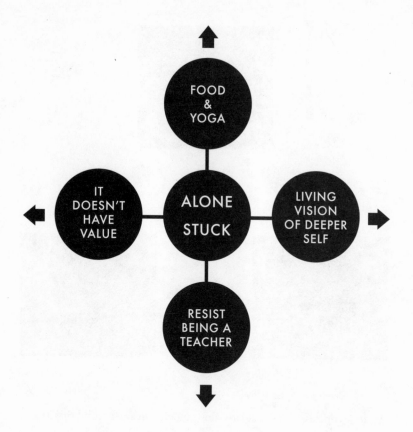

All of that felt true. I wasn't the best chef or the best yoga instructor. Some new clients hated my cooking; some didn't understand my meal concepts; some said the food was too low on the food chain. Plus the work required hard and physical labor. I no longer sat at a desk all day typing on a keyboard and taking home a comfortable salary. Instead, I worked four times harder for one-fourth of my corporate salary. Exhausted, I felt like a failure. Nonetheless, I was drawn to the work. But why? My holistic food, yoga, and body-mind chart started to look more like the one below: a feedback loop giving to and taking from each other.

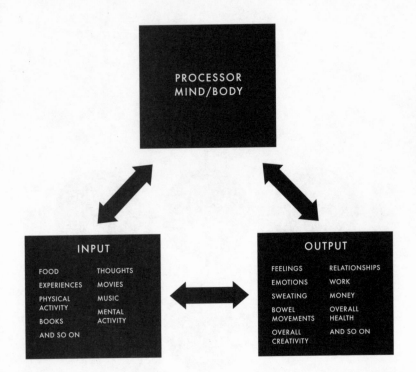

At these times, I felt particularly alone moving in and around this loop. I learned, and I made mistakes. I failed, learned some more, and made more mistakes. These were the times when I missed my dad or, more accurately, a dad.

As a child, I remember getting into bed feeling unprotected, vulnerable. In bed, I would imagine a dad, not necessarily my dad, who wanted to be with me—a dad who would read to me at night and make me feel safe, special, and loved.

I had the same feeling in high school when I did not look like other girls and the boys just thought I was weird. I needed a dad to tell me that I was pretty, strong, and powerful.

I felt it again in college when I wanted a dad to drive me to school every year and help me set up my dorm room. I wanted a dad to be there *aloneness*

to tell my boyfriends: "If you mess with my daughter, you are going to have to deal with me, you knuckleheads." I needed him to be a symbol of protection. My dad never gave me that.

After several months of managing my own business and hustling, I arrived at home one night to find myself having strong *Where-is-my-dad?* thoughts. I tried to brush them aside, but they returned after I finished preparing for the next day's workload.

I slipped into bed, and the thoughts hovered over me in the same way fog creeps over and around mountain peaks. I usually stretch myself out on my back, pull the covers over my breastbone, and gaze down toward my toes right before drifting off to sleep. But this night I curled into a fetal position and pulled the covers over my head, allowing only my nose to stick out. I took a few deep breaths through my nose, and when the initial *Where-is-my-dad?* anxiety had disappeared, a deeper spookiness disturbed me. I felt like a five-year-old, crying and rocking myself back and forth. To dry my tears, I imagined a dad hugging me. He took over the rocking so that I could fall asleep. I imagined this dad telling me, "You are successful. You are powerful. You are attempting many things most of us are too afraid to try. You're not alone, I am here."

I drifted off into a less fearful slumber.

I usually also sleep straight through the night, especially if there aren't any noises or bumps. But on this night, I woke up. With the covers still over my head, I felt a nudge coming from inside of me. I straightened up, rolled onto my back, and looked around the dark room. I decided to stop imagining a dad's arms around me because my dad has never really shown up. Instead, I started imagining God's arm around me. I was no longer a five-year-old kid or a 15-year-old girl. I was a 27-year-old woman alone in the world without a safety net, a back-up plan, and anyone who felt any sense of obligation toward me. I figured I better hold the hand of an invisible force, real or imagined.

disequilibrium

I was on my own trying to figure out how I wanted to live in this world and contribute to it. I didn't want to be a burden to others or myself. I wanted to live in this world in a safe way, a joyous way, without resistance. I needed to be a girl in action and not one of inaction.

❈ ❈ ❈

That night, I drove home from my yoga client's house looking at the bright highway lights, the green exit signs, and the white lines that divided the light 10:00 P.M. traffic. I was reminded of the writings of Theodore Roethke, who defines the word "teacher" as "one who carries on her education in public."

Then I thought of the words of Dianne M. Connelly: "She cannot be teacher-coach-awe-inspirer without giving herself away, without opening to her own astonishing aliveness, without publicly wondering and wandering in her own beginner's mind."

And again, more words from Roethke: "She lives at the edge of life as a creative act, continuous and evolving, not infrequently terrified of her own godliness; not infrequently enraptured by the joy and fun of it all; always grappling with her own humanity."

That was who I was. I was That Tao Girl living both in action and inaction, and about to live out my education in public.

Big tall trees, which reminded me of the antebellum South, surrounded Craig's house as I pulled my car into the semi-circular driveway. It was dark, with no street lamps. I emerged from the car carrying my folded yoga mat and leather Day-Timer, schoolbook style. I heard the wind blowing the summer leaves. Instead of going directly into the house, I walked up to the tree behind my car, put my stuff down on the ground and leaned my back against it, as if it could cuddle me from behind. My spine straightened, feeling the bumpy bark, and I took a deep breath. I placed my foot on the inside of my left thigh and placed my hands into a prayer position, thumbs resting on my heart. I exhaled, holding tree pose. Then I thought of my slave ancestors, who didn't know their Reconstruction fate, but did try to figure out a new way, their own way, their own Tao, which simply means a way of doing things. That's what I was about to do, figure out my own way, and at the same time I was hoping that my sister was figuring out her own way, too. I missed her.

CHAPTER 18

NOTHING IS GOING TO GET DONE, UNLESS...

I SAT IN LOTUS POSITION on Ellen's couch, looking down at the bodies. They were lying still, in corpse pose—Savasana. My thoughts wandered to that night when we discussed how yoga affected us all. Since that evening, Ellen, Diane, Nancy, and I committed to meeting once a week at Ellen's house for private yoga lessons. Each week, I'd resist. However, week after week the resistance decreased. But still, I felt dubious. I may have been insecure about my teaching abilities, but nonetheless these three women transformed to an altered state of being from their yoga practice. Their state was validated by the fact that they didn't move or twitch. It was only the rise and fall of their bellies that proved to me that they were, in fact, still alive. They are not awake, and not asleep. An eerie silence permeated the room from wall-to-wall and floor-to-ceiling. As a teacher, I've witnessed an active room full of people with busy to-do lists in their thoughts decrescendo into stillness. Dead silence. Only their bellies rising and falling, filling up with and then releasing air like balloons.

Every week, I'd bring my students back from their alternate universes at the end of class. Then Ellen, Diane, and Nancy always talked about the same thing: home renovation.

Usually, I was so tired from my long day that I would quickly pack up and go home. But this time I became curious about what they were discussing.

"What are you guys working on?" I asked.

"Nancy's house," Ellen said. "Nancy has been remodeling her house for more than 10 years."

"More like 15," Nancy interjected.

That statement sounded painful to me. I never liked the idea of buying a fixer-upper. I had always imagined that I would move into a place that was ready for me to live in.

"Nancy, you remodeled your own house?" I asked.

"Yep," Nancy said matter-of-factly. "It's been a project."

"You have to see Nancy's house," Diane said.

"Do you have before-and-after pictures, too?" I asked. Even though I never wanted to do a project like this, I admired those who did and applauded the vision of attempting such an undertaking.

"Yep, I do," said Nancy.

A few weeks later, I arranged to spend some time at Nancy's house.

When I arrived, I walked up to the white picket fence, which she had also built. The fence was quite low to the ground, but it was the perfect height for viewing the garden in the front yard. There was a lantana, a dwarf peach tree, phlox, hydrangea, yarrow, and buddleia. Nancy told me the names of the trees and plants because I didn't know much about horticulture. I knew the basics—roses, daisies, and dandelions. I also knew oak and maple trees, but that was about the extent of my plant education.

The garden's aroma was fresh and wild. And it had an uncultivated, healthy beauty. It was a short walk from the white gate to the pint-sized porch, unless you were slowed by the garden's enchantment. The few chairs on the porch invited you to sit, drink lemonade, and rock into a peaceful state.

To get into the house, I entered through a bright red wooden door. The size of the door was appropriate for the house, but it stood out like a Red Delicious apple in a supermarket pile of green Granny Smiths.

When Nancy opened the door, the red paint caught the reflection of the setting sun. The door sparkled like a red satin ribbon on a gift. Looking inside the house, I straddled the threshold, looking to another unfamiliar world. My eyes transfixed by the large gray stone standing erect in the middle of the house.

This monolithic structure served as a double fireplace, heating the living room, the kitchen, and the entryway to the bedroom and bathroom. It also gave the house the illusion of having walls. I could clearly see where each room started and stopped, even though there were no interior walls in the house. This magical stone sculpture was a symbolic pillar of strength.

The double fireplace represented *form follows function,* not the classic *function follows form.*

I particularly like structures where form follows function. This concept is true to my nature. Even today, I can only see the beauty in an object after it proves its utility. It is hard for me to see beauty for beauty's sake. My idea of beauty is holistic. Nancy's fireplace did that for me. In fact, her entire house did that for me. It was a useful work of art.

Nancy offered me something to drink.

"Wow, you worked on this house for 15 years," I said. "How did you get started?"

Nancy paused. Her face looked as though she were searching through a library card catalog, looking for the right memory to start this story.

"I graduated from college and was hired at the art museum, hanging works of art," she chuckled. "I made $15,000 a year. The 1980s were fast approaching."

"What made you think you could buy a house making only $15,000 a year?" I looked over at Nancy's petite, slender, frame. I thought: *This little lady built all this.*

"Well, the house was only $12,000, and the bank gave me a mortgage. I knew that I could do a lot of work myself. And… I had a plan," she said. "I figured if I stuck to my plan, I could make this pile of rubble into a home."

I looked around the house as she was talking. The ceilings were high and felt open, like a midnight sky. The wall colors were bright and the museum-like pictures had been hung professionally, which gave the house order, depth, and freedom.

"What was the plan?" I asked as Nancy pulled out the pictures. I grew curious about people who actually lived out their plans, especially since my parents were always preaching about building a life, a business, and a home, but not really doing it.

I thought back to a time when I confronted my father about it during a phone call: "We have to stick together," said my dad. "You need to talk to your brothers and sisters more. Talk to your cousins more. Family is important. You need to know what's going on with them. Stay close."

This was hard to listen to with a straight face. So I bluntly asked, "Dad, were you thinking that when you were beating mom at two in the morning and locking your bedroom door so that my brother Samir couldn't get in to help her?" I paused. "You missed I-don't-know-how-many birthdays, football and basketball games. The worse was waiting for you to pick me up to take me to my concert recitals and have you show up an hour late, if at all."

He hung up the phone on me. I was used to that every time I confronted him. My dad destroyed relationships. He did not build them up.

So people like Nancy intrigued me. I was interested in learning more about someone who actually followed through on a commitment, and I was eager to experience anything that showed me how to make a true commitment. My mother worked hard for survival, so it appeared to me that making any commitment beyond paying bills seemed unmanageable.

I remembered my mom telling me not to quit my job at the bank because I should have more money saved. I didn't agree.

"Mom, when did you decide to leave dad?"

"After he hit me the first time," she said. "He had come home from the Army. I was about 18 and we got into some kind of argument, and out of nowhere he hit me upside the head. I saw stars and heard a long ringing sound."

My mother and I were both silent for a few minutes, staring at the floor. It was as if both of us remembered seeing those stars twinkle and hearing that drone ring, and I wasn't even born yet.

"Mom, what was your plan?"

"I was going to save some money and get me and baby Rahima away from him."

"How much money did you have saved up when you finally left him?"

"Two thousand dollars."

There was more silence between us. Then I added, "And that was 20 years and three more kids later."

Nancy put the "before" picture album on her handcrafted-to-perfection kitchen island, while we sat on matching blonde wood bar stools. The pictures documented a dilapidated house. The structural beams were rotted. Looking at the photos, I could smell the funk and I actually saw mold. There was no functional bathroom or kitchen. *Never mind the plan, how did she live here?* I wondered.

I asked her how she did it. "I carved out one part of the house that I wanted to live in, my bedroom, and made it livable. I'd shower at the gym and figured out my meals with friends, and then started on my plan. I would budget my basics from paycheck to paycheck."

"What do you mean?"

She told me that she would buy just enough building materials to keep her busy for two weeks until her next paycheck. Each night, she had a specific focus. She tapped her hand on the kitchen counter and said that when she was putting in the cabinets, she broke the job down into small manageable tasks. For instance, the first night she might measure and record the dimensions needed for the cabinets. The second night, she'd mark all the wood pieces. The third night, she'd cut all the wood, and so on.

When I asked Nancy how she stayed motivated, she said that she was good at planning a two-week project. This way she was able to line up friends to help on specific tasks on the weekends. Because she had assigned them specific jobs to do, she then felt obligated to have her part done on time. Then she said, "Besides, I wanted the help and needed the company."

"That's amazing," I said, feeling the dedication and sacrifice.

But then she said that she wasn't always motivated. She told me about a particularly tough week. Nancy remembered coming home every day that week and being so tired of working on the house that she just stopped. She described sitting in a partially deconstructed house and just looking around at the construction. Each day, she'd come home and not do any of the scheduled tasks. Then one night she was sitting in the mess and said to herself, "Nothing is going to get done unless I do it." The next day, she came home from work and started up her regular routine again.

Fifteen years later, Nancy's house was appraised at $200,000 and her $15,000 mortgage was paid off.

What she created was so different from what my mom and dad had created. Nancy was a petite woman who lived a big life in a small physical frame, just like her house. It was solid, compact, and manicured on the outside, while the inside was an open space of functional beauty.

I felt flimsy in comparison, but maybe I could also be strong. The "before" pictures of my life felt rotted, but like Nancy rebuilt her house,

I could rebuild myself one week at a time. After watching her in action, I decided that commitment is a combination of art, attitude, and alchemy.

❋   ❋   ❋

At this point, one main difference between us was that Nancy knew that she was building a house. I wasn't sure what I was building. I knew that I wanted to live a healthy, dynamic, organic life but I didn't know what that life would look like. I believed that my foundation and building blocks included a weekly practice of yoga and eating my own home cooking. Beyond that I was a bit lost, especially because life seemed mysterious and I came from such unorganized chaos.

Sometimes I felt like the gods were playing a nasty trick on me. I imagined one of them saying, "Watch this poor soul live out her karmic challenge. Each day, she is struggling toward the one thing that will define and save her. Her only clues are: one, at the end of each class she will feel alive and whole, and two, her students gracefully remind her that her gift is supporting their lives."

Another god chuckles and says, "But by the time she is ready to teach her next class that synergistic feeling wears off and she's not sure if it is real. HA! ...Humans." At this point, the gods indulge in a hearty belly laugh and pat themselves on the back for a comedic job well done.

Every time, without fail, at the beginning of each class I resisted every step of the way. But by the end of class, I was certain that this was what I was supposed to be doing with my life.

I tried to laugh along with the gods. I tried to keep a sense of humor about my life, because it seemed that on a weekly basis a game of resistance versus certainty was being played out. Either way, I knew that I had to participate in this life because, "Nothing is going to get done, unless I do it," But, what to do is the question.

CHAPTER 19

HOTLANTA COOLS DOWN

IT WAS AROUND 15 MONTHS after starting my business that I went from optimistically having money to launch to falling behind in all of my bills. It all seemed to happen overnight. I seriously considered closing everything down and just finding a job. I became dubious about having the right combination of art, attitude, and alchemy to stay committed.

Then one late summer afternoon, while taking my afternoon power nap, I heard the phone ring. I had forgotten to turn off the ringer. I answered, praying it wasn't a bill collector.

"Hello, may I speak with Saeeda Hafiz?"

I paused, then said a polite, "Yes."

"Hello, Saeeda, this is *Essence* magazine. We got your name from a woman in Atlanta saying that you are a yoga teacher. We would like to feature an African-American yoga teacher in our wellness issue. Does this sound like something you would be interested in?"

I wanted to cheer into the phone and jump up and down and say: *Of course that interests me! I've always wanted to be an* Essence *career girl, since junior high school!*

Instead, soberly, I said: "Yes, that does interest me." I was sitting in lotus position on the floor, sounding like someone who had just confirmed what she wanted to eat for lunch. Grinning from ear-to-ear, I grabbed my three-ringed self-promotion binder. I flipped through a few pages, glancing at the newspaper clipping of me teaching yoga to kids. Then I reviewed a few client testimonials. I needed to see something to remind me that I was worthy of this interview. Also, I wanted to be prepared to answer the woman's questions as accurately as I could.

Right there, on the spot, she interviewed me for about an hour. When we finished, I put the phone down like a chef who had just put the finishing touches on a beautiful dessert.

I kept repeating to myself: *This is the break I need. This is the break I need.*

A few weeks later, someone else called from the magazine to fact check my interview. This woman told me that the wellness spread would hit the newsstands in January 1995.

I, of course, told everyone I knew—friends, family, and clients—that I was going to be in *Essence* magazine. Since I'd always wanted to be like those women in Essence, it was ironic that it was my yoga work being featured, and not my corporate work. I told myself, *Just when I seriously wanted to give up my business, this is a clear sign that everything is about to change.* I felt confident that an appearance in *Essence* would help boost my money flow, give me more business credibility, and further show that what I do does add value. As I had once heard Martha Stewart mention that "It all started to change for me once I was in print," I yearned for a Martha Stewart kind of change. I longed for a new start to my new year.

❋   ❋   ❋

In January, the issue came out, as promised. I bought a handful of copies. I flipped open the pages. I found the wellness section. I read each word carefully, but I did not see my name at all. I closed the magazine. I stared at the cover. I opened the magazine again, starting with page one. I read each page like an archaeologist excavating a section of dirt for rare dinosaur bones. I didn't see my name. Nothing I had talked about was featured. I closed the magazine. I looked at the cover and put the magazine on top of the other unopened copies. I stared at the pile as if it were a crystal ball revealing my future. Exhaling, I said to myself, "Happy Miserable Fucking New Year."

The phone rang and I let my answering machine take the message. "Hey girl," one of my friends said, "I got the January issue of *Essence* and you're not it in. What happened?"

I called *Essence*, and a woman told me, "Unfortunately, things just get cut sometimes. Every magazine has layout constraints." I was crushed.

The word "constraints" reverberated inside my head. Perhaps I should not stretch myself any further. In yoga, we often teach students to only go to a point of a stretch, not strain. In my case, I felt increasingly strained and constrained. I felt like I brought this agony upon myself. No one told me to start my own business. Hard life lesson learned—dreams can simply be cut out just because there's not enough room for them.

☀   ☀   ☀

Months later, my savings account was starting to go in the red. I did what I could to keep the creditors, student loans, and bills at bay. I felt and looked sick and exhausted, which was troubling since I was supposed to be a representation of health and wellness.

Then the phone rang again, and this time it wasn't *Essence* magazine, or a friend, or a new client, or even a bill collector. It was Child Protective Services, also known as "CPS."

"Are you related to Rahima Hafiz?"

"Yes," I said. "I'm her sister." I felt the juices in my stomach churn.

My heart boomed a Taiko Japanese drum sound.

"Ma'am, your sister gave birth to a baby boy that she left in the maternity ward. And then did the same thing with twin girls."

"I see." I felt my lungs tighten. No one had seen or heard from my sister since summer 1992. She had abandoned us all, and her Pittsburgh children missed her dearly.

"Ma'am, the children are in the process of being adopted and we would like you to provide us with some medical background. " She paused. "Can you meet us?"

"Uh, yea. Sure."

"The family that is adopting the boy would like to be there. Is that okay?"

"I guess so. Sure," My eyes were full of tears. My throat closed. My lungs felt like they did during an asthma attack from my youth.

The caseworker talked to me for about 30 minutes. I put the phone down like a bomb squad member who had just inadvertently released the triggering wire, which would make everything go BOOM.

❄   ❄   ❄

The CPS office was in DeKalb County. The offices were a lot like our banking cubicles, but the clients were children whose parents couldn't love them properly.

As we sat in a conference room, I looked at Shirley, the adoptive-mother-to-be. She was a lovely, professional-looking southern African-American woman who couldn't have children and wanted to adopt a child to complete her happy marriage. The caseworker was a young white girl trying to put the puzzle pieces together.

"We want to make sure that Malik has all known information on file in case he needs it. This way we can give him the best care."

I cooperated and told them as much as I knew. Oddly enough, I felt the same as I did in my senior year of college when I was trying to go on the pill. Planned parenthood wanted to know my family's medical history to make sure the pill would be safe for me. That is how I learned that, even though I was skinny, I suffered from high cholesterol.

I told Shirley and the caseworker about our family. I included my high cholesterol, asthma, and eczema. I included my maternal grandmother's diabetes and my paternal grandmother's alcoholism and all the other family ailments I could remember, just like I did when I was deciding to go on the pill.

As I told them everything, I realized that I was having conflicting thoughts. *Should I try and raise my sister's kids? Am I being selfish? Am I uncaring for not taking the first child she abandoned? I could have raised Daoud. Perhaps that was a reason to stay at the bank, so I could provide for my extended family. What am I doing, anyway, trying to run a business? Did I really mean what I said to my sister when she came home at 3:00 in the morning, "I will never again watch your kids." Am I a bad sister?*

"Can you tell me what Rahima was like before this?" the new mother asked.

I pulled out the last correspondence I had received from my sister and started there. I thought it would be important to have some evidence that my sister was a smart woman who made some mistakes.

"She seems really bright and the letter is well-written," the new mom said. The caseworker agreed.

"She was a good mom," I said, thinking about how she ended up in this situation. "She taught me many things growing up. I looked up to her."

Shirley smiled at me empathetically.

I continued, "She had the odds stacked against her with the domestic violence and all." I was privy to some my sister's life-changing events, but I was certain there was more to learn. Like so many families, I'm sure we had plenty of painful secrets that were never discussed.

While the social worker was preparing a few things, I stared down at the table and softly said, "My sister didn't used to be like this. My sister, being 10 years older than me, was kind enough to host my twelfth birthday party at her apartment. She paid for the cake and helped me entertain my friends." I felt myself softly smiling at these memories.

Then I mumbled to myself, "But how can this same woman leave her *children?*"

I looked up. There was silence in the room. The caseworker then shuffled through a few pages and said, "Ahh, just to let you know, there's a warrant out for your sister's arrest because she abandoned her children."

"Ummm. I see." But I didn't see. The sick feeling returned to my stomach. *How did we all get to be so bad? Rahima and Samir, my older brother, are both on drugs and have abandoned their children. They don't contact us and we don't know where they are. Omar, my younger brother, is drinking too much and not taking care of his family. And I am fucking up my life, too, thinking that I can run a business? I'm a failure, too.*

❋　❋　❋

Weeks later, the phone rang, with more disturbing news.

"Saeeda, this is the caseworker from CPS. We just wanted you to know that…" she paused, " …we learned that Rahima was picked up for shoplifting and is now in the Atlanta county jail."

"I see. … Do you know if I can visit her?"

"I think so. I don't see why not."

I put the phone down, patting it gently. I felt like the sister I had known had died.

On Tuesday, I went to the jail to reconnect with my sister, not knowing what or whom I'd find. The last time I'd her seen her was about three years ago in Pittsburgh.

I arrived at the jail and stood in a long line, waiting, briskly tapping my foot and mentally chanting my sister's name. Then I sat for a long time in the waiting area, visualizing her in divine light. At last, my number was called. I went to the window, only to be told, "Oh, honey, you can't see her today. You're a local resident. You have to come back over the weekend." I explained my situation, but the woman didn't seem to care. She just said, "Honey, come back on Saturday."

So I returned on Saturday. Again I waited in the long line and sat in the waiting area, listening for them to call my number. This time a man said, "We released her on Friday. It was a petty shoplifting offense."

"But there was also a warrant out for her arrest for abandonment."

"Sorry. She's no longer here."

Footsteps heavy, I walked back to my car. The sun was bright. The Atlanta air was warm. I opened the car door and slid in, wishing my car was a coffin to bury my already dead-feeling body. I closed the door and thought, "This Black Mecca pilgrimage is killing me."

CHAPTER 20

MOVING OUT

EARLY SUMMER 1995, I stood in line at Sevananda, Atlanta's main health food grocery store. It was several weeks after unsuccessfully trying to contact my sister in jail. I was depressed. My family was in a sad state, especially my sister, who felt lost from us. I felt like she was dead and I was a person in mourning, with no body or funeral to soothe my grief. With all this, I attempted to run my business and appear to be normal.

I refocused on the present. I was in the store to buy ingredients to make vegetable sushi and cucumber lemonade with a group of low-income African American kids. I had to keep my mind on my current work. I had the opportunity to teach yoga and healthy cooking to the kids in a local art enrichment program. In my shopping cart, I had cucumbers, carrots, short-grain brown rice, ginger pickles, brown rice syrup, brown rice vinegar, nori sheets, wasabi, and lemons.

While standing in the checkout line, doing an unassuming tree pose, first on the right leg then on the left leg, I started to mentally review the order in which the cooking and chopping needed to happen for the kids' class to run smoothly. As I pushed the cart forward, I visualized the different jobs I wanted each kid to do so that everyone could participate. I put the items on the conveyor belt, feeling confident that I had all the bases covered.

"That will be $32.38." I handed the cashier my credit card, still thinking through my class outline.

"Ma'am. The card was declined," she said, breaking my train of thought. "Do you have another one?" she asked quickly. I assumed she was trained to respond that way in this kind of situation.

I pulled out my banking card, she swiped *it*, and then the cashier said, "Do you have another one?" Her face looked embarrassed for me.

I didn't have another card. I was out of cards and money. I left my groceries on the conveyor belt, walked to my car, and got in. The bright sun turned into a spotlight glaring down on me. I was clearly on stage— the stage of shame.

"What am I going to do? I can't show up there with no food. I can't ask anyone for money. Fuck!" I said aloud to myself, closing my eyes and putting my head on the steering wheel.

I sat in the car for 30 minutes or so. The class time was approaching quickly, and I was frozen. Tick. Tick. Tick. I just sat there, staring out of the window, sweating in the Atlanta summer heat.

I turned on the ignition. I drove home slowly. I pulled into the driveway and walked into the house, head down all the way. I opened the door to my bedroom. I pulled on the cord to close the window blinds. I didn't want any light seeping into my room because everything in my life was going black—dead. I got into bed and pulled the covers up to my neck. I felt heavy and sank into my futon, and then pulled the covers over my head. I stayed there, long after the time for my scheduled class had passed.

The next day, my good friend Susan called. "What happened to you?" She was concerned, but also embarrassed. Susan was the one who had referred me to the director of the kids' program. As it turned out, there were outside visitors who came to observe the program that day, and I was not there. My actions had embarrassed the director.

I told Susan that I had fallen into a depression and just couldn't move. Susan didn't seem mad at me; instead, it was a weird kind of empathy. But all I could feel was shame. *Shame. Shame. Shame.*

❋ ❋ ❋

Days later, my friend and employer Craig came to my door.

"I know you're under a lot of pressure with starting your business and all," he said, "but I feel like there hasn't been enough cooked food in the house anymore."

"Yeah. I know. I need to sort out a few matters," I said. "Can we talk more about this tomorrow?"

Craig nodded and closed my bedroom door and walked away.

It had been 20 months since I had moved in with Craig to be a live-in chef. I went there to be a part of his healing, but now it seemed like I was hurting him.

That night I knew I had to tell Craig that I was no longer fit to do a good job. I lay awake, staring out of the window through the mauve-colored blinds. Faint moonlight hit the warm summer grass. I couldn't sleep. It was a long night. I questioned everything. After a long, long while, I finally fell asleep.

The next day, I woke up at 4:00 A.M. in the morning. The sun had not yet graced the horizon. I got out of bed, still in my pajamas, and I went to the kitchen. I grabbed some paper towels and walked out of the front door. I removed my shoes and began to walk barefoot on the grass covered in morning dew. I shivered a bit. The change felt soothing, like when you first get into a swimming pool, the chilly shock quickly becoming like a second skin.

In my holistic health classes, acts such as walking barefoot on the morning dew were encouraged as a way to keep us humans connected to the earth. Ancient teachers believed that it could help rebalance the human spirit, and my spirit needed some rebalancing. I roamed through the grass for about 10 minutes.

Later that day, I was home by dinnertime. I walked in the house and told Craig that I needed to end our arrangement. He was disappointed, but he agreed. We discussed a move out date, and then I went to my bedroom, thinking, "Shame on me. Damn!"

I was confused. It was hard for me to project how much money I would need to live on and how much money I would need to run a business, especially with my income being completely unknown. I had a business plan, but it only looked good on paper—a dream I fantasized about. I forgot the business rule that says for the first five years businesses usually don't make money; they are lucky to break even.

In my room, I sat on my futon and gazed at my appointment book. I started thinking that perhaps I was just too weak to run my own business. Maybe I couldn't do anything emotionally hard. Maybe that book, Emotional Intelligence was right. People can be intellectually smart but lack emotional intelligence, thus preventing them from achieving traditional success. Maybe I am that kind of person, one who has experienced some trauma and cannot get it together to do anything complex.

The holes in my education are abundant. I'm not entirely sure how I made it through college…Perhaps I am at the point now where I am too weak to live. Now I am hurting people in the process. Perhaps this should be the end of my road less traveled?

❋   ❋   ❋

I created my first paying job at nine years old, going around to the neighbors and asking if they had any odd jobs for me to do. One woman hired me to come in and dust her furniture every week. This job was very important to me because it meant that I would be earning my own money, and it was one less thing for my parents to fight about. I was then, in my eyes, independent. I earned my own money and I could spend it any way I wanted to. But I reinvested it by buying penny candy at the local store. At my elementary school, I sold each piece for a nickel.

At 11 years old, I sold newspapers. At 12, I babysat. At 13, I sold Avon in school. At 13 and 14, I worked government summer jobs. At 16, I was a birthday hostess at Chuck E. Cheese. At 17, I was awarded a high-paying corporate internship in computer science, where I made more per day than my mother made driving a school bus. I knew how to make money, and I was just as comfortable, materially, as any girl in school with two working parents who gave her an allowance. I had always made enough to live the kind of life I wanted to live. I had done it all my life.

So what was happening now? Why was it so hard to build a business? I had been doing it all my life.

I started feeling that my greatest strength had become my greatest weakness. Optimism was good for getting me out of bed, but I could have used some realism when it came to managing my books. For the first time, I was not earning enough to live the kind of life I wanted to live. I was failing.

❋   ❋   ❋

The sound of the phone ringing defined my life. It was usually someone wanting the car, school loan, or credit card payment. Or they were calling about some bill or another. Occasionally, it was a prospective client.

Back when I told my grandfather that I did not like my banking job, he gave me the strangest look and said, "Like? Like a job? … Jobs aren't to be liked. What you like is that you have a job. What you like is not getting a pink slip."

When I remembered this, a light bulb went on. I was the descendant of my grandfather, who believed in hard work. I was the product of my ancestors' struggles just to survive. I was now in a privileged position where I could choose to like or not like a job, and to take risks with my future. I had the luxury to follow the philosophies of books like *The Road Less Traveled*. I was afforded an opportunity to dream and believe that I could be anything! The first sentence of *The Road Less Traveled* told me, "Life is hard." The other books told me that it is my right, by divine order, to be happy, fulfilled, and doing work that speaks to my inner soul. But new-agey thinking was not my grandfather's thinking.

Historically, my people made it through the atrocities of the Middle Passage then made it through slavery, then Reconstruction—*forty acres and a mule.* Then the civil rights struggle, and now, for some, corporate American assimilation, where you could choose to be anything you wanted to be. I had these thoughts often. I was failing, and falling into a darker and darker place, especially because I was defining success as *work = my innermost personality.* How does anyone function in the midst of all this? Perhaps this was the same overwhelming feeling my sister had when she needed to soothe her mental pain with drugs. She was between a rock and a hard place.

How could I be screwing up this much? I am the successful one in the family. Everyone else is either using drugs or alcohol, or not working. I am the only child left that my mother depends on to save her from *her* poverty. I can't afford to screw up. I have responsibilities. Who is going to be there for my sister's kids, my two brothers' kids? I was supposed to be the independently wealthy one, the success story featured in *Essence.* The more I thought about this, the more I dropped lower and lower into a mental quagmire.

I went to bed that night thinking, "Perhaps this is where I start to degenerate. It has happened to nearly everyone in my family. We're jinxed." My half-sister Sharon and I used to jokingly say that we were all cursed. She and I were both superstitious at times. "Dad's family is cursed," she'd say. "How else can you explain all this deterioration?" We'd always chuckle because it felt like we'd both just spoken an honest truth about why our family was becoming so messed up.

Regularly, we would swap stories about dad. When Sharon was in college, she'd tell friends and her boyfriend, "Y'all don't leave until my dad gets here, because he might not ever show up. I need a Plan B to get home just in case he doesn't come to get me." I knew that feeling all too often. My dad had a habit of not showing up.

Sharon and I have different mothers and didn't grow up in the same household, so she was spared the domestic violence. But we share the same dad, and we both had stories of him not showing up. I was sure that I didn't tell her this one though:

I was 15 years old. My friend's dad was going to take us somewhere, but his van had just broken down, so I asked my dad to take us, and he agreed. It was a gamble, because often he would say yes but never show up. This time, he actually showed up and took us where we wanted to go. But when we were getting out of the car, he said, "Girls, rides aren't free. That will be two dollars each." He held out his hand.

I was mortified as I watched my friends dig into their pockets and purses and hand over money to my father.

I went to bed that night with the blinds slightly cracked so I could see the moonlight peeking in through the darkness. I needed to know that there was always a little light shining somewhere, especially because I didn't know who I could turn to for help.

When I woke up in Craig's house, at age 27, I felt like I had no one. My bed was warm. The house had a morning silence. The air was a little stale in my room, so I went over to the window and opened it. Fresh air found its way in. As I breathed in, I plainly realized that no one had any obligation to me—not friends, and certainly not family. I had to fix my own problems. I had to be an adult. I was no longer the child, who always had to be an emotional adult, growing up in a family of chaos. In the back of my mind, I thought to myself, "When do I get to be a kid? When do I get to have an adolescent period?" On that morning, I told myself, "That time is long gone. Childhood is over."

I remembered the 401(k) plan I had participated in when I was employed by the bank. When I left, several thousand dollars were in that account. So instead of hiding from my phone calls, I picked up the phone and made one.

"Elise, I need to cash in my 401(k)," I said to my stock broker.

"Are you sure? You worked hard to create a savings for yourself, for your future."

I told her I was sure, thinking that I might not have a future.

"Can't you get a part-time job while you run your business? I hate to see you mess with your long-term savings."

"I'm exhausted and I need some relief."

She told me she would, but that I needed to figure out a way to put the money back. "It's important for your retirement, your future." Elise said this like a big sister would. She also seemed like a big sister I wanted. She was about 10 years older, African American, and a successful stock broker.

I didn't think Elise would understand that I have never really asked anyone for anything. In fact, at a young age, I was the one providing the extras for my family. My mother saw me earning money and harped on the fact that I should be buying things for others in the family.

One Christmas, she took me to the mall. I was prepared to buy gifts for my friends at school. I was about to do my shopping, and she said, "Now that you have money, you should buy quality gifts for your brothers and sister."

I gave her a perplexed look. It was my friends at school who were there for me and made me feel loved. I wanted to buy them nice stuff, and so I did.

"Yeah. She went to the mall and bought all of her little school friends very nice gifts," I overheard my mom say to my Aunt Clair. In a tone that seemed to criticize me for being generous with my friends and not putting family first.

I was confused. It was hard to be loyal to a group that was causing me so much pain, especially when I wanted to be loyal to the group that loved me and that I loved in return.

When I cashed in my 401(k), I paid off some of bills in one payment; others I paid just enough to keep the phone calls at bay. It felt good to alleviate some of the pressure. But mostly, I was in desperate need of self-renewal. I was exhausted.

After paying my bills, I looked at the lump sum that I had left over, about $2,000 to live on, and I convinced myself that I could take an overseas trip with my spiritual teacher and group. This was the group that I jokingly refer to as the self-improvement cult that Gia, my mentor, had introduced me to while I was in Pittsburgh. There was an active chapter in Atlanta, and I would regularly attend meditation/self- improvement meetings at someone's house. Also, three times a year, Emanuel, my spiritual teacher, would come from Lexington, Kentucky to Altanta and lecture on a spiritual topic. I would always try to attend.

During the previous six months, this group had been putting together a trip they advertised as the "Power Trip." I never paid attention to it before because I knew that I couldn't afford it, but now, looking at this lump sum of cash and wanting a much-needed break, I signed up for it. It felt like part necessity and part luxury. That's how I could justify spending this money on a trip, when I should have only been focused on trying to stay afloat.

※　※　※

Just as I was packing up my things at Craig's house, the telephone rang. It was a woman from the Atlanta macrobiotic community. She had heard that I was no longer cooking for Craig. She said she knew a woman who also had lymphoma and might want a live-in chef to cook for her. Before I knew it, I moved my belongings out of Craig's place and into the new place.

This all seemed like a gift that had just fallen out of the sky. I was assured that God was giving me a second chance, time to rest and heal before I started cooking for the family. When I moved in, I was able to live there alone for a few weeks while they were away on a vacation. I relished this respite.

When the family returned, I was scheduled to leave for my trip. As our paths crossed, we were able to chat a bit about their vacation and my upcoming trip. Then, the father blurted out, "By the way, we put our house on the market and were looking to move to Mississippi. It probably won't sell right away, but when it does, of course, you can come with us."

CHAPTER 21

THE EXISTENTIAL POWER TRIP

I NEEDED A BREAK from the daily stress of my life. So, on a hot summer day, I boarded a jet at the Atlanta International Airport with just one carry-on—a gray Samsonite bag with two thick maroon stripes that looped around it to make two strong handles. I was met with familiar faces om Atlanta; Lexington, Kentucky; and Pittsburgh. Led by Emanuel (my spiritual teacher), my spiritual group and I were all on our way to meet unfamiliar faces in Istanbul, Budapest, and Cyprus.

This spiritual trip was called the "Power Trip." It was set up so that we could understand the spiritual history where Eastern and Western philosophy met. We were going to study the Ottoman and Byzantine Empires and human history dating back 10,000 years. We were looking at how events and concepts from this region and time period might impact humanity in the future, and where religious themes intersected with secular ones. It didn't make a lot of sense to me, but I wanted to be on this jetliner, going to faraway lands, hoping to stop my fall into an existential abyss.

I buckled myself in nice and tight. I took a deep breath. And I thought about how much I loved traveling. This was the first thing that helped me break my existential fall into an abyss. The possibilities were endless, from meeting the love of my life to experiencing a culture that would change my worldview forever. I felt that being an outsider on purpose was so seductive.

Traveling in a group was new for me. My idea of seeing the world was to go to a strange land by myself and talk to new and different people. My preference was to live with a local family that I didn't know, and learn how they lived. But this was not that kind of trip, and I wasn't in the right mental space for that kind of exploring.

On this journey, there were plenty of people. The woman next to me was named Kathy. I explained to her that I didn't know what I was doing on the trip. I was out of money, and I didn't really have a stable home to return to because the owners were planning to sell their house and move to Mississippi. The family didn't tell me this when I was interviewing for the position.

Kathy listened to me talk about my situation for a while, my voice quivering.

Matter-of-factly and without judgment, Kathy told me that I needed to visualize a different kind of life. In a strange way, I felt that she was showing me unconditional love. Then I had a sense that maybe this entire group loved me unconditionally.

She told me: "I remember when I was broke. I sat on the beach and I cried. Then, I said to God and myself, money is as abundant as grains of sand, and there is no reason for me to not create the kind of bank account I need and want. Then I got to work manifesting my dreams. Now, I own property and I am financially abundant."

Kathy wasn't bragging. She was merely stating facts. She was being inspirational.

I needed some inspiration because suicidal thoughts were flashing through my mind. I thought, "Perhaps it doesn't matter if I have a home or not; this might be the end anyway. Maybe that's why I'm taking this trip, to end my life on a high note, seeing the world before I go. Food and yoga can't save me."

Kathy interrupted my thoughts and said, "Even in my darkest hours, a force reared its head and told me, 'you are capable and you're powerful and you are protected.' Saeeda, many of us on this trip could write you a check to make the financial situation go away. But you are protected, powerful, and capable to create the life you want. Trust me."

Was Kathy right? Was I powerful? Was I capable? Was I protected? Her words made me think about the time when I was a junior in college. I was telling my friend's mother, Carol, who was a psychologist, how tough life had been for me. She responded by saying, "Yeah, your life does sound tough, but no one is going to feel sorry for you. No one is going to feel sorry for the poor black girl who had figured out a way, on her own, to pay for a trip to Taiwan while still in college. I'm not saying your life wasn't bad. But when you can take a once-in-a-lifetime trip to Asia at age 19, they draw the line at feeling sorry for that kind of person. Achievement always trumps hardship."

Was Carol right?

We landed in Istanbul about midday. The Istanbul air felt tight on my skin, as I waited in a comfortable chair with my one bag. The act of just sitting in that chair and watching my travel mates huddled around a baggage claim carousel made me feel like I didn't have a care in the world. When everyone claimed their luggage, we climbed onto a bus and rode into the city toward our hotel, Hotel Nippon.

In Istanbul, the hustle and bustle of the individual was easily seen, except when I saw grown men sitting in frog pose and smoking cigarettes while talking to each other. In my yoga teacher-training classes, the teachers often made reference to different people around the world who sit in frog position.

So when I actually looked out the bus window and saw the men sitting in a squat next to stone walls, smoking cigarettes, drinking hot tea in glasses, and talking to each other, I chuckled to myself and felt like the world offered countless ways to live.

Istanbul was our first and shortest stop. I was excited to be visiting a Muslim country. It was cool to be in a place where everyone recognized my name and had some idea of what it meant, Saeeda—successful and happy. I also chuckled because it reminded me of my dad when he was in one of his black power moments, he'd say, "With a Muslim name, people here [in the U.S.] will always ask you, what kind of name is Saeeda and you'll have to tell them who you are and why we are Muslims, but you can go anywhere else in the world and people will already know. The name Saeeda is common as the name Mary in many places around the world."

Turkey was a great place to be a Muslim woman; it was secular and seemed not to stifle women like other Muslim countries. In Istanbul, I was an exotic figure, unlike in America, where I'd be just another black girl or simply invisible. In Turkey, women and children were pleasantly curious about me. It was nice because, growing up, I had never felt like the beautiful one. But in Istanbul, I felt adored. This was the second thing that helped me break my existential fall.

Being in Turkey reminded me of a conversation I had in Pittsburgh at the Shadyside Arts Festival with a photographer named Emerson. Emerson traveled all over the world taking photos that he would then sell at various festivals in the U.S.. Since he had been around the world more than a dozen times, I asked him: How does a black woman, who is often considered the lowest on the totem pole, travel the world safely?

He explained that when a woman goes to another country, she should immediately find other women to connect with. He felt it was important for the woman traveler to observe how the other women moved throughout their own country. Then he said, emulate them and try to make friends with them, because for the most part, when the woman traveler hangs out with the women of that country, she will be protected.

This fascinated me and gave me insight.

He said that a common mistake for American women is trying to hang out in bars with the men. American women assume the same freedoms and customs apply. They might not like the new limitations, but until they view the country through the eyes of their sisters, they won't know how to stay safe.

※　※　※

In Turkey, I did get some mild young male attention, but I ignored it. The attention that I loved most was when some young girls in headscarves came up to me, speaking no English and gesturing to have their photo taken with me in front of a historic Sultan's Harem Headquarters. I felt honored, respected, and protected.

Leaving Istanbul, known as the port on the Bosporus Straits that straddles Europe and Asia, I boarded a plane for Budapest, the capital of Hungary.

※　※　※

When we landed in Budapest, the statement "You are protected" echoed in my mind. Only having my one carry-on bag allowed me to get out of the terminal quickly, before the rest of the group, and gave me time to sit in the waiting area. To be able to sit and wait in a new country and observe my surroundings felt like I was in control. This feeling of being in control was important to me, since the last 12 months of my time in Atlanta had felt so out of my control.

While sitting, I noticed a maroon Harvard sweatshirt. Inside that sweatshirt was a man, five foot ten inches tall, with a medium athletic build and dark straight hair. He was about 20 years old, with very pale skin. He was sitting two or three empty seats away from me.

"Do you go there?" Turning my head towards him, I asked the question in my most unaccented English, perhaps disguising my city and state of origin.

"Where?" he said, sounding a bit like Zsa Zsa Gabor from that 1970's TV show *Green Arces*, but with a male voice.

I leaned the top half of my body over the steel and vinyl armrest and pointed to the white letters on his sweatshirt.

"I was there over one summer for a six-week business intensive," he said. "Are you a student?"

I returned upright in my seat then, worried that my gesture would be misunderstood as flirting.

"No. I am here with my group visiting Istanbul, Budapest, and Cyprus. Are you going somewhere?"

"No. I'm waiting for my mother. She is coming home from a business trip."

"What kind of business?" I asked curiously.

"She sells steel to other countries," he answered.

Then he said, "My name is Gabon. What's your name?"

I told him my name. Then I got up to shake his hand and sat down next to him. I had imagined that his mother was probably selling steel to the U.S., since Hungary was moving from a communist country to an industrial power of sorts.

"Where are you staying?" Gabon asked me.

"The Thermal Aquincum Hotel. I am here for only six days." I told him that I would be visiting specific sites with my group.

When my friends, my new spiritual family, finally exited from baggage claim and customs, we boarded a bus that would take us to our hotel.

I told them that I had met a young man at the airport and he wanted to know if I could meet up with him.

Some members of the group had noticed me sitting in the waiting area with Gabon, and they encouraged me to go and meet him for lunch. A few of them commented on how cute he was.

The next day, Gabon picked me up at the hotel. A few friends waited with me in the lobby. They were visibly nervous. As he and I left the hotel, a few of them said, in unison, "Be careful." They hollered out, "Just meet for lunch and come right back."

It was nice to have someone display concern and worry about me.

I got into Gabon's car and we drove to a Chinese restaurant. I was not expecting that. He said the Chinese were immigrating to Hungary for better financial opportunities, and many of them had started restaurants.

We talked about general topics: school, work, friends, and social interests. We were similar in many ways. We both had an interest in business and seemed to have a good network of friends. Then he said, "What does your dad do?"

I didn't really have an answer that I wanted to share, but I said, "Uhh. He kinda does whatever he wants, whenever he wants to." I felt a pang of embarrassment, but I continued, "He used to work in the steel mill. He also had a cable job, and then he ran a bar business for many years. But he destroyed all that." I think Gabon saw the pain in my face. He said, "What about brothers and sisters?" I felt my shoulders round down as if a heavy yoke was placed around my neck. I told him that my siblings were addicted to drugs and alcohol. And that my sister has been missing for about a year." I exhaled, feeling the weight of my family's plight traveling with me in Hungary.

Then he said, "Hmmm. Sounds like a typical black American family." Immediately, my stomach concaved as if I was being punched in the gut. I wanted to go back to the hotel. I had lost my appetite. I barely sipped my cherry soup waiting for him to finish, trying not to show my hurt. I had never eaten cherry soup before, but was too devastated to adventure into something new.

Gabon returned me to the hotel in one piece, but my heart was broken by the truth of his statement regarding my family. This was what Gabon had seen in American movies and media, and my family confirmed his observations.

I went to bed that night knowing that what he said was painful, but he wasn't trying to be malicious. So, I decided put my hurt feelings aside and discover what else the trip had to offer.

The next day Gabon called again asking if I could get away on Saturday. He said that he would like to introduce me to his girlfriend, Edit. "We can all have dinner and go to a dance club." He suggested.

When Gabon picked me up this time he arrived with his girlfriend and a slightly older man. It was late afternoon. After we had been riding in the car for about 15 minutes, Gabon announced that his friend in the car, a local Hungarian rock star, wanted to know if we wanted to take a helicopter ride over the city.

Edit and I, sitting in the back seat, looked at each other and giggled like we were childhood friends. We both said "yeah," almost in unison.

Neither of us had been in a helicopter before, and as we approached the local airport, I was concerned that I was not dressed appropriately for the wind. We got into the helicopter, a man outside the aircraft closed the door behind us, and sounds from the motor and wind became harsher. We lifted off and up, and at that moment I felt like Charlie, in the movie *Willy Wonka and the Chocolate Factory*, when he got into the elevator after seeing some weird and delightful things in the factory. The elevator went up and up and up. It surpassed all the floors in the building and broke through the glass ceiling. I felt both the fear and excitement of it all. The sounds inside the helicopter seemed to be muted as I gazed out over the city. The historic architecture of Parliament, the Danube River, and stone towers seemed magical. This was the third thing that broke my existential fall into darkness.

After the helicopter ride, we all went to dinner, and another one of Gabon's friends met up with us. She was a woman from Cuba who taught Latin dance. Gabon really wanted us to meet, thinking we would have so much in common because we were both black. But there was one problem. I didn't speak Spanish, and she didn't speak English. He was amazed that he had to translate her broken Hungarian into English and my English into Hungarian.

Later that night we went to a dance club, where the rock star got us all in for free and we met up with two more people; one was a hairstylist and she could not get over my short hairstyle. She commented that I was brave to wear such a style, and she kept complimenting me on the shape of my head while we danced all night.

On the dance floor, Gabon didn't need to translate for Harriet, the black Cuban, or me, the black American. We were both descendants from Africa dancing with the same rhythms that survived the Middle Passage. Dancing with her and with the Hungarians, I felt like the music of life would help me survive my rites of passage.

I made it back to the hotel, and with the success of the night with my new friends once again I started to feel more protected and even more trusting toward life. And because of the love that I felt from my spiritual group, I started to feel love and care from a family. I participated in all the prayers and rituals with my group. I had most of my meals with them and did most social outings with them. My favorite outing was going to the opera to see *King Lear* in Italian, which was then translated into Hungarian. Even with my limited Shakespearean knowledge, I still understood what was happening.

I left Budapest with a good feeling: "Maybe life does work out."

❋   ❋   ❋

With one more stop, I boarded the plane to Cyprus. I had never even heard of Cyprus before this trip—again, another gaping hole in my primary and secondary education. I was told that there was a Greek side and a Turkish side, and that we were to fly in on one side and travel by bus across the island to the other side. This was the birthplace of Aphrodite—the goddess of love.

We landed in Cyprus before sunrise. Blue water surrounded our hotel. I checked into my room and, instead of lying down to rest like I usually do on long trips, I headed for the beach.

The slow sunrise was beginning to reflect the warmth of the Mediterranean Sea. I wondered if the goddess of love rose out of these waters with the same grace as this sun.

I was wearing white cotton pants and a shirt to match. The loose fabric billowed in the wind, kissing my darkened skin as it brushed against me. I held prayer position with thumbs touching my heart, my palms pushed against one other. I wanted to salute this Cyprian sun.

Inhale one. I said a silent prayer. Exhale. I lowered my arms. Inhale two. My arms went up toward the heavens as I gently arched my back. Exhale three, with a deep fold forward from my hips, I was humbled toward the earth. Inhale four, I lunged my right leg back, letting the knee rest on the ground. As my tears began to flow down, I looked up at the sun and asked, "Who am I? What's my true purpose?"

Holding my breath, position five, I held plank. Lowering my knees, chest, and chin to the ground, position six, like a lowly inchworm, I completely submitted to the will of the divine, or to the will of Allah. I prostrated to the sun, like an ancient pagan from Cyprus, a Muslim making salaat, or a Hindu yogi practicing Hatha yoga—all of these now a part of my spiritual heritage.

Snaking into cobra, inhale seven, I opened my heart again to the sea and filled my lungs with fresh air. Exhaling eight, I moved into downward dog. I paused and held the posture, looking at the world and water upside down. Then I closed my eyes, feeling the tension release from my calves and shins. I emptied my lungs, flattened my belly, and felt my hands and toes lock into the earth.

I felt like I was being born again.

Then I concluded with another lunge, inhale nine, forward fold, exhale ten, slow arch backwards, inhale eleven, and then a deep exhale twelve, a strong mountain pose. I stood still, with my thumbs resting on my elevated heartbeat—prayer position.

After doing sun salutes in Cyprus, I felt like my body was drawing mystical triangles or tetrahedrons, each movement connecting my body to the heavens and then again to the earth. In Cyprus, I still didn't have a home, but I did feel like I belonged somewhere. From the moment I set my bag down in my room, the water coaxed me to its shore to participate in the beginning of emotionally building my foundation, my home. But physically, where would that home be?

✹   ✹   ✹

Two monolithic structures protruded from the Mediterranean Sea and the space that resided between those two big rocks was said to be where mighty Aphrodite was born.

Cyprus had human history dating back 10,000 years. It was here that my Taoist, Chinese medicine philosophy became even more grounded.

On our first day of sightseeing in Cyprus, I stood in an open, cave-like structure. The multicolored clay and sea air smelled both historical and fresh. We all stood around our tour guide, a thirty-something, tanned, earthy-looking woman with curly blonde hair. We leaned forward, our hands resting on the wooden fence surrounding the structure, as we listened to her explain the symbolism of the mosaic embedded in the floor.

The mosaic depicted the four seasons, and the energy that the people of 10,000 years ago believed each season to have. It sounded a lot like the 5,000-year-old Taoist philosophy, except that it was 10,000 years old. It was comforting seeing life repeat itself, evolve, and grow. It made it all the more meaningful. We humans were always trying to practice a practical as well as spiritual way of living. We human beings connected with the things we understood, and honored the things we didn't understand.

I continued to listen to the lecture. The tour guide referenced different symbols in the open cave. There were symbols and pictures that depicted a virgin birth. She explained that the story of Christ was not the only virgin birth story, and the way she said the word "story" made me think that perhaps she did not believe that the Christ story was real. To her, it was just that, a story. Then she said, "There are many traditions that use the virgin birth story."

My face must have looked stupefied because my mind was saying, "You don't know anything about the world or history." I had never heard that said before. "The virgin birth story is older than Christ? Did everyone know that the Christ story wasn't that unique?" I thought. I was too embarrassed to ask the guide or my travel mates what they knew.

The tour guide went on, "The cross also appeared before Christ. It has a long history. One of the earliest explanations for the cross was simply as a symbol bringing union between two polarities," she added. Goosebumps appeared on my arms because this was exactly how I viewed my yoga and food practice.

I felt ignorant, but it also freed me up a bit. I realized that everything evolved and oftentimes repeated itself like the virgin birth story. Life was more than my little world of successes and failures. Maybe my life would also be an evolution of stories; some would repeat, and some would evolve.

The next day we went to the historic spot where the goddess of love was born—Aphrodite. I, of course, envisioned an AFROdite. I was learning that being on the Cyprus Island, we were smack dab in the middle of the earth. Cyprians like to tell you that. Literally, we were between Europe, Asia, and Africa, and its geographical position easily explained why this crossroads had a turbulent past. I understood that, being in the middle of it all and having turbulence follow. That was exactly what I felt about my world. I was on the margins of everything meta-geographically. I was in the middle of rich and poor, drug addicts and physicians, illness and wellness, educated and uneducated; the list could go on. But I had another thought while I was absorbing the history of Aphrodite; I pictured her wearing a small, shortcut Afro like mine. I smiled and then chuckled to myself. It was nice to laugh for a change.

Cyprus may have been divided between the Greek and Turkish sides, but because I identified with it as the birthplace of the goddess of love, it represented for me a place with the healing powers of love.

We listened to the Aphrodite lectures and did a prayer ritual there. We went for a walk afterwards, and as I was walking a little distance away from the pack in a meditative stroll, Kathy called out my name. She walked toward me with the confidence of a queen. Her body was athletic, yet soft. Her hands cupped, one hand was over the other, as if she had just caught a firefly. Then she extended her arms out in my direction.

"I have a gift for you," she said smiling.

"Oh," I said, pleasantly surprised. She lifted her right hand as if she was taking the lid off of a light blue Tiffany gift box. It was a rock. I took it from her and gently ran my fingers over it. On the topside, it was smooth and tanned with engraved dark lines. It appeared softly wrinkled. Underneath, my fingertips caressed the rough sandy texture. Being sharp on one end and smooth to the touch on the other, it felt like it could be an ancient cooking or carving tool. I didn't want to appear ungrateful, so I smiled and put some light behind my eyes and said, "Thank you, Kathy!"

"Saeeda, let me tell you what this is," she said, excitedly, apparently guessing that I thought it was just a rock. "It is an ancient turtle. I was walking along and saw it standing in the middle of my path, slowly moving as turtles do." She was giggling. "This rock is your symbol. It is a turtle, and a turtle is never without a home. It carries his home with him all the time. You will always have a home, no matter where you go. You are protected."

The inside of my nose started to tingle and my eyes welled up. I put the turtle-rock on my heart and smiled. I looked into her blue eyes, and then opened my arms wide, holding onto the turtle-rock, gesturing for Kathy to come toward me so I could squeeze her tight. I hugged her while taking a long, deep breath. I felt whole.

At the end of the trip, I boarded the plane knowing that I no longer wanted to vanish into that existential abyss, and that my falling into it had stopped. I felt capable and protected.

Much in the same way that Savasana gave me a trust in life, this trip gave me a sense of a protected life, a life that would be filled with unpredictable adventure and healing.

As the plane jetted toward the sky, I thought: "I do have a home; I just don't know where it is yet."

CHAPTER 22

ALMOST MISSISSIPPI

WHEN I EMERGED FROM BAGGAGE CLAIM, Atlanta's night air blew hot on my skin. The atmosphere and the air smelled of struggle.

With my single carry-on bag in one hand and the turtle-rock that Kathy had given me in the other, I went to the curb to meet my co-worker from Peachtree Center Athletic Club. Tony was a fitness trainer. He offered to make one month's car payment in exchange for using my black Nissan Sentra for three weeks. I'd felt grateful, as it was one less bill for me to worry about. Besides, it was easy; I trusted him.

I opened the car door to the backseat and put my gray bag down. I felt a little culture shock. We exchanged polite chitchat, and I noticed that my car was nicely detailed. The dashboard sparkled. Perhaps it was a symbol that my life was about to shine again. Tony detailed my car, and perhaps the trip detailed my spirit.

We drove into downtown Atlanta to drop him off at Peachtree Center Athletic Club. He got out of the car and I hugged him a thank you goodbye. Then I got back in the car and headed toward what was my new home.

My stomach churned a bit when I glanced into the rearview mirror, watching the center of Atlanta get smaller and smaller. I merged from Highway 75 onto Highway 85, and then I drove past perimeter 280. When I glanced in the rearview mirror again, I could no longer see the bright skyline.

I told myself, "This is meant to be. You barely put any effort into finding this new live-in situation with this new family. They seemed like nice enough people, and maybe your journey does include moving to Mississippi."

But for the present, I kept driving to the suburb outside of Atlanta where they lived. It was nighttime, and the highway grew blacker and blacker. The farther I drove out into the suburbs, the darker it became—with only stars and a few headlights in the darkness. I tried to think positively about my situation.

I drove my car to my new, gated community. It was said that the famous football player who had dated Left-Eye, from the girl group T.L.C., lived in this same community. It was weird for me to move so far from the main city and urban life. I didn't know exactly how I felt about needing a key, a security gate code, and a familiar nod to the security guard sitting in a watch booth just to get in and out of the house. These things didn't help me feel protected or free.

I walked into the house with my bag and turtle-rock. It was picture-perfect. But it was different from Nancy's house, which was the dilapidated house my student Nancy remodeled to perfection. The best way I can describe it was that Nancy's house seemed authentic, while April's house felt like keeping up with the Joneses' or What would the neighbors think? Don't get me wrong. It was beautiful, but manufactured beauty. Nevertheless, I had agreed to try this house and this family.

It was late when I arrived. I softly let myself in and went straight to bed.

The next morning after waking up in a beautiful bed and showering in a modern floral bathroom, I felt timid about what to do. I talked with April, the woman of the house, about what she wanted. I made a few dishes, including a kabocha squash pie with oatmeal crust. The pie was specifically for her husband and five-year-old daughter—my way of making something healthy and sweet for the family. However, the pie was off limits to April because I used a simple sugar, brown rice syrup, and that could enhance the growth of her cancer cells. But when she saw it, she allowed herself one forkful. "Yum. I won't eat any more, but yum. This is good."

After a few days, I finally settled into my role. But it was not to last. I learned that the house had sold. Everything was happening so fast; I expected it to take six months or so. I was invited to come to Mississippi.

For the next few days, my life followed a rhythm: I made good food, ate a few meals with the family, and had some good conversations with April about her cancer and healing. But it was all interrupted.

"Saeeda, can I speak to you for a minute?" Mr. Smith said one evening.

"Sure," I responded.

"Let's go outside on the back deck."

During the short walk to the deck, there was a long pause. Mr. Smith and I both sat down, and I began to shake.

"I went to get a new phone line in Mississippi, and I was told there is an outstanding bill, totaling $213.97."

I started to cry. I had inadvertently let my phone bill lapse. It was still in his name, and I was thinking I would take care of it when I returned from my trip. I was embarrassed because it looked like I was deliberately taking advantage of them, when in reality it was just an oversight.

"...and I want you to pay me by the end of the week, and I want cash!" Mr. Smith demanded.

Damn! I hadn't meant to hurt this family, and especially not with a phone bill.

But I was so unsure of myself. Was I sabotaging myself? Was I mad that they didn't tell me about the house being for sale when I interviewed? Did I just not give a fuck anymore?

I packed up my life there as quickly as I had unpacked it.

When my yoga checks came in, I paid him in cash. I said my sad goodbyes to April, her daughter, and Mr. Smith. Feelings were hurt all around.

With the last bits of my belongings packed in my car, I got on the highway. I was not headed to Mississippi. Instead, I went to my friend Stacey's house, again, for a quick refuge. Part of me was relieved. Part of me was embarrassed for botching up this situation. Part of me still felt that I had a protected life. But mostly, I felt sad and scared.

CHAPTER 23

BUT I AM NOT
YOUR MOTHER

AT STACEY'S HOUSE, I woke up in a pitch-black room. Nothing stirred; I felt like I was in one of those sensory deprivation flotation tanks, minus the water.

The room had a north-facing window, but it also had window blinds that blocked out any incoming light. With no noise or light, I felt like I was suspended on Pink Floyd's *Dark Side of the Moon.* I started to let that music play inside my head.

Alone in that dark room, I thought about the first time I stayed there, two years beforehand. I was full of magic and hope then. Atlanta was full of possibilities.

I lifted up from my already low-to-the-ground foam mattress bed. I found something to eat in the kitchen and turned on the TV. After a day of watching dumb TV, I turned on Oprah. I was hoping Oprah would give me some inspiration as she had done when I was in college. But mostly, I marinated in my own personal failures and lack of direction. I couldn't even make myself do sun salutes or cook anything substantial.

I had no idea that this last experience would immobilize me, especially after such a positive international trip.

Late afternoon, I took a bath, where I created my own flotation tank. Sitting in the hot water, my mind drifted to Stacey. Even though Stacey and I were the same age, her life was at a different level. She was already in the middle class and grounded in its values. She was able to build a nice starter home for herself with property given to her by her dad. Instead of being jealous, I was fascinated. I was always curious about how other people lived and made decisions, and what influenced those decisions.

Stacey's dad constructed things with his property and education, but my dad deconstructed things. My dad could have had my grandfather's modest property to manage, but it all seemed downhill after he, at age 21, married my mother when she was 16. My father lived a different kind of life than the one he said he wanted to live.

My father was the son of two people who built a decent lower-middle-class lifestyle. My grandparents bought a small starter house in a countryside neighborhood near a suburb called North Versailles, east of Pittsburgh. It had a rural feeling to it: not too many people, and houses not too close together. Trees, grass, and fresh air were plentiful, so plentiful that my grandfather was able to plant a southern-style garden every year. Next to my grandparents' home, my grandfather and his brother George built another small house. These were good beginnings for young black men who migrated from the south. My grandparents seemed to be doing okay, but their marriage appeared loveless at times. My dad confessed to my mother that he often witnessed my grandfather beating my grandmother. My dad pledged to my mother not to be that kind of man, telling her that he wouldn't do that to anyone.

When my mom told me all that, I felt angry, confused, and deeply saddened. My dad had wanted to do better, but didn't do better. In fact, he did worse than my grandfather. I wondered if I would do worse than my parents and my grandparents.

Floating in the warm tub, I remembered hearing my mom tell me that my dad never wanted to abuse his wife. Where did it all go so wrong? Was James Baldwin right? "Children have never been very good at listening to their elders, but they have never failed to imitate them."

My family was complicated and confusing. I know that my dad wanted to do better by me, but couldn't.

I am 11 years old. I am on a rare visit at my dad's house, the bar-house he owned. There was a mahogany door that separated the house from the bar. I had to go into the bar around 9:00 P.M. in the evening to ask my dad a question. I opened the door, got to the first landing, and saw that he was at the end of the bar near the street entrance. I looked over and saw my father talking and gesturing firmly at some guy, and then, all of a sudden in slow motion, he leaned back, drew a fist, and hit the guy square in the jaw. And just like in a boxing match, the crowd went wild and the guy was flat on the floor.

I was thinking it could have been worse, because my father owned a gun and kept it with or near him for unsuspecting bar trouble.

Later, the man fought and took my dad to court. I was called in to testify. "Dad, what should I tell the judge?" I was ready to say whatever my father wanted me to say. Strangely enough, I wanted to please him.

"Tell the truth," he said knowing that what I might say could hurt him. He seemed resolved that he had done wrong.

I testified. I told what I had seen. My dad had to pay all of the guy's dental bills, and then some.

I sat in the bath. I turned on more hot water to heat up the water, which had started to go cold. I figured that I was statistically doomed. I had read that children of domestic violence were likely to be victims of physical, mental, or sexual abuse. These children also had increased risk of drug and alcohol abuse, and even of committing crime.

I was probably doubly doomed, since it was then two generations of domestic violence, and who knows what beatings my ancestors before that had to take. I wondered if the true fight is the fight we have within ourselves to find peace, but our pain is what often wins. I continued staying at Stacey's house, and I felt more and more hopeless each day. After Stacey went off to work, I repeated my new routine. I crawled out of bed, found something to eat, and watched dumb TV.

One day Stacey, perhaps tired of seeing me so sad, came home with a rose for me. It brought a smile to my face. It was like seeing a rainbow in the midst of a storm.

"Stacey, thank you for being so good to me. You nurture me like a mom," I said softly.

Stacey looked at me kindly. Our brown eyes locked, and she said, "But I am not your mother."

I felt a chill crawl up my back like a centipede.

Stacey was right. It was not her responsibility to nurse me back to health, even though her hospitality was impeccable.

I didn't need to be reminded that there was no one in this world who had any obligation toward me. Where did someone like me go when broken? I felt like I needed my real mother, but I remembered her explosive emotional outbursts any time me or one of my siblings disappointed her. I just wanted to be accepted unconditionally, not broken down further.

I always had my own money, made good grades, had good friends. I had never really shown weakness or neediness. Even though my birth order was next to youngest, I felt like the eldest child, even more mature than my parents. But at that point in my life, I was the weakest and terrified to face my mother. Yet, I didn't see any other option.

I knew one thing for sure, Stacey was right; she was not my mother. So who was?

CHAPTER 24

AN ATYPICAL PRODIGAL DAUGHTER

IT WAS SEPTEMBER 1995—over a year since I had seen my mother. I had flown to Pittsburgh, where the fall weather was a lot colder than the weather in Atlanta.

I stood on the corner of Beaver and Butler streets and looked at the familiar old white house. The lawn sloped downward. The grass needed to be watered—or, in Pittsburghese, one would say "The grass needs watered." But as I looked around this financially depressed area, it was clear that watering the grass was not anyone's priority.

With my same bag in hand that I had taken on the Power Trip and my turtle-rock inside, I walked toward the stone stairs that led to the front door. I stood at the bottom of those stairs, only two short flights. I could see the white metal screen door and the rickety letter-sized mailbox, a muted red color in need of paint. The house looked the same as it did on the day my mother purchased it—dim and in need of repair.

Although it wasn't remodeled like Nancy's Atlanta home, this house did have some similarities. It was a symbol of blood, sweat, and tears.

Nancy's house yielded a better aesthetic return, but my mother's house yielded a shelter for a broken woman, a single mother trying to possess something of value in the world. It was a symbol that said she did something good for herself. All my life, I knew how much my mom needed her life to turn out "good," as she would state it.

I don't know if this knowledge of "life turning out good" started the day my parents separated, or the day my paternal grandfather evicted my mother, my younger brother, and me from our home.

With my bag in hand, I opened the door. My mother greeted me with a light hug and a look of disgust. I expected as much, considering it was an unwritten rule for all of my mother's children: *Don't come around here needing and wanting anything because I ain't got it.*

Defenses, on both sides, went up.

❋   ❋   ❋

The best way I can describe returning to my mother's house would be in the same way pet experts tell cat owners about introducing a new cat into a home that already has an older veteran cat. They say that it can be tricky, because you have to take many factors into consideration—*territory, age, background, and the personalities of each cat.*

I wish I had read an article about that before I went back to my mother's house; it might have helped my situation. I would have known to set up a comfortable "safe room" for myself. Instead, I didn't know where to sleep, my old bedroom or the couch. I went to my old room, which was filled with my old bedroom furniture and had a drafty ceiling and a dim overhead light. I put my bag down and went into the living room. I sat on the couch and thought that this might be a better place to retire. The living room had a warmer feeling than the bedroom. I sat on the 15-year old secondhand couch and looked up at my senior graduation picture. My face was puffy in the picture because I had dental work done a few days before, and that was the last day the photos could be taken. The light blue background and my puffy face, no smile, summed up how I felt about my seventeenth year—I had survived life thus far, but it was not pretty.

When I gave my favorite high school teacher, Mr. Nee, a photo, he asked me why I wasn't smiling.

I shrugged and said, "I didn't feel like smiling that day."

I looked up at my photo and stared at all the family's high school graduation photos. I decided to stay on the couch, surrounded by my phantom family, and the real support I felt against my back from the somewhat firm 20-inch sofa cushions. I sat there thinking that these cushions might be the only support I would receive here in my mother's house.

The next day, I woke up on the couch. I sneezed uncontrollably and I picked up the same routine I had at Stacey's house, minus the bath. I watched dumb TV, then *Oprah,* and then ate cold cereal and ordered cheap pizza.

That first afternoon, while my mother was at work driving the school bus, I laid down on my mom's couch and took a good look around my new sleeping quarters. Bits of the fabric were worn out in the couch, so much that I could see part of the wooden frame. I stared at the things in the living room—the Goodwill-purchased crocheted blanket, the vintage television that didn't work, the only coffee table I had ever known my family to possess. If that coffee table could talk, it would have told a painful tale.

Next, my eyes became fixated on a royal blue velvet chair. The chair looked like new, but it must have been 12 years old, even older because my mother bought it secondhand. I remembered when she purchased the chair. Its seat cushion had the stuffing oozing out of it. You could see the spring coils. It was a dingy beige floral fabric. It had scratched up wooden legs. The chair looked like it had been in a fight and lost.

My mother, at the time of purchasing the tattered thrift store chair, was taking reupholstery classes. She wanted to learn a useful trade that could add extra income to her work in the bar my parents owned. My mother knew how to sew clothes and wanted to learn how to fix up furniture.

After my mother started that chair project, she would show us pictures every few weeks documenting her progress. I remember when she finished it. On that day, I thought to myself, "This woman knows how to transform a beaten down object into a work of art." I must have been six or seven years old.

Next, I sat up and shifted my eyes from the blue chair that never seemed to age. Then through the archway that separated the living room from the dining room, I gazed at the dining room table and chairs. This was also a secondhand furniture set. I remembered the seat cushions had been ripped, but mostly the wood was badly scratched. My mother again performed magic. The seat cushions were replaced with a sturdy, bright teal woven fabric. The material was wool. The wood was re-stained to a dark, earthy color. When I rubbed my hand along the finished wood, it felt like a furniture set that I would touch when walking through the furniture section of Gimbel's department store at the mall.

I laid back down, my back against the seat cushions. I prayed, "God, I need the mother that can turn these frayed furniture pieces into functional objects, not the mother that was so beaten down that our home felt like a refugee camp for women and children surviving domestic violence. I need the mother who can make a home for her children in the same way Nancy made a home for herself. I don't need the frightened woman who needs her kids to take care of her; I need the woman who can sew two pieces of cloth together into a stylish, wearable outfit like she did when I was in the fourth grade and needed a Halloween costume."

After praying, I turned on the TV.

My mother and I had our routine. She'd wake up early and go to work. I would slowly wake and examine my life. She'd come home for a quick lunch, then go back to work. Some nights she would go bowling or attend some kind of academic class. We didn't ignore each other, but we also didn't talk much. Funny, how when there is so much to talk about, hardly anything is said.

At night when my mother came home, we would have simple conversation. I told her about Nancy and the house she remodeled, week-by-week. But, overall, we didn't know what to say to each other. We were, like that cat expert said, sniffing around each other through small holes left unguarded. At night, we retreated to opposite sides of the house. My mother was in the upstairs north bedroom, and I was in the downstairs far south living room. Suspicious goodnights were exchanged.

On the third day, I woke up on the couch, once again sneezing my head off. I repeated my daily routine. I made sure the curtains were tightly shut so very little light could get through during the day. My daily schedule was being set by what TV show came on at what time. The news at 12:00 noon, *Family Feud* at 12:30 P.M., *All My Children* at 1:00 P.M., *Guiding Light* at 3:00 P.M., *Oprah* at 4:00 P.M. , the local news at 6:00 P.M., *Jeopardy* at 7:00 p.m., *Wheel of Fortune* at 7:30 P.M., some sitcom or TV movie at 8:00 P.M., and asleep by 11:00 P.M.

On the fourth day, again I woke up sneezing. It was the weekend. I overheard my mother on the phone, "Yeah, that's her. She sneezes like that every morning." By the way she was speaking on the phone, I knew that she was talking to my Aunty Clair. They talked on the phone every day. My mother also had a familiar tone that I recognized. The tone was, whatever poor health you are experiencing right now, it better not cost me money or time. It was not the June Cleaver, "Ward, I better go and check on the Beav," tone.

I sat up and looked at the walls. There were cracks in them. The ivory-colored curtains were graying. The IBM electric typewriter was on a metal cart with wheels. "Which mother lives here? The refugee mother, or the restoration mother?" I slid back down into sleep mode and waited for her to leave the house so I could continue my depression routine.

On the fifth day, I woke up sneezing. I hadn't showered in days. My neatly close-cut signature hairstyle was no longer a low-to-the-scalp Afro. It was a scare-fro, like the one Don King wore into the boxing arena, wild. Both my pajamas and my body had an odor. I walked upstairs to shower and freshen up.

As I was getting dressed, I stumbled upon my turtle-stone in my bag. I thought of Kathy, who offered to connect with me whenever I decided to come to town. I called her.

"Hello. Kathy? I'm in Pittsburgh. Everything fell apart. That family moved to Mississippi and I let go of all my other clients that I had in Atlanta and came to Pittsburgh to figure out my life."

"Saeeda, here's what you do. Listen. Give me your address. I am going to send you something. I know the kind of space you're in. When you get my package, call me." Kathy said this with the same enthusiasm she had when she gave me the turtle-rock. "Sorry that I can't talk right now. We'll talk later."

Without fail, the next day I woke up sneezing but I also heard the mailman. I went to the mailbox, and Kathy's package was there. This was back at the time when the post office tried to deliver mail in the same city overnight. I opened it, and inside were two books, *Think and Grow Rich*, by Napoleon Hill and *The Greatest Salesman in the World*, by Og Mandino. I called her, immediately.

She told me to read *The Greatest Salesman in the World* first. I took a long shower, got dressed, grabbed my turtle-rock from the suitcase, and placed the rock on the coffee table. For the first time since I had been staying at my mother's house, I didn't turn on the TV. I sat down on the couch and opened to page one.

Hafid lingered before the bronze mirror and studied his reflection image in the polished metal.

"Hafid," I thought. "That name is close to my name, Hafiz." Perhaps this was a sign. It was rare that I would open a book and read an Arabic or Muslim name. Most names were European.

I reread the first sentence. It gave me the same feeling I had when I was in college and befriended an elderly woman in Philadelphia who said to me, "Your name is Hafiz, Saeeda Hafiz? Hafiz like the Persian poet Hafiz?"

I didn't know the Persian poet, but when she started to describe him as a master Sufi who writes about love for the divine by using wine and the wine bringer as symbols to explain his intoxication, I too felt a mysterious satisfying inebriation.

This was unlike when my dad talked about our name, Hafiz, saying the name means "master," one who masters or memorizes the Qu'ran. Then he further explained that the name Hafiz made white America notice that he was not accepting the slave names forced upon us. But my father taking on this name angered my grandfather, who saw it as a blatant rejection of him, not the white man.

I reread the sentence again. Then I read the next line, and then the next line. I was off and running. The story was a quick read. I read the whole thing in one sitting. I called Kathy that night.

"It was an interesting story." I said. "It made me smile quite a bit."

"The affirmations really do work. You should try them, since you are feeling so down. For instance, the affirmation, *I will greet this day with love in my heart*," really helped me when I was starting to build my business and rebuild my life after my divorce. Now start the second book. Keep reading inspirational stories. It will really lift you up."

I went to bed that night, again on the couch, feeling a little less depressed, and I felt a whisper of hope in my heart. Kathy's action of love was the kind of mothering I had craved.

The next day, I woke up to the phone ringing. My best friend Buddy was calling. He asked if I had been asleep, and he was right. He reminded me that Pittsburgh makes me depressed.

Then I started sneezing. "Are you sick, too?"

I told him no, but that every morning I wake up sneezing. Then as I was talking to him, I realized that it was my allergies. I am allergic to dust and mold. My mom's house was damp, and the rooms were cold. The carpet was frayed, and there was so much clutter.

"I gotta get out of here." Then Buddy graciously invited me to come visit him in Washington D.C. He was there on business. When I told him that I didn't have any money, he offered to pay my fare as an early birthday present. He invited me to come to the hotel and just chill out. He said I could order room service, take those long baths, and enjoy the fact that housekeeping comes every day—no dust, dampness, or mold.

Then he confessed that he and his partner Manuel and just broken up and he needed someone to talk to as well.

※　　※　　※

A few days later, I boarded an Amtrak train at the newly renovated train depot in downtown Pittsburgh.

On the train to Washington D.C., I saw my life's history moving from one sad memory to the next.

I thought long and hard about the state of my nuclear family and how it felt more like a nuclear explosion, all of our lives scattered in toxic radio-active particles emitting poisonous ions.

The latest reports on my dad were that he was experimenting with crack cocaine. He had used different kinds of drugs and couldn't believe crack was as powerful as people had said. So, as a challenge to himself, he started smoking it, too.

This should be shocking, but it was coming from the same man who once had faked his own death to see how people would react. I will never forget telling my boss at the bank that my dad was dead. My boss coached me along in my grief as I searched for meaning. Then I found out months later that he was alive and well in Cleveland. It was some kind of test or hoax. When I explained it to my boss, he must have thought that I was a freak and a liar.

My sister, then with a total of six children, was nowhere to be found.

My older brother was destroying his life. He went from college graduate to radio announcer/journalist to fireman to divorced-deadbeat-dad-crack-addict to father of three children.

My younger brother was struggling from job to job, with alcohol problems sprouting up in between. He was losing touch with his daughter, which was breaking his heart.

Now, my life was coming undone.

In a D.C. hotel room, I woke up between Egyptian cotton sheets, 600-thread count. The day before, I didn't know the meaning of a thread count.

The light streamed through the window. I listened to my friend Buddy take a shower, while the smell of sandalwood traveled underneath the bathroom door. I chuckled to myself and thought about how he didn't have those fancy soaps before he came out. Since he had come out as gay, I realized, he had become more stylish.

I looked around the room at the wooden desk, the small brass desk lamp with the green lampshade, and the mirrored closet door. Yesterday, I had awakened in my mother's living room on the couch, sneezing my head off. Today, I wasn't sneezing and my surroundings were much improved.

As I listened to the water go down the drain in the shower, I couldn't help but think that the same force of gravity that was draining that water was the same force pulling me down. I was convinced that it was some dark force dragging my family down. I felt doomed, so I put the soft feath-erlike pillow over my face and went into a deep sleep.

"Hey! Wake up!" Buddy was standing in the open doorway wearing a slick dark suit and Kenneth Cole shoes. He was all ready to leave for work. "I wanna know, *What sustains you when all else fails?*"

"What?!" I said, as I turned over, half waking up. "Go to work. Leave me alone."

"I'm serious. When we go to dinner tonight, I wanna know, *What sustains you when all else fails?*"

When I finally woke up, I sat up in bed, and that question floated around my head and in my brain like an illuminated fairy. Of course my belief in God is what sustains, but as soon as I said that aloud it didn't feel true. If that wasn't the truth, what did sustain me?

I took a shower, a long hot one, thinking the steam would help reveal what sustained me. The shower was great, but it didn't help me produce an answer.

I unfolded my yoga mat. I hadn't done yoga in many weeks. I did slow sun salutations, thinking that as I held each posture I might hear that same voice that I had heard in my first yoga class. Perhaps that voice would tell me what sustains me when all else fails. I did round after round, but no voice spoke to me.

I sat down to meditate. I also hadn't meditated in weeks, but surely this would be where the answer would come. I stared into blackness, softly repeating Om. I started to feel more at peace, but I was not any clearer on what sustained me.

I left the hotel room and went for a walk. I found a restaurant that served some healthy items. I had a veggie sandwich on whole grain bread. I practiced my meditation chewing techniques, thinking perhaps this would put me in touch with my sustainability core. The chewing was very relaxing, but that was all it was.

I returned to the hotel for a nap and woke up disappointed. In the past, my dreams had always helped me solve my soul-searching queries. Exasperated, I began to run some bath water. I called room service to bring me two cups of table salt. Waiting, exasperated, I hollered out,

"What *does* sustain me when all else fails?"

Then, a knock on the door, and a male voice said, "Room service."

I laughed. I added the two cups of salt to the almost scalding water. I slowly got in. I wrapped two dry towels around my shoulders to contain the heat. Submerged and sweating, I asked again, softly. Staring at the shiny metal faucet, I could see my distorted reflection. I closed my eyes, and my mind whispered, "The present moment. The present moment is what sustains you when all else fails." I continued sweating and felt relieved. "Taking an authentic action in the present moment is what will always sustain you." Gentle tears fell from my eyes. PRESENT

I took my time getting ready to meet Buddy for dinner because I wanted to savor the richness of that statement, repeating to myself, *The present moment is what sustains me when all else fails.*

At dinner, Buddy talked a bit about his job appraising commercial real estate. He opened up about his heartbreak with Manuel. We ate well. He enjoyed a glass of wine and a cocktail. Then he looked at me and asked, "Do you have an answer for me?"

"Yep. The present moment is what sustains me."

I told Buddy about my day and what had happened, and I concluded with, "Now, I know what the phrase *All Men are Created Equal* means to me. We all have the same opportunity in the present moment to choose how any event will make us think, feel, and act. We don't all get the same kind of life, but mostly everyone has this ability to choose in the present moment."

Buddy smiled, and said, "Aw, Bunky," using our pet name for each other.

"I might not be doing well at my business, and it might be failing, but that doesn't mean that I'm worthless. I might come from a family with lots of unfortunate situations, but that does not mean that I don't have value. I can choose different thoughts, words, deeds, and intentions that will redefine my situation." I paused. "I am curious. Where did you get that question anyway?"

"When Manuel broke up with me, I was falling, spiraling down, fast. Once when I was at a Radical Faerie meeting, someone read this famous Native American poem called "The Invitation." Before getting on the train from NYC to D.C. afterward, I grabbed it. I wanted to think about what would sustain me now that my life with Manuel is over."

✻　✻　✻

After three days in D.C., I returned to my mother's house in Pittsburgh. I didn't know what I would do, but I did feel empowered to do *something*.

The next day I woke up and, without fail, I sneezed and sneezed.

"What is wrong with you? Why do you sneeze every morning?" she said, stuttering a bit. She had an occasional stutter.

"It's all the dust and clutter in here. Why do you have all this second-hand knick-knack stuff, anyway?" I watched her nose wrinkle. Her round, slightly pointed nose held up her glasses. Her light brown skin made her full face glow. It was weird seeing how much we looked alike, especially since many have commented that I look like the men in my family.

"Look, you weren't invited here. You just showed up," she said in a low, sassy tone. My mom looked fatter. I paused. I was quickly reminded of all the times I had heard my mother say, "I didn't have to give you life. All the sacrifices I made for you." To which I had always secretly thought, "Why didn't you abort me when you had the chance? You think I like living through this misery with you?"

We weren't raising our voices, but it was clear that we were fighting.

I was ready for this fight. I had always rehearsed what the not-so-good girl would say to her mother if she felt entirely free to do so, and if she were not always trying to protect her mother from another awful life situation. Somewhere along the growing-up way, I decided not to be a problem for my mother, just a joy. It was clear that she had too much of the other stuff.

"Why are you messin' up your life?" she said, wringing her well-used school-bus-driving and bowling hands. Her hands looked like she could pack a punch, too. Once when I was a teenager, she did slap me across the face for not hanging up the phone fast enough for her liking. I can still hear that ringing in my ear.

"You know, I've hardly ever asked you for anything. In fact, I have contributed a lot to the family since I was nine years old. I have always worked and have never caused you trouble. The one time I need you, I get, "You, weren't invited here." As long as I'm what you want me to be and you can brag about it, all is well. But as soon as you have to put some effort into being a mother, then it's, "Why are you messin' up your life?""

I felt total relief. Everything was coming out so clearly. I had run this conversation in my head with her ever since I was 15.

"You don't think giving you a roof over your head and food to eat is being a mother? Girl, some folks don't even do that. You better go'on somewhere with that foolish. You have no reason to be messin' up your life like this. You had opportunities that I never had."

"You had opportunities, too. I resent that you always try to live through my life. Get your own life, Mom, live your own life."

"I have my own life. Sy, I think all that new-age stuff has screwed up your mind. Since that diet change, you have been trying to drive a wedge between us. You have been exposed to lots of religions and doctrines, and I think you are all confused and mixed up."

"Mom, it's my new-age training that keeps encouraging me to try to fix my relationship with you, to love you unconditionally. Which is hard, because that is not how our family loves one another. Everything has always been conditional. You and Dad love us, conditionally, so we can make your unfulfilled lives look better.

You both keep saying we have no reason to be messed up. You don't know why Rahima and Samir are drug addicts. Ma, they are addicts because they are in a lot of pain. They are hurting from all the beatings you suffered. They had to hear it and watch them up close. You don't think listening to our mother scream at the hands of our father has no effect on us? We're all messed up behind it. How can you not understand that?"

"That was a long time ago."

"Yeah, but we all still feel the pain. Some times are more painful than others. And you live in a way where you ask us, all the time, to suppress it, but it gets expressed in one way or other. Mom, almost all of your kids are addicts. And what drives me crazy is, you constantly say things like, 'I didn't have to give you birth.' And "All the sacrifices I made for you.'

"That's true, I didn't have to give you birth." She paused. "And I have made sacrifices you don't even know about."

"But the thing is, you did give me birth, and still I'm made to feel like a burden on your life. Not a good thing for a kid to grow up with. You gave birth to me, and yet I feel like you and Dad abandoned me. Then you and Dad try to live through our accomplishments but never take the blame when things go wrong. Your love has always been conditional. And I resent that the most."

"If you don't like it here, you can leave," she said while she leaned back and pursed her lips. I recognized that confidence; it usually came with the old-fashioned statement in African American culture: *I'm the HNIC—Head N-word in Charge.*

I went to bed that night thinking that this is not the mother who reupholstered that ratty chair and that scratched-up dining room set. I wanted the mother who knew how to transform a beaten down object into a work of art, but perhaps that mother was long gone. The next morning, I woke up sneezing, but I knew that I was not to blame. And, more importantly, I knew that I needed to be in a place that wasn't toxic, physically as well as emotionally. I packed up my bag and put my turtle-rock inside of it. I walked past the red mailbox and down those stone stairs to catch a bus.

CHAPTER 25

RED AND MR. ROGERS

I LEFT MY MOM'S PLACE THAT MORNING and arrived at my friend Red's apartment that afternoon. Red and I had become friends when I first started my holistic health study, and we frequently shared meals together.

When I entered her building, my breath was short and the pulse in my neck was strong. I was nervous. I didn't want to be judged, again.

Red opened her door and stretched out her long arms, wide. She stood close to five feet four inches, her dancer's body lithe, yet strong. She looked like Tilda Swinton, except Red had long, curly red hair. Her hug held me so tight that I was filled with gratitude.

"Thanks for coming," Red said.

"Thank you for having me."

Red had been in a minor car accident and thought that she might have a fractured hip. She wasn't sure if she should be standing or walking on her leg.

I offered to cook her meals, and she offered me a place to stay.

The first night, over cups of Sleepytime Tea, I brought Red up to date on all the details, from my failed business in Atlanta to my visiting Child Protective Services, to my failed attempt to visit my sister in jail.

Red watched my tears flow. She listened, and I trusted her. She allowed me to break down. This was great for me because I was never allowed to have a breakdown growing up. My feelings were always minimized. I was told, "Stop crying, you don't have problems."

Red shared her life with me, too. She had finished her master's degree program, worked at an overwhelming job as a counselor, and had some troubling family issues of her own.

I went to bed that night on Red's couch, and I woke up at 5:00 A.M. in a room that felt warm. I was not sneezing, and it was easy for me to bounce into the bathroom and prepare for my day. I went into the kitchen to make breakfast for the two of us. It was brown and sweet rice combined, cooked slow and topped with an applesauce fruit compote. While I was cooking, I woke Red up to the sounds of soft Zen music playing. She prepared herself for work and, once she was dressed, she sat down to a candlelight breakfast. We chatted over our morning porridge and then went about our respective days.

Next I practiced my yoga routine, showered, and visualized a one-step-better future for myself: for example, to cook more and watch less TV. Then I sat down to plan the week's menu according to my seasonal food education. It was fall; the leaves were changing colors and the morning air was crisp. This was doubly important because, according to traditional Chinese medicine (TCM), autumn was the time to strengthen the lungs and large intestines through food and exercise. TCM believes that emotional problems can show up physically and there is a season when that ailment is more pronounced. If a person had grief or abandonment issues, it could adversely affect the lung and large intestines. I found this philosophy compelling because all my life I suffered from asthma, and have always felt abandoned by my parents. Considering this vulnerability,

I made sure that I ate according to the season and practiced the appropriate yoga postures.

I went to shop at the East End Food Co-op for some staples and fresh produce. I saw some familiar people and places. My heart smiled, even though prior to leaving Pittsburgh, in my mind, I had arrogantly sworn that I would never return. But now here I was again, humbled.

When Red returned home, I had dinner all prepared: carrot-ginger soup with a miso swirl, arame strudel, collard green ribbons, brown rice and lentil pilaf, and apple kuzu pudding for dessert. We ate slowly and talked even more slowly.

Red was one of the smartest people I knew. She was well-read on Spinoza, Kant, and other philosophers. She once told me that, as a little girl, she would spend hours lying across her bed, just thinking. She was the first person that I had ever met who didn't automatically buy into the "pursuit of happiness" model. I really liked that. This was somewhat similar to Buddy's philosophy of "becoming more of who you really are," but happiness mattered a lot to Buddy. Perhaps Red and Buddy were more alike than unlike. They both helped me understand who I wanted to become. I enjoyed the option that a static state of happiness was not necessarily the goal. I was open to happiness being a byproduct, not the whole story. We chatted until 10:00 P.M. that night.

I went to bed, satiated—mind, body, and soul.

A few days later, Red found out she didn't have a fractured hip.

Since her hip was fine, she didn't necessarily need me to cook for her; but we continued our breakfast and dinner routine. Red said that this routine fed her, too. She knew how tough it could be to prepare a good quality meal when she was working full time. She appreciated waking up and coming home to a candlelit breakfast and dinner.

During my new regular routine, I watched only three TV programs. I was hooked on *Mister Rogers' Neighborhood*. I watched *Oprah* sometimes.

And from time to time I would tune in to the O.J. Simpson trial.

Dinnertime, on occasion, was filled with talk about the trial, which transitioned into a bigger discussion about the human condition and how we love and obsess.

The Mr. Rogers' show inspired me. I had watched it as a kid, but this felt different. I loved the simplicity of it, the subjects, and the care he showed toward the children. I loved the Land of Make Believe, the Trolley and that whistle, Prince Friday, and the daily guest stars knocking on the door. I felt like I was being re-parented properly.

About a week after staying with Red, I woke up at 5:00 A.M., repeating my new routine without resistance, and I caught myself singing, off-key, Mister Rogers' theme song, "It's Such a Good Feeling." Without shame, I sang it when Red sat down for breakfast, a morning serenade:

> *It's such a good feeling*
> *To know you're alive*
> *It's such a happy feeling*
> *You're growing inside*
> *And when you wake up*
> *Ready to say,*
> *I think I'll make a snappy new day*
> *"Snap Snap."*
>
> *It's such a good feeling*
> *A very good feeling*
> *The feeling you know*
> *That I'll be back*
> *When the day is new*
> *And I'll have more ideas for you*
> *And you'll have things*

You want to talk about
I…will…too.

She smiled, laughed, and joined in. Weird, I know, but it felt lovely. It was the lullaby that I needed growing up. Red and Mr. Rogers fed my soul a different kind of holistic health dish.

Each day I felt stronger and stronger. I was growing more into who I really was. I gained more weight, which was good. Life was starting to feel abundant. I started returning to my spiritual group's weekly meditation meeting and world peace visualization sessions. What I like about my spiritual group was their belief that if you create a better you, then you will create a better world. So there was a lot of self-help going on and with this group we created a place where we could be vulnerable as well as safe.

During one of our weekly meetings, I found myself sharing my Atlanta journey.

At the end of the meeting, a woman named Pamela approached me and asked what I did specifically for Care International and The Bank.

I told her that I programmed and managed their marketing database, which was set up for clients in various stages. "Hmmm. I have a hunch," she said. "You should come by and interview with our company, Aaliyah. It's a strategic planning company. We have a software package that helps businesses create dynamic strategic plans. The strategic plan evolves and changes as the company is introduced to new stimuli. We're expanding our marketing efforts and could use someone who knows how to set up and manage a database."

I told her that I would love to interview for the job, but that I had left all of my professional business attire in Atlanta. I only had my tattered blue jeans and long-sleeve T-shirts with me.

"Come as you are," said Pamela. "We're not like that. We're looking for talent and how you dress doesn't matter. We're professional, but not corporate."

The next thing I knew, I had agreed to go in for a job interview. During my first meeting with Aaliyah, I watched a presentation about their company. The first thing that flashed on the screen was 🜨. When I saw the first slide and noticed that their business logo was the female version of my food and yoga logo, I excitedly interrupted. "Your logo is the Egyptian symbol for woman. My food and yoga business logo 🜨 is the Egyptian symbol for man!"

The president of the company explained why he uses this symbol and name for the company. "The name Aaliyah means to take things to a higher level in both Arabic and Hebrew."

I smiled, thinking, "This is where I'm supposed to be, taking my life to a higher level."

A few days later, I was offered the job.

✻   ✻   ✻

In October 1995, I was temporarily living with Red in her cozy environment. I had a job at a company that sold software to help businesses function more holistically. I still made the daily meals for Red and me. More and more each day, we worked and ate well, and lived out the lyrics of Mr. Roger's song: *It's such a good feeling, to know you're alive. It's such a happy feeling, that's growing inside.* I stayed with Red for five weeks. It was one of the happiest times in my life.

CHAPTER 26

CARO-LION!

LEAVING RED'S PLACE IN NOVEMBER 1995 was bittersweet. I was happy to be moving on and making enough money to get my own apartment, but I was deeply sad to be giving up that daily bond of friendship.

I thought about the last two months. I had traveled from Atlanta to my mother's house to Red's place, only to land in my own attic apartment on Broughton Street. The apartment was right around the corner from my new full-time position at Aaliyah, Inc., where I was a marketing database manager. I had officially moved back to Pittsburgh.

The street was lined with big oak trees, shady and colorful. Every so often, the leaves made a crackling sound. The house sat on a round corner, and every time I made a smooth turn, whether I was walking or biking, I would think that my life was definitely rounding the bend, too.

I started my new life with very little, but the puzzle pieces slowly began fitting back together.

Red did for me what I had wanted my mother to do. I had hoped for healing time between a mother and her daughter, but instead our mother-daughter relationship was strained. Now that I was back on track with a daily yoga practice and eating my own home cooking, I could see that I got what I needed. It just didn't come from my mother. It came in the form of friendship instead, and for this, I was grateful.

If Red and her friendship nursed me back to health, then it was Caroline and her friendship that trained me for life's marathon.

Caroline and I had worked on the same floor at the bank. She was an international banker who spoke Spanish, Portuguese, and English. She and her Scottish boyfriend (soon to be her husband) Derek would invite me over for sports activities and dinners with their friends.

She told me that when she first saw me on the tenth floor at the bank, she knew that we would be friends. She said she assumed that because I was long, lean and wore my hair in a style that most African-American women didn't, a short natural. Caroline said that she hadn't heard me speak, but was sure that I was French-African, particularly because my walk was graceful, elegant, and confident.

I have to say, I was skeptical. I wasn't sure why she wanted to be friends with me, especially once she knew that I wasn't French-African. I wasn't sure we had much in common, with the exception of our both being in our mid-twenties and working at a bank.

Caroline was a sports activity enthusiast. She would do 60-mile weekend rides on her bike, for fun. She lifted weights, ran, swam, speed skated, rollerbladed, and windsurfed, just to name a few. Her athletic body was beautiful in a dainty way, like a southern belle. She had long, blonde, curly hair, a wide smile and a laugh that was unapologetically loud, playful, and contagious. I didn't think I could keep up with her, but the first thing she gave me was the gift of acceptance. When it seemed that some people commented on my being "weird," she made me feel extraordinary. She was interested in me, and my views on food and yoga. I started going on 60-mile bike rides with her and her other friends. I enjoyed this crowd.

But I wasn't like her at all. I wasn't a sports activity enthusiast. We were from two different worlds. Her parents were well-educated and professorial. When she was growing up, her dad made pancakes on Sundays. Her family had real vacations. She knew about the U.S. firsthand because her family traveled throughout the country during her childhood.

Although she was altruistic toward me, I didn't know if I could trust her. I feared that once she got to really know me, she wouldn't like me. I also didn't want to be anyone's exotic "black" friend. I had heard that highly educated, white middle class women longed for that. You know, the black friend that lets them confirm for themselves how cool and liberal they are. Besides, in general, it took me a long time to trust people, but I didn't know that about myself at that time. I knew that I could be close to people and even love them, but still not trust them.

But there were wonderful moments that made me want to keep our friendship alive.

When I moved to Atlanta, Caroline was sad to see me go. She had missed me, and when I returned I felt welcomed and wanted.

Every few weeks, Caroline had a formal dinner party, Martha-Stewart-like.

The meals had plenty of food options for me to eat—no dairy, no sugar, and no meat. She made fish and meats for the other guests, but always had a few dishes that were Saeeda-friendly.

After Caroline married Derek, she would often invite me over for dinner and make the foods that I really liked. One night, Derek said, "Why all these macrobiotic dinners? Let's mix it up. Caroline, what happened to the great chicken and lobster dinners you made before we were married?"

We all laughed. In that moment, I realized that he was right. In the food department, Caroline mothered me. She wasn't making the meals that she and Derek really liked. It was Saeeda-focused. I appreciated it and could see Derek's frustration. Derek, a true Renaissance man, ate whatever she prepared, but even he had his limits. He wanted some spicy meat dishes to go with all the whole grains and vegetables.

One day I heard Caroline describe me to one of her friends: "Saeeda is my best friend, and if she were a man, I would've married her." Caroline had a unique way of making me feel precious.

One weeknight, while her husband was working a late shift at the hospital, she and I were having dinner alone and we shared even more personal stories about our childhoods, our families, and our imperfect mothers. She said, "Sy, it's okay. We can mother each other." And that felt good. I didn't fully trust her, but I did trust life. I thought, "Maybe it's okay to fully let my guard down with Caro-Lion.

❋   ❋   ❋

Caroline was usually doing something constructive, and that example taught me the best. One day we went to the art museum. I didn't know if she invited me to go with her because she knew that I needed to see this city in a different light, or if she just wanted some company.

The day we went to the museum, a peculiar spark ignited inside me. I watched visitors, people who paid money to be there, enjoy our city and its history. I decided to start living in my home city as a visitor. I didn't know how long I would be staying in Pittsburgh, but I was going to do the things that visitors did when they came to town.

So when I heard the docent say, "People come from all around the world to visit Pittsburgh, to study its landscapes, rivers, and industrial age," I thought, *That's me, a tourist. I'm not going to focus so much on my family's history but, instead, enjoy all of this city's documented beauty.*

I visited the local parks. I went on walks and nearby hikes. I toured building architecture exhibits. I went to the theater, plays, and dance performances. Mainly, I found myself going to the art museum at least twice a week for a docent tour.

I loved learning more about the world through art history. It was a good way to fill in the holes in my education. For instance, I learned that the August Wilson play, The Piano Lesson, was influenced by Romare Bearden's collage with the same title. Bearden documented Pittsburgh's history and black experience, and I was being re-educated there. It was at the museum that I was introduced to a deeper understanding of Rembrandt and the lithographic etchings of Albrecht Durer. I studied the history of Kodak's importation of photography to the U.S. I saw the steel mills in a new light. I learned about Old Norse tapestries and myths and paintings of Europe's Enlightenment age. All this was new to me, but seemed to be a refresher for Caroline.

Caroline was unlike anyone I had ever met. I'd seen pieces of her in different people, but not all rolled into one. She could easily do over twenty-five male pushups at any given moment and make the silkiest Apple Buttercup Squash soup. Her soup was sweet and tart with a nutmeg surprise. She was her name—Caro-Lion—strong, ferocious and nurturing. She protected me while I was in my fragile state.

When I returned to Pittsburgh with my tail between my legs, it was Caroline who told me that my business hadn't failed; it was just taking a pause. She instructed me to make a list of all of my accomplishments since starting my business. "You will see how successful you really are," she said. I believed her. Life was just taking a pause. Life was a marathon full of hills and valleys to tackle.

I did what she asked and, unbeknownst to her, that list helped me craft a letter to Mark, the group exercise manager at Club One. I was asking for an audition to be on a yoga substitute list. I wanted to get back into the yoga world and to earn extra money so that I could pay off some bills faster.

I sent Mark a cover letter, a résumé, and the only newspaper clipping I had, an article featuring me teaching yoga to kids.

A few days later, the phone rang. "I got your letter," Mark started, laughing. "I can't believe you sent me a letter. Nice. You could've just called me. I know who you are. And I do have a class that is looking for a permanent instructor. It's the Sunday class at 9:00 A.M. If the members like you, and I know they will, it's yours."

All week long, I practiced my sequence to an imaginary group of students in my unfurnished living room.

On Sunday morning, I arrived early. This was the same club where I had taken my very first yoga class. I watched the students come through the door, giving each one a nod and a smile. Some faces were familiar, since I had practiced yoga there from 1990 to 1993, and some faces were brand new. But both sets frightened me.

I walked onto the studio stage and started to teach. The 90 minutes went by fast, particularly because when I step into my yoga world, parts of me vanish. I was still there, of course, but I was more than just little ol' Saeeda. I was part of something bigger.

I hadn't taught a yoga class in three months. I had forgotten the part of my teaching that I enjoyed the most, giving myself away and being with my own astonishing aliveness.

The next day, Mark called me, "They loved you. Let me read you some of the comment cards:

Keep her!

She's great. I hope we have her every Sunday.

Saeeda's style fits our Sunday morning practice.

So, if you want it, it's yours."

I was elated, and I accepted on the spot. Another piece from my shattered life was completing the puzzle. Caroline started coming to my class, too. I would be her first yoga teacher. It was nice to be able to give to her, because from day one of our friendship she had always given to me. Things were moving in the right direction. Up.

CHAPTER 27

YOU CAN'T PICK YOUR FAMILY, BUT...

IN MY ATTIC APARTMENT, I stood in the kitchen doorway. Its cream-colored painted ceiling sloped, making the culinary island, which I built myself, the central focus. In the background stood an old range. The sound of the pressure cooker was hissing. I could see steam sneaking out of the stainless steel pot. The lid was tilted. In the oven, I was baking a carob cake. The kitchen was hot.

When I cracked the window, the brisk outside air rushed in. In the middle of my kitchen was a well-stocked open pantry. Everything had a label according to its season. It was the middle of autumn 1995, and I felt grateful and abundant. I hovered over the cutting boards that sat on top of a wire rack. I peeked between the wire mesh at the glass jars. The jars contained different color beans, black and purple seaweeds, jewelry-shaped grains, and Japanese and Italian pastas.

I was cooking and eating well, working full time, spending time with friends, meditating with my spiritual group, and teaching yoga. These fruits felt like they came from the seeds I had perhaps planted in previous spring seasons.

On Sunday mornings after yoga class, I had a ritual that I performed with two of my students, a husband and wife team. We would go to the 61C Café for tea, coffee, and a breakfast snack. I was partial to their raspberry granola with steamed soymilk.

One day Zed, the wife, said, "Would you be interested in making a yoga video?"

"I dunno. I don't have the money to make one. Perhaps, one day."

"If I could get the equipment and you didn't have to pay anything?" She paused to take a bite of her biscotti. "Would you be interested, then?"

I was interested, but timid about doing a project like this. I didn't want to let anyone down. Was I good enough to do a video?

"I just think that you have such a gift. It would be nice if you could share it with others, in a more… ," she paused and sipped her fancy bowl of coffee, "in a more permanent form."

Zed had the fingers of an artist, fingers that said, *We are used to paying attention to details.* Fingers that said, *We are used to turning the abstract into the concrete, trash into treasure, and function into form.* Zed always seemed to wear comfortable black clothing that accentuated her auburn short hair.

She and her husband George were a bit older than I was, not quite parental figures, but definitely guardians. I felt safe around them and I was in love with both of them. She was artistic extraordinaire, and he was *über* intelligent.

George was a professor. He worked on math and string theory Roger Penrose, the mathematical physicist, mentored him. George had gray hair that danced on top of his head like he was always thinking about something electric. His body was round and strong.

He and Zed were matched perfectly. I liked that they included me on Sunday mornings, and sometimes Friday and Saturday nights.

"Sure. I'll do a video with you," I said, pausing between eating my delightfully warm cereal. I also thought this might be good practice for me. Who knows what my yoga destiny was?

"I just told someone in my water aerobics class that she should come to your yoga class. And when she asked me what you were like I told her, 'She's a cross between Mr. Rogers and Martha Stewart.'"

I laughed and told Zed the story about Red, Mr. Rogers, and me. I told her about my following Martha Stewart's career and the time when *Essence* magazine called and interviewed me, but the article was never printed.

She laughed compassionately. Most of our Sunday mornings were like that, satiated with humor and insight.

❋   ❋   ❋

From week to week, life lifted me one step higher. Finally, I was empowered to do the video with Zed. Then I had the thought: *Perhaps I could do the same with audiotape, since my students often asked me for a tape of my class.*

I knew someone who had a high-quality home recording studio where I could buy recording time. One of my students, Liz Berlin, was a member of the band Rusted Root and she offered to provide original background music for both my audio and video.

With the help of all these people, I was able to make a low-budget audio and video to sell to my students.

At the same time, yoga was becoming more popular, a revival from the 1960s. Phil Jackson included a practice for the Chicago Bulls basketball players when they were NBA champions. Sting graced the cover of *Yoga Journal.* Local newspapers did articles about yoga coming to health clubs. I started to get phone calls from these newspapers, interested in my knowledge and perspective.

My friend Caroline called me a local mini-celebrity because when we walked along the streets of Shadyside people recognized me, and acknowledged us with a wave or a friendly chat.

Over the next year, I also started to teach more often and at more places.

One day, out of the blue, I received another call from *Essence* magazine.

They told me they were doing a spot on wellness, and asked me if I would do an interview.

"How did you get my name?" I said defensively.

"You're in our files as a yoga expert."

"Really?" I said, stunned. "Well, the last time you interviewed me, I..." I stopped myself and instead said, "How can I help you?" At first I wanted to say how I was robbed regarding the previous opportunity, but then I realized I shouldn't let my past disappointment block a future possibility. In that moment, I switched. I decided to become an optimist.

The woman interviewed me for about 40 to 45 minutes. I was happy to get the call and do the interview. But this time, as I hung up the phone, I decided not to tell anyone that I was interviewed, just in case the story needed to be cut right before it went to print. I applied the Caroline marathon strategy: in it for the long haul. I decided to look at this *Essence* phone call as my passing a pleasant milestone. And who knows where it would end up? I stayed focused on the steps in front of me—work, food, yoga, and friends. My life was abundant.

The next day, I woke up and smiled as I thought, "I'm in the files at *Essence* magazine as a yoga expert."

❋　❋　❋

Late winter, we finished the video and the audio. Now I understood why movie credits were so long. A creative project requires the overwhelming support of others. It was an eerie feeling seeing how much we needed a community to complete it. I didn't want to think about needing so many people because I was used to thinking that nothing is going to get done unless I do it myself. And now I was faced with a new possibility: Nothing is going to get done *well* unless we work together.

To celebrate the video and CD release, Soba restaurant catered a space with complimentary appetizers that were Saeeda-friendly and a cocktail for each of my guests. Tom, the owner of Soba, was supportive of what I was doing. His restaurants offered healthy alternatives for people changing their diets and still wanting fine dining. I felt good about referring my clients to his restaurants.

I sent out formal invitations to friends, students (both yoga and cooking), and my spiritual family. I also invited my mother and other members of my biological family, including aunts, uncles, my maternal grandmother, brothers, sisters, and cousins. I would have invited my father, but he lived in Cleveland. I was excited to celebrate with everyone, regardless of the past.

A strange thing happened to me right before the video and CD release party. I was getting dressed, putting on black high heels, dark hose, and a chocolate brown mini-dress, then adorning the outfit with brass arm jewelry, simple earrings, and a big smile. All of a sudden, a flood of happy tears poured from my eyes. It was what I called "rainbow weather." That's when you have two opposing weather conditions, sunshine and rain, which make it a perfect time to see a spectrum of all colors.

I don't think I had ever experienced tears of joy before. I had laughed until my eyes watered, but that was about it. I had experienced painful crying, but that wasn't what I was feeling. I cried tears of joy, hard, then I laughed, hard, and when I finished, I checked my appearance, reapplied my makeup, and left my apartment. I put on flats and walked over to Soba.

I arrived at the restaurant about 7:00 P.M. I did a walk-through and then chatted with the bartender and the server just to make sure that I understood the flow. Then it was 7:30 P.M. and guests started to arrive. At 7:45 P.M. I was selling and signing videos and CD cases and answering questions about my recording journey. I was happy watching everyone climb the stairs; when they got to the top, each person entering gave me a congratulatory hug. Time flew by. I was elated. It was going well, and then I noticed not one family member had come to the party, even though I had sent them all proper invitations. Every time someone walked up the stairs, I was hoping it would be one of them: my brother, my cousins, my nieces and nephews, or my mother and Aunt Clair. I wanted them to be proud of me. Each time someone entered I was excited, but also somewhat let down.

At 9:30 P.M., Lucky, my younger brother's best friend, came in. I smiled and looked around him, expecting my brother too. He wasn't there. I thought, he must be parking the car.

Lucky gave me a big ol' hug. "Omar wanted to be here, but he couldn't make it. He sent me instead. He wanted to make sure you knew that he wanted to be here.

"Thanks, Lucky. " I felt my throat close up a little. "I appreciate the update." Lucky gave me the explanation in such a vague way that I didn't dare ask why he couldn't make it and, to this day, I don't know the story.

It was 9:45 P.M., and a small group of us decided to have a late supper at Soba. This seemed like the perfect time to sit down with close friends and take it all in. One friend counted all the cash that came in from the sales. We had sold all the videos and CDs.

We finished up our meal, and it was close to 11:00 P.M. Overall, I felt satisfied and very lucky.

Then Caroline, Derek, Norm, Cindy, Zed, George, Esther, Marcia, Theresa, Paul and I all debriefed about the success of the night. "It was cool listening to people talk about their experience with you as a teacher," Zed said.

"You're special, babe," Paul Schwartz said. "You know good people. Superstar. I'm so proud of you."

"Ha!" Caro-Lion said, "And people started asking for signed

copies. That was great!"

We all had smiles on our faces and laughter in our hearts. And then, in walked my mother. I may have seen a rainbow of color before the party, but now I only saw RED.

Caro-Lion must have seen that I saw red, because she quickly got up and welcomed my mother and found her a seat away from me, at the other end of the table. Caro-Lion gave her a menu, explained to her where we were in the evening, and introduced her to some of the people at the table.

I, on the other hand, exhaled a long slow and deep breath. Zed's artist hand held mine. I was shaking. I wanted to scream across the table, "Now! Now, you show up! Now!" Zed squeezed my hand in comfort. Derek tried to distract me from my own tension by saying something else successful about the night, but I couldn't hear anything anymore. I was back in the world of thinking how I come from such fucked-up people. I was angry. I wanted to yell at my mom and express my disappointment. Instead, I swallowed my anger, like I had done so often in childhood. I also didn't want to wreck my own triumphant night. So I exhaled a long, slow, and deep breath and continued talking and laughing with my friends and spiritual family.

❋   ❋   ❋

The next day, I went to Caroline's for a celebratory brunch. I was upset, but her husband gently said, "You had a great night. Don't let your mom ruin it. Keep achieving what you want in life."

Derek was right. Maybe my biological family wasn't there, and I shouldn't have expected them to show up. But more importantly, all the people who had been showing up in my life—and the list is long—were there. To name a few: Kathy, my spiritual big sister; Zed and George, my guardian angels; Gia, my mentor; Cindy and Norm, the happiest couple I know; Paul, my father figure; Leilani, my sister-like friend; Daniel, my romantic interest; and my best friend Caroline and her husband Derek.

I had always heard, "You can't pick your family, but you can pick your friends." And on that night I realized that I had in fact picked my family, and I couldn't have felt luckier.

CHAPTER 28

BUT YOU ARE NOT
A CHRISTIAN

I MET DANIEL at an INROADS holiday function in 1996. He was fastening his name tag to his suit when he turned around and introduced himself.

Daniel waited for me to stick out my hand for the shake. He seemed to purposely go out of his way to gently "win friends and influence people," just like Dale Carnegie suggested. I could tell mingling with new people didn't come naturally for him. I liked that he was trying. I too remembered having to acquire the gift-to-gab.

Daniel had just started working for a Big Eight accounting firm as an accountant. He was a small-town boy, but I learned that his small town world was growing bigger whether he liked it or not. We became fast friends. During the time when I was treating myself like a visitor in my hometown, he allowed me to show him the Pittsburgh that I was newly discovering.

We both had a childlike interest in life and were wide-eyed about what it could offer. I loved the safe space Daniel and I were in. Each week or so, we would have dinner with friends or alone, go to a museum, or take a city culture walk, and sometimes even take a day trip away.

Daniel regularly went to the Carnegie Museum of Art with me, listening intently to me repeat facts that I had recently learned about art. I felt like my thoughts were being valued, especially when we discussed each other's point of view.

While walking with Daniel in the museum one day, one piece in particular struck me. It was called "The Peaceable Kingdom," completed in the early 1800s by Edward Hicks. I explained how this artist was a Quaker and a self-taught painter.

"I like that the painting addresses what they call the four humors of man," I said. The four humors were often used as a guide to health. Kind of like my holistic health work, keeping in time with the four seasons." I told him how I loved the quote, "The wolf and the lion shall dwell with the lamb, the leopard shall lie down with the kid, the calf and the young lion and the fatling together and a little child shall lead them." I explained that when I stared into the painting that represented the animals and the child, I felt more peaceful, like yin and yang finding balance.

Daniel and I did quite a few things together, such as seeing the musical *Miss Saigon*. It was the first live musical he'd seen. He explained that his family didn't do cultural things together, although they were close-knit.

"Did you know that I still live at home with my family?" he asked. There's no need to move out." He made a clear declarative statement that blocked me from judging or questioning why he still lives at home. The truth was, I didn't care either way.

"I could not wait to move out. I never really felt at home with my family." I said.

"Wow." Pause. "That's hard for me to imagine. Growing up, I only played with my brother and my sister. And we kept to ourselves at school.

We're a religious family."

"Huh." Then I paused. "My family's definitely different." I didn't explain too much. But I did say, "I'm not that close to them."

Daniel shook his head as if to say, *I feel sorry for you.*

The look on his face frightened me. I liked our friendship and realized that I wouldn't mind it developing into something romantic. But that I-feel-sorry-for-you look brought up my insecurities of, *Who would want to be with a girl from a drug-addicted, broken home?*

* * *

After hanging out with Daniel for several months, I was certain that we were starting to feel romantic toward each other. So when he asked me to be his date at his company's holiday party, I thought some magic would happen that night.

He picked me up at my house; I was in a particularly good mood.

"You look...nice," Daniel said with a gentle smile, handing me a single red rose. His brown eyes told me that he was pleased with my choice of formal dinner wear. He was initially worried because he thought I should wear a long dress, not a cocktail dress. But I didn't have a fancy long dress and didn't want to buy a new one because I already owned a $500 cocktail dress.

Daniel had a boy-man look about him. His honey-brown skin looked nubile, innocent. He was about six feet tall and dressed in a tuxedo. Think leading man in a black romantic comedy, like Boris Kodjoe or Shemar Moore.

We left my house to go to his firm's holiday party, and I felt like we were a younger version of Claire and Cliff Huxtable, from *The Cosby Show*, going to the high school prom.

I never went to the prom. This felt like my belated prom, a private fantasy inside my own head. It was a fantasy because I didn't know if Daniel and I were just taking it slow, doing our own version of an old-fashioned courtship, or if he was just being a good friend to me. What I did know was that I wanted to try and find out more, even if I was afraid.

At the party, he introduced me as his date. I got a small shiver up my spine as a grin expanded across my face. It felt like he was saying, *This is my girlfriend.*

At the table, we easily and naturally talked with his colleagues about our weekends.

Over dessert, he and I shared stories about our favorite day trip, to Falling Water.

Falling Water, by Frank Lloyd Wright, was like a hidden goldmine located right in my own western-Pennsylvania backyard. I remembered feeling dumb when Caro-Lion put this famous house and architect on my radar. Even her Scottish husband knew about this house and the architect. I couldn't believe that I didn't know anything about them. I wanted to share how clueless I was with the table guests, but I didn't. I wanted to explain to them how I thought it might be due to a combination of race, class, addiction, violence, and poverty. The more I functioned in my new world, the more I realized how my upbringing colored my education and experiences, or lack thereof.

At the table, I just tried to enjoy that I was finally in the know. It was nice to not feel dumb or like an outsider. Daniel and I, two new Buppies (Black Urban Professionals), had a lot of catching up to do if we were going to fit into our new world. The nice thing was that we were doing the necessary activities to catch up, and a nicer thing was that we were doing it together.

Then one of the executives' wives broke my train of thought by saying, "Saeeda, I love your pearls, and that dress."

"Thank you," I said humbly. I wanted to immediately reply with "I had nothing to do with this outfit today. Caro-Lion lent me her expensive pearls, and my friend Frederick picked out the dress." I didn't want any-one to think that I was a phony, or posturing. I was having fun, but part of me did feel like a little girl playing dress up.

When the evening ended, Daniel pulled up to my apartment and we talked a bit in his car before he walked me to the door. I opened the door to the ground floor of my building, and then he reached out to give me a hug. "I had a good time," he said. Thanks for coming with me."

"Me, too," I said, leaning more toward him and wondering what would happen next.

He turned around and left me there in the doorway, thinking, "I was certain that he was going to kiss me today."

※　※　※

The following week, we went out again to do some things in the city and then go out to dinner. During dessert, I said, "I've been really enjoying our time together over the last few months." His face started to twitch a bit, communicating that he wasn't sure what I was about to say. He leaned back in his chair, but I continued talking while the butterflies in my stom-ach began to flutter. "I really like you and thought maybe…we could start dating …romantically?"

"Well,…it crossed my mind. Once. In the beginning, but…" he stopped and looked down and then said, "but you're not a Christian."

"I know, but I'm very spiritual. I love what Christ stands for…"

He shook his head to communicate, "No, I have to be with a Christian woman, my kind of Christian."

I was holding back my tears and lost my appetite. I didn't finish my dessert.

The server bounced over and said, "All finished?"

"Yep." I croaked out the answer like a frog.

I caught sight of Daniel's silhouette, but gave him no eye contact. He didn't look like a Christian to me. He told me his answer with no compassion in his voice, no reaffirmation of our friendship. He gave me nothing. Just like that, it was over.

I cried all night and the next day, too, and part of the following day. I lay in bed that morning and thought, "My romantic life and my family life are two areas where I suck." A deep part of me felt that I was doomed that no one would ever want me.

❊　❊　❊

Even though Daniel and I weren't meant to be, I still had my spiritual family. The next day, I called Caro-Lion to help me through my heartache. She listened closely, and helped me once again view life as a marathon and this experience as just one more hurdle to jump over.

CHAPTER 29

GOING TO A HIGHER LEVEL

AFTER DANIEL REJECTED ME, I decided to focus on what was going well. I found my heartbreak manageable. Spiritually, I understood that I was not doomed because he rejected me; I was just not going to be with him. I focused more on my great connection to friends, my spiritual family, and my new job as a marketing database manager.

※　※　※

Aaliyah, Inc., used a statistical model that helped organizations evaluate the health of their business. The mathematical algorithm was a unique way of asking Jungian-type questions about what drives a business market, asking all the pertinent questions that relate to the holistic health of a business. At the end of what they called "pairwise comparisons," executives and managers better understood their priorities, obstacles, and what actions they needed to take to grow.

After I had been working at Aaliyah for several months, I asked if I could be added to the new sales and marketing team. I wanted to use the business side of my college degree, not just my computer side. I wanted to use my gift-to-gab, corporate insight, and natural ability to market and promote products that I was excited about. Caro-Lion often said that I was a natural marketer, so I was interested in practicing the art of cold calling and discovering what it felt like to hear "No" over and over. I had done the solo business thing. Now I wanted to know what it was like to build up a business in a team environment.

The energy of a start-up was like a primal adrenaline rush. It demanded that we work hard while being creative and innovative at all times, something that big corporations didn't necessarily demand. Everyone was hungry and excited about the possibilities of the future.

Aaliyah was the most diverse place I had ever worked. It had about twenty employees, representing five different religions, new-agers, single mothers, four races, liberals, conservatives, young, old, and some who were relatives of each other.

One day the printer broke down and the president's son made an announcement on the intercom: "Can we have all major religions say a prayer for our printer so that we can send out this proposal on time?"

We all laughed and prayed. The printer did eventually start working. I enjoyed the love and acceptance of our multicultural environment.

Another thing I loved about Aaliyah was that we had to think strategically for our clients and ourselves. Abdul, the president of the company, had a brilliant math-engineering mind. It made this 5'7", pudgy, olive-skinned Egyptian with a swollen, red nose very attractive.

His knowledge, drive, and charm closed quite a few business deals, if not all the deals. We all rallied behind him.

Abdul and Pamela, the other principal owner, started taking private yoga lessons from me. They both said they wanted to use yoga to personally grow and de-stress from the pressures of owning a start-up. It not only helped them, but it also felt good to me because they were supporting me.

*   *   *

When I joined the company, Aaliyah was expanding their marketing and sales reach. Now they were including Fortune 1000 companies, not just the Fortune 500 companies.

Lakshmi, an Indian woman with an MBA in marketing and a Master's degree from the University of Pittsburgh, was hired to help us grow. Bright and tenacious, she was in charge of creating a marketing team. She trained us to keep the conversation moving toward a sell or a sales meeting, and she showed us how to interject enthusiasm and smarts when it got tough.

The marketing team was excited to get started and take Aaliyah to a higher level.

One day, Abdul called the entire company into the conference room so he could watch us, the new marketing team, give a preview presentation of what we were going to do to bring in new business. He wanted the company to decide if we could convince a business manager to review our product. Lakshmi proudly went through all of the steps, showing how her campaign would increase business. We did a mock customer role-play so that each employee could see the behind-the-scenes conversations that lured the customer into the doors of Aaliyah. When we finished the presentation, the room was quiet and all eyes were on Abdul to comment first.

"Lakshmi, what the hell was that?" Abdul shouted. "This was not what I asked for!" Lakshmi's eyes looked stunned as they welled up, but she didn't cry; she just stared at him.

"Abdul…" I chimed in, "How did Lakshmi miss the mark? Is there something specific you can point to that's wrong?"

Abdul stood there for a minute or two in silence, looking like he was searching his mind for an answer.

"This is NOT what I want!" he shouted.

"What do you want?" I said. "What's not working here?" By now the conference room was morgue quiet.

Then Abdul started yelling again, "Lakshmi, I gave you a lot of time to get this right. This is not good enough."

He was yelling, but he couldn't give us anything concrete about what was wrong. I was confused.

Later that night, I meditated on what had happened. I sat down at my altar and allowed myself to get into a trance: A thought floated throughout my brain: "Abdul has a brilliant math-engineering mind, but I think he doesn't understand how this part of the business works. And he might be embarrassed to say so. He then makes us wrong and traumatizes us."

At the end of my meditation, I opened my eyes and told myself to keep an eye on this behavior. It could be dangerous.

I watched Abdul blow up from time to time. It always made me tense, but I wanted to hang in there. I enjoyed the work and the people.

One day, a little more than a year later, I was on the phone with a prospective costumer. Abdul had walked into the sales and marketing room and heard me on the phone with the prospect. When I hung up the phone, he gestured me into his office and started yelling. I apparently said something incorrect and he was chewing me out for it. He got close, in my face.

I left his office and went back to my desk. Our office manager came over and said, "Are you okay?"

I nodded as my eyes watered. I was shaking. I went home that night and planned my exit strategy.

When I went into the office the next day, the dust had settled. I decided not to use the "I-quit" card too quickly. I wanted to talk things through with Abdul. He was one of my yoga clients and I knew that he wasn't just a businessman; he was also a spiritual man whom I had seen do things to improve himself on mind, body, and soul levels. Perhaps Abdul and I could talk through things. We could discuss where we were both at fault, and then we could develop a new way of working with each other, a more peaceful way.

I arrived at work that morning. Put my things down. Turned on my computer. While it was booting up, I went to Abdul's office. I stood in the doorway and said, "Can I talk with you about yesterday?"

He nodded and said, "Have a seat."

I sat down on the black leather couch. I was wringing my hands, one of the things I do when I'm nervous, especially when I know things might end badly.

"I might have made some mistakes yesterday on the phone, but I don't think you should have yelled at me. That's not..."

He interrupted and shouted, "If the situation happened again, I would do the very same thing."

"Okay," I said and went back to my desk.

I sat down and started to listen to my voicemail messages, and that's when I had a flashback.

I am 17 years old. My mother and I are leaving our house and getting into her car to go somewhere. While I am opening the car door to my mother's silver Chevy sedan, I see Greg, our 28-year-old neighbor, grab Carla, his live-in girlfriend, by her hair and start pounding on her. My mother gets into her car, turns on the ignition, and motions for me to get in, too. We drive off. My stomach feels sick. My mom says, "I don't know why she would let some man hit her."

Having a knee jerk response, I say, "Why did you let Dad hit on you all those years?"

She doesn't respond. We ride together in silence.

That night, I went to bed knowing one thing for sure. If I stayed in that environment, I was essentially saying it was okay for Abdul to yell at me. I would be like Paula, allowing some man to punch me in the head in the middle of the street. I would be like my mother, stuck for 20 years with four kids and no self-esteem.

The next day, in my heart, I was done with Aaliyah. I decided to take myself to a higher level. It took me six weeks to leave Aaliyah and make my next move.

CHAPTER 30

MENTOR, MAGAZINE, AND MOVIE

IN FALL 1997, Gia owner of Holistic Wellness, asked me, "How do you stay so calm all day?"

I had been working for her for about a week.

"I do what you taught me. I eat soft cooked grains in the mornings."

Gia smiled, grabbed her messages, and went into her office.

I stayed in the reception area, my new workspace. I had left Aalyiah, Inc. and started working for my mentor Gia.

I was hired part-time as an office manager to answer phones, make appointments, type up letters, develop the monthly newsletter, make bank deposits, and do other clerical duties as needed.

Gia often called me into her office to do a sitting meditation with her. She and I had the same spiritual teacher, Emanuel, who taught us how to do a five-minute meditation on giving and receiving. It helped us set the spiritual intention for the day: attracting clients who needed and wanted our services, eliminating our fears and living in the present moment with courage. Then we could get down to the business of making our intentions a reality. We worked hard.

Gia also gave me the opportunity to teach yoga classes, especially since she had just secured a holistic health contract with the Women's Hospital. Since her business was growing, she trained me to teach her natural weight loss class, which was successful, and she allowed me to develop my own food class, which wasn't so successful. I needed practice in this area.

Overall, I didn't make lots of money, just enough to cover my bills—and sometimes not. It felt good to take a stand when it came to how I was going to be treated in the workplace. I was happy to be working for someone who cared about performing "loving, right actions."

Again, my life was filling up as it had when I had my Atlanta business—but with a few improvements. I still taught yoga, but I only had six to eight classes a week, which was better than teaching 12 to 18, as I did before. I prepared food for others, but not as a live-in and not full-time. Working at Holistic Wellness allowed me to naturally market my services. For example, when I appeared in the local magazine Shady Ave, it attracted some independent clients for me. I was also featured in the local city paper, the *Pittsburgh Post-Gazette*, as well as an Internet publication that also featured Sting. I offered my new clients general counseling, but sometimes people needed more intense solutions, and at that point I referred them to Gia.

It was at this time that I came to understand that I liked being a holistic health generalist, rather than a holistic health specialist like Gia. In addition, I learned that success at a business depended on knowing what you can and want to provide, instead of trying to be all things to all people. I realized that I wanted to inspire individuals to take care of themselves, not prescribe specific remedies in a one-on-one session. I didn't want to take on holistic health cases in the same way Gia worked with her clients.

One evening, I returned home from work to find a message waiting on my answering machine. "Saeeda, this is *Essence* magazine. We would like to fact check your interview. Please call."

I thought to myself, "Here we go again. They're fact checking my interview, just like they did last time."

In the morning, I called *Essence* back. I confirmed my interview.

"We expect this article to go to print in six months, summer," she said.

"Great," I said unenthusiastically. I hung up the phone, and right then and there, decided not to get excited about the possibilities in life. I decided to conserve my energy for actual events. I walked out the door of my apartment and continued about my normal day.

Money was low, but good things were happening. I started to have a more substantial marketing binder that held all of my press materials and accomplishments. The sound of the phone ringing and messages on the machine were more likely to be opportunity knocking rather than a creditor, and this was a welcome change.

One day a woman named Donna called me and said, "We're starting our yoga program here at Carnegie Mellon and I wanted to know if you would be interested in teaching yoga for us?"

I had been in love with Carnegie Mellon University since 1983. During high school, I had attended a college-prep summer intensive there. I was thrilled to be asked to do anything for them. I wanted to be around those unique and innovative thinkers again, and I wondered if I could really have something to contribute.

I told her I was interested, and I began teaching there. The CMU yoga classes were different than other classes I had taught. They were three times the size—about 60 people. I was used to 20, maybe 25 students. I was nervous the first few times, but I adjusted.

Each time I entered Skibo Hall, I remembered entering that building 16 years earlier as an 11th grader. When I walked up the stairs, my past and my present merged. Then it was 1983 and I was a scared high school student who was studying physics, chemistry, and calculus on a college campus. Now it is 1998 and I am a scared yoga instructor who is about to lead classes. Classes that felt metaphysical. Classes that felt like I was manipulating the chemistry of these great minds with physical yoga postures which allowed each person to relax into a deep state, Savasana.

The Dean of Mathematics, the Associate Dean of Mechanical Design, professors and students of physics, medicinal anthropology, English, drama, and art all came to my yoga class.

The floor resembled a mosaic, with colorful mats placed on the floor like tiles. Each body stretched out in the relaxation pose. I dimmed the lights and started the class with: "Listen to your body. If something hurts you while in a pose, gently come out of it and relax, and on the contrary, if something is not going deep enough, challenge yourself to go deeper."

At that moment, I began to teach the postures. I started to get to know my students and what their daily lives were like so that I could reference why a specific posture might be helpful, in a general way. For instance, there was a student getting his masters in art and mathematics. He explained that he was taking yoga to enhance his creativity and decrease his stress level. I gave him hand postures to help keep his fingers nimble.

A second student blew out her knee from too much running. A third student had a bad shoulder from overuse in gymnastics. One student was so anxious that she always needed extra Savasana time. One professor was trying to get pregnant, so I let her know which postures generally help with reproductive health.

I was meeting people from so many disciplines, from abstract scientific artists to musical theater performers to artificial intelligence robotic programmers. The 75 minutes passed quickly.

I ended the class the same way I started it, with everyone in the relaxation pose, Savasana. I took the students on an inner journey. It created stillness in the room, reassuring them that this was the time that their bodies would feel the benefit of each posture completed today and previously.

I told each student this was their time to heal every single cell in the body. It was the time to keep what they needed and wanted for better health, yet it was also the time to let go of what the body no longer needed. I affirmed for my students that each of them was whole, powerful, and peaceful.

At the very end, I slowly brought each student back, suggesting that it was time to return to the body instead of in that ethereal space between being awake and asleep. However, some people fell asleep. Some students even snored, giving themselves the much-needed rest they often deprived themselves of. I, too, left the class restored and refreshed.

One evening after class, a young woman approached me, introduced herself, and said, "I would like to invite you to a dinner. It's a dinner honoring you as one of the most respected female role models on campus." She handed me an invitation.

"Really? Wow. Me?"

"Sure," she said matter of fact. "Will you come?"

"I would love to come," I said, humbled. "Thank you." I walked away thinking, "How could this university and its students think that I should be honored in this way? I'm only here twice a week."

When I arrived at home, I called my friend Buddy and told him what had happened. "This request came from the young women on campus, out of the blue. This is the greatest acknowledgment I have ever received. It's an award that I never applied for. I didn't market for it or do any self-promotion to be noticed in this way."

Quick-witted Buddy said, "Saeeda, you may not be a supermodel, but you are a super role model."

"Imagine that," I said, grinning and terrified, thinking again of the quote from Roethke, "She lives at the edge of life as a creative act, continuous and evolving, not infrequently terrified of her own godliness; not infrequently enraptured by the joy and fun of it all; always grappling with her own humanity."

Just then, I froze. I realized that I had resisted teaching all those years because I knew that people on some level were watching me. To live this life is to be a role model, and whether you are a super *role* model or not, someone is watching and that frightens me. I still resist teaching to this day, but each class, I find that I resist it less and less.

❄ ❄ ❄

Another phone call came in a few months later.

"Hi. We received your name as one of Pittsburgh's top yoga instructors."

"Well, I do teach at quite a few places in the city," I replied.

The voice at the other end asked if I work with high-profile clients.

"I can," I said. I was thinking, "Who in the hell is this? Is this a joke?"

"Would you consider coming to teach in a hotel room?"

I told them I would, and that I was flexible on the times and dates.

"Okay, I'll get back to you in a couple of days," the voice said.

Again, I didn't get too excited, nor did I speak to anyone about the call, since I had agreed to conserve my energy for actual events.

Later that night, at home, I had a strange premonition. I was reclining on my futon bed and I saw the vision of me teaching yoga to an actor that I was not too familiar with. In fact, I had only seen her in one movie, on video at Stacey's house in Atlanta. The film was called *The Last Seduction.* I shook my head and immediately told myself, "You're crazy," and then I pushed the thought out of my head.

The next day, I received a call from the personal assistant of the high-profile client, "Are you available on March 25th at 11:30 A.M.?"

"Hold on, let me check. ... Yes, I'm available."

"Come to the William Penn hotel and ask for...." It was some name

I had never heard of.

But I did just that.

I knocked on the door carrying my yoga mat and CD player with its small speakers. I waited a few minutes, but no one came to the door. "Is this a hoax?" I thought to myself. I checked my paper with the notes I had taken down while on the phone, and then I knocked again. No one answered. I went to the phone in the hallway and called the front desk.

"I am at room 301 looking for Laura Bailey. Is this Laura Bailey in room 301?"

"How did you get that name and number?" a hostile front desk attendant said.

I hung up the phone and went back to the room, knocked again, and thought, "I'll wait a few more minutes and then I'm outta here."

I could see someone peeking through the keyhole, and then slowly the door opened.

It was a dark-haired woman with a case of bed hair, but not like anyone I had ever seen who has just woke up. Her straight, medium-length hair was more like the hairstyles I had seen in movies, where the hair was made to look disheveled, yet sexy. She wore loose-fitting pajama-style pants. Her skin was white, yet it had a mysterious tint to it. It was what I called "rich-people skin." It was the kind of skin that had seen numerous facials, lots of rest and relaxation, and secrets only rich people knew.

She extended her hand, gracefully. "I am Linda Fiorentino." She said it in a way that seemed rehearsed, a way that superstars are told to introduce themselves to the general public to make them feel at ease just in case the everyday person felt too star-struck and speechless. I must've had a dazed look in my eyes, because it took me a slow second to lift my hand to shake hers. I'm sure that I was uncomfortably staring at her.

"Come in." She turned around and I followed her, trying to be cool about it, but my voice was a little shaky. Next, four other people walked in.

They were introduced to me, and most of them were personal assistants to someone in the film—*Dogma*. Linda's makeup artist was also there.

"Do you think you can teach us in this room? We are six or seven people today."

I surveyed the room and said, "If we move this table to the side and push back these chairs, we should all fit."

"I am so glad Kevin let me bring my own make-up artist for this shoot," Linda said. Later, I understood "Kevin" to mean Kevin Smith, the director.

"Linda, I bought you a gift," her make-up artist said, handing her a brand new yoga mat. I had a few extra mats with me just in case anyone needed one.

Then there was another knock on the door. In walked this five foot three inch Latina woman, in good shape and well-built.

"Leeenda," she said in a Spanish accent, "I hope I'm not late."

"Salma, this is Saeeda, our yoga instructor." Linda introduced us.

"Hello, I'm Salma Hayek." She extended her hand and said her name in the same way Linda had said hers, a way that was to make me feel at ease. They were both so nice that I did begin to relax. I told myself, "You can only be who you are and give them only what you have. Relax. Breathe. Teach."

I taught the seventy-five minute yoga class. I learned that they were working on a Kevin Smith film with Matt Damon, Ben Affleck, and Chris Rock, and that the people on the film smoked too much. During the class, they suggested that maybe I could come to the set and watch them film.

"That would be cool," I said, smiling, while I continued teaching.

When I finished teaching, I returned home and immediately called Stacey. Stacey was the one who had introduced me to the movie *The Last Seduction*.

"You're not going to believe who I taught yoga to today," I paused.

"Linda Fiorentino. Had it not been for you, I would not have known who she was."

"You do know that she was in *Men in Black*," Stacey said, probably shaking her head.

"No. I haven't been to any blockbusters lately, just independent films."

"How did she contact you?" Stacey asked.

I explained the whole setup and then said, "And who is Salma Hayek?"

"What?! You taught Salma Hayek, too?" Tracey paused and said, "Well, she's only Mexico's Spanish novella superstar. She is like the Marilyn Monroe of Mexico—sexy, sultry, famous."

"What are novellas?" I asked.

I could feel Tracey's head shake over the phone even more.

She sighed and said, "They're Latin-style soap operas."

I called a few friends that night and told them what happened. This was how I liked using my energy, celebrating something that had actually occurred. In fact, that day, two things actually happened: Linda and Salma. I went to bed that night quite happy.

At the second class, they bought a six-week package, and when the pre-paid check came in I celebrated even more with my close friends Caroline and Derek, and Cindy and Norm.

A few days later, I was talking to my younger brother, updating him on all the events. There was a slight pause, and then he said, "I had no idea that yoga would have you teaching superstars. We all thought you were crazy for quitting your corporate job."

During the course of the next six weeks, I gave some private, one-on-one classes with Salma and the same with Linda. In fact, Linda had invited me for dinner twice, once she treated me to dinner at a local bar and grill, and then she made me a home-cooked meal. Although I don't regularly eat chicken, that night I ate baked chicken with rice and veggies. Through my teaching Linda and Salma, I learned that even though they were rich they didn't waste money. They didn't always order room service. They moved into nice, cost-friendly homes instead of staying in expensive hotels, and no one was afraid of hard work or domestic chores like laundry and cooking. I felt privileged to receive this insight. It balanced all the tabloid hype one hears about superstars.

❋ ❋ ❋

It was May 1998.

"Girl, I just got my June copy of *Essence* today in the mail, and you are in it! Why didn't you tell me that you were going to be in *Essence?*" Ly was the same friend who asked me, in January 1995, "Where are you? I looked through the entire issue and you're not in it. What happened?"

"Girl, I learned my lesson the last time. Magazines can interview you, fact check, and still not have room to print your comments. This time, I decided to let the pages speak and keep my mouth shut."

"Word," Ly affirmed, fully understanding my situation. We were roommates in college, where she majored in journalism. As a successful Olympic track and field star, she understood both sides—the interviewer and the interviewee. We cheerfully shared this moment of success.

"Life is starting to look up," I said, smiling, as I put down the phone.

❋ ❋ ❋

Things were going well for me. I was eating well, doing yoga, teaching regularly, working steadily, meeting weekly with my spiritual group, spending time with friends, and progressing professionally. But because of my low emotional intelligence or ability to handle life's emotional hurdles, I wanted to prepare myself for any great changes that might happen, whether they be tremendous highs or rock-bottom lows.

Whenever my phone would ring, it had the spirit of a Las Vegas ino roulette wheel.

I'd often asked myself, where was my sister? Where was my older brother? How was my younger brother *really* doing these days? *angst*

Every time I received painful family news, I personally felt assaulted, ashamed, and mad. It was like something inside of me died again and again. I was afraid of becoming a shell of myself.

Now that I had taught to a few movie stars, was my name on the list as the one to call when making a movie in Pittsburgh? Many big budget films were mostly made in New York City, but Pittsburgh was a cheaper alternative. Was I now part of this culture?

Was I Super Role Model or just a person grappling with her own humanity in public? My life was not about taking a drug or denying my family's past situation. My lifestyle made me face my entire life: the good, the bad, the really bad, and the ugly—the really ugly.

One essential thing I learned in my holistic health food classes and my Sivananda yoga training is that healthful food and yoga can be a gateway into helping an individual define for his/herself *what good health is.*

Yoga taught me that asanas can go beyond the muscular and the skeletal adjustments. Sometimes the poses can open up emotions and psychic experiences. We were trained to refer students and ourselves to good therapists when the mind is disturbed. We were encouraged to seek professional advice when and if we needed or wanted to take a deeper look at life.

Even my cooking teachers spoke of having a team of people help us fully heal. "Food is only part of the story," said chef Tim Atkins, an instructor at the Natural Gourmet Natural Foods Culinary School.

Knowing this, I felt ready for psychotherapy. I actually felt strong enough to look at my family issues a little more closely without them smothering me. I also wanted to be prepared to handle the unexpected, since I never knew when the family's drama would surface.

Dr. Tory Butterworth was a therapist who rented office space in Gia's building. I'd see her repeat clients come in and out of her office, and their physical bodies seemed lighter, each time they left.

In casual conversation over several months, I surmised that Tory might be able to understand the multifaceted Saeeda. It seemed that she had a spiritual acumen and a clinical grounding that wouldn't make me feel like a freak. I felt like Tory could hear, without judging me, that I am an African-American woman who was raised Muslim by parents who engaged in domestic-violence and poverty. I felt confident that she might be the one who could process that I was finding my inner wisdom through holistic food and yoga practices without boxing me into a prescribed way of being. I hoped that she could see that I was earnest in my journey and I needed a non-biased partner to assist in my restoration.

In our first meeting, I explained to Tory, "I want you to help me define what good health means to me. I want a life that can merge the past with the present so that my future can be better than what my siblings have created. I want to prevent the destruction I see around me. I want a full life and a fulfilling one."

Taking what I learned and believed about holistic health, I explained to her that I wanted life to be abundant in time, money, friends, pleasurable work, and romantic love. I wasn't sure about family at that time.

Overall, Tory seemed to understand that I needed to feel good enough to create a better life.

I left her office knowing that I had to work on reconciling the past into the present. I left feeling that she and I were on the same page. We both knew that this work would be complicated, and messy.

CHAPTER 31

SIBLING TRAUMA DRAMA

ON A DAY LIKE ANY OTHER in spring 1998, I came home from work, prepared dinner, and settled in for the night. The phone rang and I picked it up. On the other end, the operator said, "Hello. I have a collect call from Samir Hafiz at the Petersburg City Jail. Will you accept the charges?"

"Yes." I said, thinking, "What now?"

"Sy, I'm locked up." My older brother explained how it wasn't his fault, but I thought to myself, "It probably was." I was kind of relieved that he was in jail, because this meant that he just might sober up from his crack addiction and stop living on the streets. I couldn't remember the last time I had actually heard from him. We talked a bit about his situation, our family, and the fact that he had missed the news about granddad passing away. I filled him in on my experience in Atlanta, and what was happening in Pittsburgh. The conversation ended with, "Can you send me some money?"

"Why do you need money in jail?"

"They give us some of the basics here, but there are still things we need to buy. I want to write people, so I need stamps. I need a new tooth-brush. Also, there is a guy here who is teaching me how to draw and I want to buy some art paper."

I exhaled and asked him how much he wanted. I wasn't making that much as an office manager and yoga teacher, but I felt obligated to help my brother, even if my financial state was poor. I thought, *If I don't help, who would?* I didn't have confidence in the fact that my mother would support him. In fact, she had always said, "If you go to jail, don't call me."

I hung up the phone thinking about what it had been like for me having my two siblings addicted to crack. I realized that I had a special pocket in my heart that loved them. But I also had a special place in my brain that grieved for them as if they were already dead. I was always preparing for the worst news, and I recognized that I had to work on that final stage of death and dying—acceptance. I had always hoped that it would turn itself around, but studies show that kids with our kind of upbringing don't do much better than our parents did, or do worse. I was prepared for their death so much that, when I got a phone call from one of my siblings out of the blue, I spoke with caution and not too much excitement. I didn't want to emotionally get too reinvested.

I was always happy to hear from them, but I also knew that the connection wouldn't last. The return of my siblings was like seeing an apparition. This was a weird place for me to be; nonetheless, when it came to my older brother and sister, this was where I lived.

❊   ❊   ❊

Days later, I sent my brother the money.

One night after teaching a yoga class, I collected my mail and walked into my house. I noticed a letter from my brother. The return address said "Petersburg City Jail," but what I noticed on the ultra-thin envelope was my brother's stellar penmanship. I always admired his clear handwriting, the curls in his cursive r's and n's and the confidence in his capital H's and lowercase z's. It was definitely a younger sister's admiration for an older brother's ability to do things better. Weird, I know, but his penmanship was something I had always aspired to. I always thought, "How does a boy write so neat? I thought boys were messy."

I put my things down. I went to my window ledge. I liked sitting on that ledge and looking out onto the street. It made me feel like I was sitting on a tree branch, up nice and high, like a bird. I cut the end off the envelope like I had watched my dad do with his letters. I'd always thought that was super cool.

His letter started off by saying that he never thought he would end up a "bad man." I stopped reading, looked out the window, and thought, "I didn't think of him that way, either." This was the same brother who wanted me to be an orthodox Muslim when he was embracing our childhood faith on a deeper level. This was the same brother who was recognized in the Petersburg community as the next Iman (the holy man in charge of the mosque), who had a good wife and two children that all followed his leadership. This was the brother who sent me letters when I was in college in 1985, about how some *Essence* readers were finding peace through Islam. We had friendly discussions about my feeling a deeper connection to the woman meditating than with the woman making Salat (the prayer one does five times a day). My conversations with him let me know that I was capable of making a compelling argument regarding why it is important for an individual to be able to choose his or her faith.

Thirteen years later, who would have known that I would be sending the very same article and letter to him in jail with the hopes that his own words would inspire him to clean up his act?

He wrote back and, to my surprise, he started telling me his story in the form of a memoir.

CHAPTER ONE

When I first got to jail after being busted for possession of cocaine in 1991, I was mentally and emotionally traumatized. There I sat in the Petersburg City Jail in an isolated cell-block for 24 hours thinking my life was ruined for being a "bad man." I considered myself a loser, a total failure, a disgrace to everything I had previously represented. It was hard for me to accept that I was a well-known drug addict, an accident waiting to happen in the eyes of local police officers. The visible job I had as a firefighter had accentuated my drug habit and the lifestyle I was living. Like a man riding on a white horse dressed in white attire, I naively had been riding and stopping at all the well-known drug areas buying and smoking cocaine, thinking that I was not being noticed. Meanwhile, fire officers, the city police and even my wife and neighbors knew what I had been doing. I'd been on and off the stuff and back on the stuff since late 1987 after being turned on and turned out by an ex-junior high school teacher who had become a "so-called" trick girl. I will never forget the day..........

It was a hot, humid and sticky Friday evening in July. I had just received my semi-monthly paycheck. The sun was threatening to disappear, but it hung on the horizon appearing as a smooth gigantic basketball with no lines. I was driving a new and shiny two door navy blue escort complete with air-conditioning and an AM-FM cassette stereo. When I rode through the city in it, I was as confident as Nat Turner was when he mounted and rode his horse, convinced that his mission was backed by GOD against what was perceived by his contemporaries as insurmountable odds. Unlike Nat though I preyed on prostitutes who in desperation, and most of the time of my race, did whatever I wanted them to do for ten dollars, or sometimes less. Most of them were crack-addicted women who hung on street corners flagging men in cars hoping for a catch to feed their habit. I had already been with most of the ones I had seen on this day, when out of nowhere, or so it seemed, appeared a shapely, fair-skinned woman from a flower shop who I had not seen before. She looked far more well-kept than all the other women I'd done business with and when she flung her arm in the air, lifting her hand like a woman needing a taxi-cab, I brought my buggy to a schreeching halt.

"Damn," I said silently, "she's a sexy mother _____." Smiling like a cheshire cat, I reached over and unlocked the passenger-side door. She jumped in the car and flexed a soft feminine look at me.

"You looking for some pleasure? I hope so, cause I aim to please," she said.

Immediately I felt my nature rising and my heart began to race. "Where to and how much?" I asked, barely able to keep my eyes off of her face and breasts.

"You know where the football field is?" she asked, anxiously. "By the way, I hope you got at least $20?" she continued

"Yea" I answered. As I spoke, she began fumbling through her purse. I had no idea why and frankly at the time I didn't care. All I knew was that I was about to get my thang off and I could hardly wait.

As we pulled away from our meeting place enroute to the field, she requested that I pay her half the money up front. She had closed her purse by then, having pulled nothing from it. Still somewhat in awe of her appearance, I reached in my pocket, pulled out a ten and gave it to her.

She looked at me _____ and said, "Can you do me a favor?"

I thought, oh no, here we go with the bullshit. She's gonna try to fanagle her way out of the business at hand. She began to direct me to turn down certain streets, and like a taxi driver unfamiliar with the city I followed her lead.

"Stop here," she demanded anxiously. Now we were sitting on a side street about midway down just off of one of the city's main one-way streets. She jumped out of the car and trotted toward what appeared to be an abandoned duplex apartment. "I'll be right back baby" she said reassuringly.

In less than five minutes she was re-saddled in my car and we were off again. I got us to the football field in about ten minutes and I was all set again to let her do her thing. I looked over at her as I began unbuckling my belt. Before I could say anything to prod her attention toward me, I was distracted by her. Again she was fumbling through her purse and I wondered what the hell she was doing. Then *suddenly she looked at me and asked, "You ever smoke crack before?"*

"Naw," I said curiously.

I had heard about it, but I was green to how destructive it had become for those who were using it. I was also confident that crack was no different than any other drug that I had tried, a mild mood-altering substance that I could use and stop using whenever I wanted.

Seconds later, I found out differently. Homegirl knew it would affect me unlike no other drug I had. Instantly, upon taking a deep take of rocked-up cocaine from a rigged-up crack pipe the woman had put together using a plastic soda-pop bottle, aluminum foil and a rubber band, I was addicted.

Now I was interested only in how I could get my hands on more of this drug. I remember fervently asking her to take me to get more of the drug. Also my desire for sex was astonishingly pre-empted by my need to pump more of the stuff in me. That pleased her. The woman knew that she had a new addict under her wing and handled me for the rest of the night until I was almost out of money. On our last run to buy more drugs, she sensed that I was at the end of my rope and about to go home, so she took ten of my dollars and never returned anything to me for it. Though I was a little pissed off about that, I was ignorantly grateful to her for showing me how to achieve the most splendid sensation I'd ever had. It was a feeling that I have never since considered a "high." Whatever it is. It became and is now, as I write, the ugliest enigma I've ever confronted, a feeling I wished I had never felt. It is a personal monkey that jumps on my back without warning, aiming to destroy anything that I try to do positive....

When I read the beginning details of my brother's memoir, I almost fell off the window ledge. My mouth gaped open not believing what I had read. It had never crossed my mind that a crack addict, my brother, wasn't looking for drugs at the time. He was looking for sex, a different kind of high, an escape from something. It was eerie, because just as I wasn't looking for yoga to save me, he was not looking for crack to destroy him.

I stared out the window, hard. I was sad and angry. Life has so many unknowns. So much depends on luck and preparation. It just depends on what you are prepared for or are susceptible to, and in my case my family background really didn't prepare us for success. It prepared us for ways in which we needed to not feel the pain of our situation.

❋ ❋ ❋

A few days later, I got another collect call from my brother.

We discussed his letter, his memoir, and my reaction. He talked about how our family was so messed up. We repeated my sister's Atlanta story, her drug use and how I almost had contact with her. Without warning, he blurted out: "You know, Rahima was raped when she worked at Zayer's."

"What?!" I almost dropped the phone, just stunned.

"Yep, and Dad beat her when she told them about the situation."

I felt sick. I had been sitting on the windowsill, staring out the window, and all I had wanted to do then was free fall to the floor. I felt like an unsuspecting bird that was just hit by rock.

There was a long pause between my brother and me. Then I said, "Well, that sure does explain why she has so much pain and why doing drugs for 20 years might feel so good or numbing." My sister must have been about 19 then, and I was about nine.

My brother and I didn't have much to say after that. We just hung up.

❋ ❋ ❋

A week later, I received another chapter from my brother's memoir, and then another phone call a few days after that. He again asked for more money, I sent some, but also had a bright idea: I would pay him a penny a word for his writing.

"You're just like Mom. You always wanting somebody to work for it."

That was true. I agreed with him but he also had a great story to share and I wanted to be encouraging and show him that he had value.

He did this for about 7,500 words and then just stopped sending his letters—but he didn't stop asking for money, and I didn't stop sending it and accepting his expensive phone calls.

✺   ✺   ✺

"Hello. Collect call from Rahima Hafiz at the Atlanta County Jail. Will you accept the charges?" said the operator.

"Yes." Here we go again. First my brother, now my sister. I thought. This was the first contact I'd had with my sister since 1993, five years earlier. I believe she found my name in the phone book. I stayed listed so that my family could connect with me. I always felt between a rock and a hard place when it came to my siblings.

My sister was picked up on theft charges and was in a place where she could perhaps get clean. She and I had a few phone calls every week before I was able to bring up the fact that she had been raped.

"Samir told me some disturbing news. I wanted to ask you about it, if it is okay with you. If you don't want to talk about it, I completely understand."

I asked her if she had been raped when she worked at Zayer's.

"Yep," she said in a very cold, matter-of-fact way. We paused. I could feel her pain through the phone.

"What happened?"

"I was working the late-evening shift that night. I needed a ride home. Dad didn't pick me up." When she said that, I thought, yep. He was out and about, and didn't make time to pick her up. "So when another employee in the strip mall offered me a ride home, at midnight, I agreed."

"Then about ten minutes into the car ride, he pulled the car over and then pulled out a knife. He told me, 'Here's how it's gon' be…or I'm gonna kill you."

"Oh my God! Rahima. I am so sorry." I started crying, silently. "Samir said that Dad beat you after that."

"Yep," she said again, but now in a defeated tone.

"When I got home that night and told Mom and Dad what had happened to me, my Dad started beating me." I was silent, remembering how men in some cultures blame the woman for being raped.

I was speechless and shattered. We talked more, but all I could do was wonder if my dad beat her the way he beat my mother—or worse? Discovering these brutal stories that were hidden from me made my throat feel as if it were stuffed with cotton. I just didn't know how to heal us from all this brutality.

When I reviewed my family history, I always had a new reason to add to my already mile-high pile of reasons why I didn't want to live in this family. As a matter of fact, many times I felt that I didn't want to live in this world.

I kept up my daily food and yoga diet, but I did notice that I walked around town less alive, more depressed, and many days, numb. Some days I didn't cook at all, especially breakfast. This news made me never want to start a new day.

My father's actions made life a perplexing place for me. He was a monster toward my mother, my sister, and his girlfriend. Yet he was the same man who used to tell my younger brother and me stories about how slave owners used brutal tactics to instill fear into the Africans, to make them easier to control. Was he like them?

When I was 11 years old and my younger brother was eight, my father told us historical stories of how slave owners would have their overseers grab a slave woman who was late in her pregnancy and make the other slaves watch as this woman's belly was sliced open with a machete. All of them would see the baby fall out. During these stories, I couldn't help but wonder, was our history the reason why my dad was so brutal?

I intuitively knew that my dad was trying to empower us with these stories to make sure we could shut up white kids at school when they started talking about how inferior blacks were. My dad, representing the militant black America, wanted those kids to know that if our ancestors were inferior it was because their ancestors were barbarian devils.

My mom did the same, but in a softer way. She gave us comic books about black inventors and important figures. Benjamin Banneker designed the first clock at the White House. Garret Morgan invented the gas mask and traffic light. Madame C.J. Walker, the first black millionaire, made a fortune developing black haircare products. Dr. George Washington Carver was a botanist who invented peanut butter and lots of practical uses for peanuts.

Both our parents had their own way of trying to elevate us. But what we read and heard were polar opposites of what we witnessed and felt on a dail basis. I wished my parents had modeled the behavior they wanted us to follow. Like James Baldwin said, *"Children have never been good at listening to their elders, but they have never failed to imitate them."* My parents' "Do as I say, not as I do" philosophy confused everyone and made the shame of our upbringing more damaging because we knew that they knew better.

I remember a day when my dad beat my sister because she was sleeping in too late for his taste. Out of nowhere, he took a belt and started wailing on her. I remembered thinking "That makes no sense." Perhaps that was the morning after she was raped.

※　　※　　※

My sister and I were rebuilding our relationship through her collect calls. One day, she told me that she would be getting out in October 1998 and that she needed a place to stay.

"I will need you to be my big sister," she said.

I felt a weight on my shoulders. I didn't feel like I could be her big sister. I was trying to keep my own balls aloft. Besides why couldn't our Mom be a mom and let *me* be a little sister?

"Maybe Mom's house might work. I can give her a call," I offered.

"Thanks," my sister replied.

I didn't think my mother and sister had really been in touch. My mom worked a lot, and it was possible that she wasn't around to get the collect calls.

I called my mom.

"I don't know what condition Rahima is going to be in," my mom said, putting up her boundaries.

"Well, I don't know if she can stay with me," I responded, not wanting to take on the caretaker role for my mother or my sister.

Then my mom built her case. "You know, Rahima has been on those drugs for years. I don't know if I can have her in my house."

I felt my defenses go up. When was my mom going to step up and be a mother to her daughter when she needed it most? I was mad at my mom and myself for not being able to give my sister the care she needed.

"I'll call Aunt Jean. Maybe she can help." My Aunt Jean is my mother's younger sister, and a year younger than Rahima. She is also a recovered crack addict herself who put her life together and became a nurse.

I picked up the phone. "Aunt Jean, Rahima gets out of jail soon. She wants to come back to Pittsburgh and start over. I don't think I can have her stay here with me, and my mom is hesitating, too. Can she stay with you?"

"I don't know, Sy. I have to think about it. Crack addiction is tough. I don't know if I want to put myself in that kind of situation where someone has access to my stuff and can sell it at the drop of a dime, just to get high."

"Right."

"And, I'm not gon' lie. I think about getting hiiigh every day. I just don't. When I was gettin' high, people would come over to my apartment and say, 'Jean, you still have furniture? Girl, we sold everything a long time ago.' Sy, I don't want to lose everything. I already lost Hawthorne (her son) behind gettin' high."

Hawthorne, my Aunt Jean's son, at age 10, called CPS on his own mother the day she and some friends locked themselves in the bathroom to smoke crack.

"Let me think about it for a day or two. I'll call you back," she said.

The phone calls went back and forth, round and round. Everyone had a legitimate reason for not giving Rahima a place to stay. Then, finally, my Aunt Jean called me and said that Rahima could stay with her. I had to laugh when she said that if Rahima doesn't do right by her, "It's gon' be on." My aunt meant that she was willing to fight over keeping her life in recovery a success.

Aunt Jean had a finished basement and said that my sister could stay there until she got herself together with a job and could afford her own place. I assured my aunt that I would communicate her requests, especially the part about "It's gon' be on." We laughed to ease the tension of the unknown.

❋   ❋   ❋

Rahima told me the date and arrival time of the Greyhound bus she would be on. She was excited, and so was I. I told her kids about her coming and staying with Aunt Jean. We were all happy.

On a Sunday evening a few weeks later, we all met at the bus station to give my sister a warm welcome. We looked on the notice board to find the platform number unloading passengers coming from Atlanta. We all walked over to the door. A few minutes later, we heard the bus pull into the station. Our hearts beat fast with pleasant anticipation. A couple of people started to get off the bus. Our necks stretched with eagerness as each passenger descended the stairs. More people got off the bus. I could see from my peripheral vision that people were hugging and greeting their loved ones, but I kept my primary focus on the people getting off the bus. It had been over six years since I had seen my sister. The last person exited the bus—and no Rahima.

I watched every single one of us, a bouquet of balloons, swelling up with exhilaration at the thought of a mother being reunited with her children. When my sister didn't get off the bus, I could see us all deflating, as if the air had suddenly been let out. Each of us fluttered aimlessly up and down, then ultimately flattened to the ground with disappointment. Then worry.

"Maybe she's on the next bus," my Aunt Jean said to the kids.

"Yeah, maybe I got the date and time wrong," I said. "Sorry, everyone. I don't know what happened." I knew I hadn't made a mistake, and now I was scared of what the real story would be.

The next day, I got a call from my sister, "I didn't take that bus. I wanted to see Khadijah and her dad before coming to Pittsburgh." Khadijah is the youngest of my sister's seven kids. I had never met this child and I didn't know if that was the truth. Why didn't she call me in advance so that we wouldn't all be waiting at the bus stop for her? Of course, I thought that she went to go get high one more time.

Rahima finally did arrive a day or two later, without the fanfare. My Aunt Jean still allowed her to stay in her basement, and slowly my sister started to put the pieces back together. She found a minimum wage job. She made deeper connections with her three children living in Pittsburgh. Things were looking up for a while.

❋   ❋   ❋

My older brother had a similar tale when he returned to Pittsburgh. He called me and said, "I'm getting out of jail next month. I will be taking a bus to Pittsburgh. Can I stay with you until I get myself settled?"

"Samir, I can pay for you to stay in a hotel. I'm not comfortable with you staying with me in my small one bedroom."

"If I go to a hotel, I'm gonna use again."

"Where's a safe place for you to be, then?"

"I don't know, but if I go to a hotel, I'm going to use."

"Let me call around and see what I can do."

My brother had a childhood friend named Chet who was able to help set up something for Samir in Pittsburgh. Chet was doing some ministry work that helped down-and-out men turn their lives around.

Both siblings back in Pittsburgh. Both putting the puzzle pieces back together. They were doing better. They both had jobs and were in treatment programs.

This time, the special pocket in my heart was not for grieving. It was for hope.

CHAPTER 32

THE HAIRCUT

IT WAS SPRING 1999. One day when I was in the hair salon a woman called my name. I didn't have my glasses on, so I couldn't see who was talking to me, but I answered her, "Yes?"

It was Brenda from INROADS; we had met a few times at events.

"Right. You're the Executive Director."

"Was. Now I'm with YWCA, second in command. INROADS has been following you. Weren't you in Essence magazine?'

"Yes, that was me," I said, feeling my posture straighten and my face brighten.

She told me that she had seen me in a few other local magazines.

"I didn't know that INROADS Pittsburgh was keeping track of its alums."

It made sense that INROADS would follow their alumni, but since my professional path detoured quite a bit from their mission statement, I was surprised that they were still following me.

"Listen, you've been on our radar," she said. "The YWCA is looking for a new health and wellness director. You should send us your résumé. I'll tell the CEO that I met up with you."

Meeting Brenda in the hair salon seemed like divine intervention.

I called my friend Buddy and asked if I should send her my résumé. I wasn't sure that I wanted to work full-time. I had quite a few things going on and wasn't sure that I could handle a new full-time job on top of it.

I had just signed with ......a New York literary agent for my how-to food and yoga book idea. I liked the freedom of working on projects, scheduling clients, and having part-time work with Holistic Wellness. My latest celebrity client was the group Barenaked Ladies, and *Essence* magazine had called me again regarding another magazine piece.

"You know that I am not impressed by that stuff," Buddy said. Then he paused as if he were trying to solve a math equation. "If the job was part-time, it would be perfect. You probably could get health insurance, the one thing missing from all of your freelance work."

I agreed.

But I wanted to make sure that I could discern the difference between an acceptable opportunity and a possibly overwhelming workload.

I decided to ask my agent what she thought about my taking a full-time position, if I were offered one. She told me with emphasis: A book coming from a YWCA Health and Wellness Director has a better chance of selling than one from an independent food and yoga instructor.

❋   ❋   ❋

I went to the interview. Gia wrote me a glowing recommendation, which felt like she was giving me her blessings. She said, "I would prefer that you stayed here, but it does sound like a good opportunity."

A week later, I was offered the job.

Two weeks after that, I started a full-time job as the YWCA's Health and Wellness Director of the Greater Pittsburgh Area.

CHAPTER 33

THE BAMBOO TREE

IT WAS AN INDIAN SUMMER IN 1999. On my first day at the YWCA, the temperature approached 100° Fahrenheit. I was dressed professionally, corporate style. I wanted to be official, and convey power and authority because I went from being an office assistant one week to having a staff of over forty women and volunteers to manage the next week.

The bottom two floors of the YWCA were my new domain. The basement housed the Health and Wellness department, known as the new Women's Holistic Wellness Center. Due to construction, I hadn't seen my office when I interviewed. The YWCA's wellness image was being renovated, literally and figuratively, and my new position was part of it.

I didn't mind the heat or the construction, mostly because I felt like my life had been under construction, too. And I wasn't quite restored either. Perhaps the YWCA and I were meant to go through this next stage together.

The YWCA hired me to bring holistic health concepts and services to the organization, as a way to stay current with national health trends. It seemed like the entire nation was transitioning. It felt like America was finally willing to acknowledge that holistic health might have a valid place in traditional medicine and fitness. I was happy to be at the forefront.

I walked around my office and thought, "Is this the right job for me?" Part of me felt excited about the work, but another part of me dreaded the demands of a full-time job. What would happen to the book, my food and yoga clients, and the time to take care of me? I sat down at the desk. I looked at the mint-colored cinder block walls, imagining where I could put my office artwork. I opened the filing cabinets that stored over a decade's worth of health and wellness programming. The smell of old paper greeted my nose each time I pulled out a manila folder.

I don't usually sweat. But that day I was sweating because it was hot and because I was nervous. I was excited about the new possibilities that I might create; yet, I felt my heart quicken because I wasn't exactly sure how to do that. And I had to walk around and talk to all the people that I knew were judging me on some level. I could feel the whispers, "Who's this new director?"

"Breathe, Saeeda, breathe. Smile. Show them unconditional love and enthusiasm. You know how to do that," I said to myself.

First stop, the pool, two floors below street level, in the lower basement. An Olympic size pool was used to teach women and their families how to swim, for water aerobic classes, and for lap swimming. I wasn't a good swimmer and thought, "Maybe one day I will take lessons here, even though I am terrified of deep water." The pool staff seemed pleasant and capable, but later I learned that the aquatic director had been at the YWCA for a while and had applied for my job. She was mad about not being selected. Which explains why I thought, "I hope this job goes well," as I shook her hand.

After a departmental tour, I walked into my office, sat down in my new chair, and thought, "I wasn't looking for this job, but becoming the Director of Health and Wellness for the YWCA feels like a job that I have prepared all my life to do. Yep, this job definitely puts me farther down the holistic health path."

I glanced at all the files, the components, and thought of all the people I had to manage. I sat back in my seat and took off my shoes. I cracked my toes. I stood up on my tippy toes and gazed out of the window that overlooked the pool. As I watched the swimmers swimming back and forth, I realized that I was now in a position that would please just about everyone in my life.

Ted, my banking mentor, could respect this position. I was no longer domestic help in his eyes. I had a non-profit professional career with a path that could lead me in the direction of becoming the CEO of the YWCA, locally or nationally. My INROADS training was about to be used and their mission fulfilled: *to prepare minority youth for positions of leadership in business and in the community.* I was being asked to do a job that combined my college degree, my childhood fantasies, my holistic health passions, and my experiences in corporate America, small business, and self-employment.

Seemingly overnight, I was doing all of this for an organization whose mission was to empower women and girls and eliminate racism. Even extremist black America could be proud of me for this kind of job. And here I was hired to help empower these women and girls through holistic health teachings and practices.

Can you say, "DREAM JOB"? I thought that if I had to work for a living, this was a great thing to be doing. I had become the thing that I was I hired to facilitate in others. On some level, it was the thing that I longed for—to be a healthy, holistic African-American professional woman who made a social and spiritual impact.

All of this happened when I wasn't looking. I felt like a bamboo tree. For four years after bamboo trees are planted, they show no major signs of growth. Then in the fifth year, if the soil and the temperature are right, they shoot up 80 to 90 feet. Maybe folks on the outside would not describe me that way, but, on the inside, that's exactly how I felt.

Bamboo trees are able to shoot up so high because in their first four years they anchor their roots firmly into soil. I was frightened each day because I didn't know if my roots had been anchored deep enough for such growth. Even though Caro-Lion helped me see my successes, I still felt like I had failed at owning my own business.

I already had a pretty full life before this job. I worked part-time at Holistic Wellness 20 hours a week. I taught four to six yoga classes a week, another 12 hours. I taught the occasional food and yoga workshop, another five to six hours. I made most of my meals from scratch, another 10 to 15 hours a week. I saw my friends regularly and still explored the city as a visitor, another 10 hours.

Now my life was all of the above, minus the 20-hour-a-week job, which had been replaced with a 50- to 60-hour a week job that I didn't think I knew how to do.

But when this job appeared, I thought this time the gods were giving me a break, instead of playing tricks on me like they had in the past. So I psyched myself up for what I call the *Behind the Music* story. You know, the story where someone like Jay-Z or Missy Elliot is featured. This VH-1 show depicted how the artist made their way to the top, from point A to Z. I told myself that this was my time to work like hell and…create the life that I could define as successful: a healthy, holistic African-American professional woman who makes a social and spiritual impact.

✷　　✷　　✷

In August 1999, I was living proof of what Traditional Chinese Medicine philosophy says about the late summer season. The best way that I can describe the late summer energy is to use the word *pull*. Late summer is central to all seasons. As Dr. Elson Haas states in *Staying Healthy with the*

Seasons, "It is between the two solstices and the two equinoxes. For about two to three weeks, it can be a time of intense metamorphosis in nature and within ourselves. This period of time has aspects of all the seasons and often weather which is very hot, cold, or some other extreme." Just like the temperature in the basement of the YWCA.

Indian summer is the time of being pulled in all different directions, up and out as well as down and in, which can either create total chaos or a profound centeredness.

At this time I looked at my life from a witness point of view. I had no idea what was going to transpire. I was in a position where I had to show up and execute quality. I was also in a position where I had to surrender to the natural laws of the universe and accept how it was all going to turn out. My life was more public than it had ever been. I was a long, tall, and skinny bamboo tree in a community position for all to see.

❋   ❋   ❋

I was featured in the *Pittsburgh Courier* newspaper with the headline, "Hafiz is Putting the 'w' in Holistic Health." *The Pittsburgh Courier* is one of the oldest African-American newspapers in the U.S. When the article appeared in print, I received lots of phone calls from various friends and colleagues all over the city. I was also in the *Pittsburgh Business Times* and the *Pittsburgh Post-Gazette* in sections like "People on the Move." I was definitely on the move with my new schedule. My days were long and full of minutiae, but I was also busy doing the thing that I valued.

What I loved about my job was the opportunity to create holistic health workshops, sell the YWCA to corporate ladies downtown, teach yoga classes to women all over the city, and strategically plan the department's future. I enjoyed coaching the women who worked for me. I wanted everyone to reach their highest potential in their jobs and in their lives.

What I didn't like about my job was the daily operations. I didn't like it when the clean towels were not delivered on time. It wasn't fun not having towels available for members who just finished a sweaty work-out—or worse, a warm shower. I didn't like when an instructor didn't show up, or when people complained about the temperature of the pool.

Most of my days, I felt like a human Atari, zapping very small and very large space invaders. I was scared to miss a target because that target reserved the right to gobble me up.

My days started early. I was often up at 4:30 A.M. I chose to open up the facility, so I had to be there at 5:30 A.M. The morning gave me a chance to enjoy quiet. It was the perfect time for me to get some things done. I also bonded with some members one-on-one without being over-whelmed by a sea of faces. I usually ended my day around 4:30 P.M., so I could go home during a light commuting time. This gave me time to eat an early dinner and prepare for any night classes I might be teaching.

When I wasn't putting out work fires, I could focus on marketing and program development.

One of my first assignments was to work on my letter to the members. I had enormous fun writing my first newsletter column from the director's corner.

From the Health and Wellness Director…

Dear Members, Volunteers, Board of Directors, and YWCA employees,

As an African-American woman, I am very excited to be a part of this wonderful organization whose mission is to empower women and girls, and whose imperative is to eliminate racism. Because of the mission and im-perative, I feel the YWCA of Greater Pittsburgh is committed to helping each and every woman be empowered, supported, and her personal best. To further that commitment, the YWCA Women's Holistic Wellness Center pledges to provide a comprehensive health and wellness program for all of you. As we move into the 21st Century, YWCA Women's Holistic Wellness Center is enthusiastically committed to being a premier organization for every woman to begin and to continue developing as a whole person—body, mind, and spirit.

Now that you know that we are committed to the whole health of every woman, let's define what we mean by "holistic health" and how it relates to our mission and imperative. Because holistic health is a buzz phrase today that is being used, abused, and misunderstood, I would like to set the tone of how we are using the phrase "holistic health" in relationship to your own personal health, as well as to our mission and imperative.

After spending 10 years in the field of holistic health, I have become familiar with many holistic health definitions and philosophies. To make it simple, holistic health is knowing that you are a whole system and part of a whole system (i.e., the universe, the world, the community), and that you affect that whole system and that whole system affects you. The responsibility of the Women's Holistic Wellness Center is to provide you with experiences that will strengthen all the parts of you as a person, which will then strengthen your communities and the world as a whole. Our philosophy is that by doing positive physical activities for your body, challenging mental activities for your mind, and rejuvenating activities for your spirit, you can continue to create a whole-balanced woman.

So why would you want to be a whole-balanced woman? I know the answers might seem obvious; however, I would like to point out that when you ask that question and listen to what your answer is, you define or redefine your purpose in life. So ask yourself, "Why do I want to be a whole-balanced woman and what are the benefits?"

At the YWCA Women's Holistic Wellness Center we have asked ourselves this question, and our answer is this: We believe that when you are not a whole-balanced woman, you are more likely to judge, complain, and

spread negativity to others. You are more likely to feel separate from your family,
your community, and even your SELF. And when you are feeling separate,
you are in more danger of experiencing the diseases of this world, like colds,
headaches, stress, fear, depression, injustices, racism and all the negative "-ism."

However, when you are a woman who is whole and balanced, you are
more likely to be happy and experience oneness with the universe and nature.
Isn't it funny that happiness is described as a oneness with everything? This
means that you are connected—you are not separate from yourself, the com-
munity, or the world. You are more likely to share, love, and be helpful to
yourself and others. This is how the Women's Holistic Wellness Center feels
that it contributes to the mission and imperative by conditioning a woman's
body, mind, and spirit to be whole, helping her to remember that she is not
separate from the world, that there is no such thing as "us" and "them," and
to remember it is always all "US."

I was excited to tell them what the organization and the department meant
to me. I learned that, historically, the YWCA's initial intention at the turn
of the 20TH century was to function holistically. The organization chose
the name "Young Women's Christian Association" for obvious reasons,
except for the Christian part. I learned that Christianity was used because
it happened to be the most popular faith at the time. The organization
targeted young women who were working far away from their families, be
it across the Atlantic or in a rural area in the U.S. The YWCA was not
linked to the YMCA, despite its name, but was developed in the same
spirit of providing a place for those working long hours in the factories
during our industrial revolution.

Now, 100 years later, the YWCA was defining itself as a place for
a woman at every stage in her life, particularly a woman who was transitioning from the industrial age to the information/technological age.

The YWCA was getting back to its initial holistic health roots: a place for a woman to renew her body, mind, and spirit. I made some really good friends there, women from all backgrounds, religions, ages, races, and professions. I genuinely belonged here.

At the YWCA, I didn't feel like an outsider like I had in the banking world. I was in a place that accepted a woman at every stage of her life—the good stages, the bad stages, the high and low stages.

❋   ❋   ❋

When the welcome letter to the members was complete, I sent out the newsletter to a widespread group of contacts, including people I met through Holistic Wellness, Gia's company.

With excitement, I gave Gia a copy of the newsletter. I was so proud to show Gia that holistic health work was living and breathing even more fully in Pittsburgh, especially now to low-income women. I wanted to show her that I was applying what she had taught me and, secretly, I wanted an "attagirl" from her.

A few days later, I got a call. Gia asked me to meet her for tea.

CHAPTER 34

MENTOR VS. MENTEE

WHEN I MET GIA FOR TEA, she was quick and to the point. "I can't believe you called the women's center, the YWCA's Women's Holistic Wellness Center."

"I didn't. They had that name before I knew there was even a job at the YWCA." I paused, feeling defensive and uncomfortable. "They already had pens printed with that name on it when I interviewed. I thought I showed you one."

"And your article…in their newsletter… Well, one of my clients came in and asked me, 'Aren't you livid?'"

I sat there, across from Gia, like I had done a thousand times. The other nine hundred and ninety-nine times, we were usually agreeing about life and how it unfolds. But this time was different.

There I sat, disappointed, sad, and confused. Gia seemed to feel the same, and she was also angry. I have seen her angry before, but never at me.

"What would you like me to do?" I asked.

"Stop using the name."

"Okay. I'll go back to my bosses and ask them to change the name, so it isn't confusing. We could probably just stick with Health and Wellness Department."

"And your article…It just sounded too much like me," Gia continued. "And the product and services are very similar, too."

I knew Gia well enough to understand that she thought I was being disloyal to her, and I knew myself well enough to know that I didn't do anything intentionally against her. I really thought that I was flattering her, her teachings, and holistic health teachings in general. But instead I had apparently threatened her.

"I should've made you sign a non-compete clause," she said, as I saw her neck tighten. She was livid. I looked into my teacup, not knowing what else to say.

"I'm sorry," I muttered. "Do you want me to quit?"

She didn't say anything. Gia held her head down. She swallowed her tea, but I could feel that she could not swallow the hurt and disappointment. I knew she loved me, and I loved her, but I also knew that in her eyes this was the ultimate betrayal.

I was shaking. She was visibly upset, too. Tea came to an end. We grabbed our things. I got to the door and opened it for her. She walked through and then turned around and said, like she had a thousand times, "Do you need a ride home?"

I shook my head no.

Gia had always offered me a ride home. I don't know if she was on just automatic when we walked through the door and asked if I needed a ride, or if she really did want to drive me home. Either way, I refused. Then she bolted toward her car. In that moment, I knew our friendship was over. I walked home stunned, thinking: I know that I ultimately trust life. But how could I lose a mentor and friend over my dream job opportunity?

❊   ❊   ❊

My friendship with Gia was over, but my work at the YWCA was in full swing. After all the newspaper articles were written, and the headshots were snapped, the day-to-day work remained.

It had been four months. Each day I kept my routine of getting up at 4:30 A.M. and finishing work by 4:30 P.M. I lived in my attic apartment, on my beautiful tree-lined street in a big house that sat on a round corner. It felt like the puzzle pieces of my life were finally clicking into place, even without Gia.

The Gia "breakup" was neither comfortable nor easy. For many reasons, I wanted our situation fixed. Besides, we moved in the same circles. I was so conflicted that I reached out to a mutual, trusted friend in our spiritual group and asked if I had just screwed up.

Tammy said, "When I got your newsletter, I did the happy dance in my kitchen. It was great to know that you were reaching more people who would not be exposed to this lifestyle. You're following your path. This helps more people seek peace." Tammy's words made me feel grounded and willing to move on, even though I was sad that my teacher and mentor felt that I had intentionally done her wrong.

Unsolicited, our friend Kate, another member of our spiritual group who specialized in conflict resolution, offered to work with us for free to help us resolve our contention. I called Gia and left her a voice message, but she never returned my call.

I talked with a few more people about this situation. One of our friends, Christine, said, "Now that I'm 50, I'm more fearless. I'll talk to Gia and see what I can do."

Gia again refused to meet with me.

Because I trusted the wholeness of life, I didn't want to give up, but I knew that it might take time. I knew that Gia believed there was enough out there for everyone. It wasn't so much about stealing clients away from her, but more about her believing that I was extremely disloyal.

Then, one winter day in 1999, I rounded the corner, walked up the stone stairs onto the big Victorian-style porch, and grabbed my mail. I noticed a legal letter in my hand.

I opened the letter. It was a cease and desist letter from Holistic Wellness, which I saw was also sent to the YWCA.

I was nervous. Immediately, I called Buddy.

The next day, I went to work. I prepared myself to be fired or asked to resign.

I sat at my desk and answered emails. I decided to show my assistant fitness director, who had a legal background, the letter.

"You're not being sued, yet. But…I am certain that the lawyer is looking for the right avenue to make a case."

I felt nauseous.

Later that morning, the YWCA's CEO walked into my office with our human resources director.

"Hi, Saeeda," she said.

I looked at both of them. They looked neutral, but I felt faint. I had only fainted one time in my life. *I was 14. I had been home sick from school, with asthma or allergies. I had gotten out of bed to go to the bathroom. I was walking down the hall and my mother was on the phone with Aunt Clair. I heard her say, "Clair, I gotta call you back. Sy is turning white." And then my legs gave out and I fell to the floor.*

I felt like falling to the floor right then and there.

When I said hello to them, my voice quavered. "Did you get my message and the letter from the lawyer representing Holistic Wellness?"

"Yeah. We got the cease and desist letter. Our lawyers are looking into it. Don't answer it personally; let us handle it."

"Keep working on providing wellness products and services to our clients. Keep thinking about ways to get new business."

"Oh. Okay. Thanks again for dealing with this."

"Of course. Don't worry. We'll handle this … misunderstanding."

I was sure that the look on my face was one of both confusion and relief.

After they left my office, my assistant fitness director came in, "What'd they say?"

"They are handling it." The CEO was so calm. I wanted to be that calm. She just stood tall and gave me the impression that this was just one more thing a busy CEO has to deal with on any given day.

"Well, until they decide to sue you, you don't have much to worry about."

I was still trembling because this battle wasn't over.

We all got back to work. I sat at my desk. I lit a candle and decided to just do paperwork that day. I thought over and over, "What have I done? What did I do wrong? I can't believe this is happening."

This kind of situation had never happened to me before, but I did recognize the popular theme. *The master gets upset when the student branches out with the knowledge the master has bestowed upon her. The master feels the student is ungrateful and disloyal to the teacher and the teachings. The student feels that she was applying the teachings the master taught her, and that she is just being a part of the larger intent of sharing the teachings. The student is confused and the master is angry, and they never speak again.*

Didn't my teacher sound like her teachers and like the teachers before them? I read the books she told me to read. Weren't they all saying the same thing in their own words or quoting the material exactly?

I went to get my lunch: basic Chinese vegetable takeout with brown rice. I returned to my office, which was like a safe den, and thought to myself, "Who owns the knowledge, anyway? Or does the knowledge own us? Aren't we just stewards, each one teaching another?"

Letters from the YWCA to Holistic Wellness went back and forth a few times. In the meantime, I picked up the phone and called Gia.

Gia and I had the same trusted spiritual teacher. I imagined that we would go to our teacher and tell him what had transpired between us. I thought she and I would both be coached back to a middle ground. I had fantasized that Gia and I could even deepen our mentor-mentee relationship.

"Gia…" I said on her voice mail. "Perhaps we can go to our spiritual teacher and tell him about our conflict and he can help us solve this matter?"

I never heard back from her. We never went to see our spiritual teacher. I was never sued, but the matter between us was never resolved.

To this day, I'm stunned. I was, once again, convinced that my mentor, who taught me to seek the "highest good" resolution, would be eager to resolve our issues with one of our most skilled spiritual counselors. But that wasn't the case.

Maybe one day Gia and I will go see our spiritual counselor for guidance. In the same way, perhaps one day my mother and I will go to counseling to heal our past.

In the meantime, I went to my mat and practiced yoga daily. I went to my kitchen and practiced home cooking. I used these tools to keep me on an authentic path. The path sometimes felt painful and sometimes pleasurable, but mostly it felt like real progress toward a home within myself. And like any long journey, I hoped I would have the endurance to march along.

CHAPTER 35

HOME BASE

AFTER A YEAR WORKING AT THE YWCA, I moved to a new apartment. It was in Pittsburgh's Squirrel Hill neighborhood, on a brick road called Phillips Avenue. The road wasn't yellow, but it was light in color and it felt like the road to follow, just like Dorothy did in *The Wizard of Oz*.

Each time I approached my apartment from the street, I could see my white painted door. The door had a little heart-shaped mirror on it. The mirror had light pink trim, and my morphed reflection danced when I got close. Kathy had given me that mirror as a housewarming gift. I had the mirror on the outside and the turtle rock that she gave me on the inside, and each time I arrived home, it was a door I wanted to enter.

It was a small apartment, but it felt limitless. I had never been someone who knew the difference between variations within a single color. In this apartment, my eye became much more sensitive to variations as I lovingly decorated. Green used to be just green, but now it was forest green, teal, or chartreuse.

My house was a no-shoes apartment. In my two-by-two foyer, when

I took off my shoes I noticed that the white Berber carpet was speckled with colors of beige, light brown, and gray.

For the first time, I enjoyed creating a home. My prized possessions were:

- A print from France of African Colonial French women, given to me by my friend George;

- A photo of five Muslim women from Senegal, in a matted bronze frame; and

- A table and chairs, farm-country style, that matched the kitchen cabinets perfectly.

In my bedroom, I had a basic black futon bed that was low to the ground. Above the bed hung a print of Klimt's "The Kiss" and a photograph of a stone carving of a couple in Kama Sutra poses. My friend Zed, with her artistic hands, had created the picture for me.

My newly remodeled modern apartment was nestled tightly between two brick buildings, but it had a mysterious way of harvesting light. The windows filtered in the sun with an intense sparkle that filled my Zen rooms with a heavenly aura. It was my sanctuary, a physical representation of Savasana. I might not have considered Pittsburgh my long-term home, but inside me something shifted. It was important for me to be at home wherever I was living.

❋   ❋   ❋

I loved my apartment so much that I started to entertain friends and colleagues to small holistic health dinner parties.

All of my life burners were turned on. My life was cooking. I continued therapy, even though Dr. Butterworth had to move me to another workplace since her official space was a rented office from Holistic Wellness, Gia's business. Tory decided that it would be best to not meet there anymore. I was seeing Tory at least every other week, if not weekly. Our body-centered psychotherapy helped me feel less crazy as I navigated through my life.

"Tory, I have all areas in my life moving. I want to see how I can make it all work better, more efficiently, more effectively."

Dr. Butterworth let out a deep exhale. "I don't know why I haven't seen it before. You're a perfectionist."

"No, I'm not," I said. "Perfectionists are people like Martha Stewart who create beautiful things. I'm not like that. It doesn't have to be perfect for me, but I do want to do a good job."

"Yeah, but you want it all to be correct and working…perfectly. I see that now. I see that it affects how you approach situations. This is something to look at."

At the time, this statement offended me. What I heard coming out of her mouth was, "You're not good enough to do something well."

"What does she know?" I thought to myself, defensively.

❋   ❋   ❋

A couple of weeks later, I was back in Tory's office.

"In our last session, we were talking about you being a perfectionist."

I bristled, again.

What I liked about our sessions was I felt like I could be me. I could cry when I needed to cry. I could say that I didn't love my mother, and Tory could hear it without judging me. I could tell her about my hopes and dreams. I could tell her what I loved about Ben and the sexual passion he instilled. I told her most, if not all, of my secrets. So I was surprised and miffed when she said, "I'm not sure you trust me."

"Of course I do. I tell you everything."

"Maybe you do tell me everything, but I'm still not so sure you trust me."

"You can be intimate or open with someone, but that doesn't mean you trust them," she said.

It was like a mysterious click that went off inside my heart. "This explains it. This explains my puzzling behavior," I thought to myself. I could flash back to all those times I was telling Caro-Lion intimate details about my family, but knew that I didn't fully trust her, or anyone for that matter. I saw myself at childhood sleepovers, talking and sharing with the other girls, and all the while knowing that it did not mean we were close. On some level, throughout my life I had known that people could use the information I gave them to hurt and betray me.

Tory's words were a big revelation. She said, "The people close to you hurt you the most. So why would you trust someone who claims to care for you? It takes you years to trust someone. You might be on the verge of trusting me, but I don't think you trust me yet, even though we have worked together for two years."

I felt like Tory "got" me. This was when I decided that Tory, my therapist, was my home base. She wasn't my mother or father, but she was that one place which consistently provided a sensible rudder for me to steer my life. And to know that I didn't have to trust her or love her unconditionally was a relief. I liked that my home base was someone whom I paid for, session by session. Strange, I know, but it was comfortable. Paying made it feel like she didn't have a pre-designed agenda for me. It emancipated me.

Maybe for the first time ever, I felt physically at home in my house and in my head. It didn't feel quite normal, like I had imagined normal to feel. I still felt different from others, but I did feel that I could build a new foundation for myself, and perhaps even find love…reciprocal romantic love.

But, if my dad didn't show up for me, why would any other man? Also, how was I going to not repeat the statistic that predicts that I will have my mother's romantic life? These questions burned at the very core of my being. I didn't know if I would ever be able to answer them.

CHAPTER 36

NICK

IN MY YOGA CLASSES at Carnegie Mellon University, I was in the habit of asking proficient students to demonstrate the poses. There was one student in particular who often demonstrated for me. His name was Nick.

Nick had a square jaw like Superman. He had a lightly tanned face. He looked gentle, yet strong. He was strong. He held difficult poses with ease. He attended class regularly but still seemed shy. He didn't speak much.

In his silence, I often found myself studying his physical features. His shoulders were broad. He had a T-shaped build. I thought he was Indian. Maybe Kashmiri. I imagined that he was able to do yoga poses so well because, when he was a little boy, he studied with his grandfather in the Himalayas.

Periodically, I invited yoga students to my home after class for macro-biotic-vegetarian dinners. This was a great way for me to continue making home-cooked meals for myself. After working full-time at the YWCA and teaching an additional four to six yoga classes per week, cooking was the last thing I wanted to do. I was often tired and wanted to order pizza or go out to a restaurant and be served. But this way I created an external reason to prepare well-balanced meals.

Following my Caro-Lion method, which lets each person know that he or she is important, I had my dinner party system in place. When we arrived back at my house, I put the vegetarian sushi rolls made from brown and white rice, and the premade wasabi and soy sauce-ginger dips on the table. Then I'd heat up a soup. (I usually had two soups in the fridge—one bean, and one vegetable or grain.) Last, while people were eating and talking, I'd heat up the grains, beans, greens, and other vegetables to serve as entrées.

The more confident I became in providing a meal for my students, the more frequently I invited non-students on non-yoga nights to my house for a holistic meal. Sometimes I tried to play matchmaker at these dinners.

One night, I invited Anjuli, her brother Sanjay, and Nick for dinner. In the back of my mind, I thought Nick and Anjuli would hit it off, both being Indian (I thought) and attractive. Plus, I thought Sanjay was cute.

Anjuli arrived, but without Sanjay, and then Nick arrived. We started dinner, and all seemed to get along.

At one point, Anjuli asked Nick where he was from in India.

He smiled, swallowed, and then wiped his mouth. I waited to hear the story that included studying yoga with his grandfather.

"Uh," he chuckled, "I'm not from India. I'm not even Indian."

"What?!" we both said in unison.

"I thought you were Indian, like me," Anjuli said.

Then I confessed to Nick that I was certain that he was Kashmiri. I explained to him that I told myself this whole story about him having studied yoga with his grandfather, and that he found my yoga classes good enough to attend, even though it was not exactly how his grandfather taught him.

Again, we all laughed.

"Nope. I did gymnastics in high school and college. And I'm half Colombian and half white guy."

"Boy, did I get that one wrong!"

We finished dinner, and I suggested that we have dessert and tea on the porch, where they should try swinging on the old-fashioned porch together.

Nick and Anjuli went outside, and when I came through the door with the tray of tea and pear tarts, they were moving and swinging. But the chemistry and conversation between the two of them seemed stagnant. An hour or so later, we all said our goodbyes.

❋   ❋   ❋

Weeks later, I invited a different set of friends, along with Nick, to my house for dinner. Right before dinner, everyone called to cancel, except Nick. I thought about postponing, but I was certain that he was already on his way.

The doorbell rang. I exhaled and opened the door and said, "I hope you are hungry because it is just the two of us. Everyone else canceled." I didn't know what he was thinking about the new situation, but the night was enjoyable. When he left, I felt like I had made a better friend that night.

Nick and I started hanging out more as friends. He invited me to do things with his friends, and vice versa. We would often find ourselves alone, but I never felt any romantic pressure between us.

In October 2000, Nick asked me if I wanted to go to a Halloween dance with him. I agreed. We went to a place called The Attic. I don't remember the type of music they played that night, but I do remember his makeshift costume: a bathrobe, a fake sword, and a towel over his head like an Arabian prince. I was dressed in simple black tights, black short shorts, and a gray turtleneck sweater. I put a vending tray in front of my sweater and short shorts, and transformed into a candy-cigarette girl. Sometimes he and I danced together, and other times we danced with the group. Then it softly hit me, during one of our one-on-one dances. I was starting to find him attractive. I could feel myself tense up at the thought. Then I thought, "This attraction will pass." I chuckled to myself, kept on dancing, and reminded myself that we were only friends.

Nick and I kept hanging out, at least once a week, and my feelings toward him increased each and every time I saw him; in class, on an outing, randomly on campus, and at coffee shops. My feelings were so strong that I almost felt dishonest not telling him how I felt. I told myself this was nonsense. It was just as nonsensical as my thinking that he was Indian. But each day I couldn't stop myself from believing that if I didn't say something I was committing a big mistake.

So one day, I told one of my best girlfriends that I was going to confess my feelings to Nick.

"Ooooo gurrrl. You're brave," said my friend Holly.

I explained to her that I wasn't being brave, since I deeply believed that he didn't like me in that way. I was counting on him not returning my attraction so that it would be easier for me to stop my attraction toward him.

"What are you going to do if he says he likes you, too? Do you want to be in a relationship?"

I told Holly that I wasn't sure if I wanted to be in a relationship.

I remembered enjoying the slow pace of my relationship with Daniel and now feeling the same pace with Nick. It gave me a chance to manage any of my relationship fears. Even though I believed I wanted companionship, relationships never really seemed to make anyone happy, and I wasn't sure it would make me happy. I didn't mind going slow, since the relationships belonging to my parents, grandparents, sisters, and brothers have never worked out. I guess a part of me didn't mind pretending that I was dating someone. This way I could have the benefits of male company without being fully invested in maintaining a real and active relationship. In fact, part of me preferred it. Who needs the real thing anyway?

Then Holly said, "I don't know, Sy. You better be prepared for more than one kind of answer."

❋   ❋   ❋

The night I decided to come clean to Nick, I invited him to one of my favorite Saeeda-friendly restaurants, Kaya. The food was easy to work into my holistic health plan, and the atmosphere was cozy and elegant.

I wasn't sure why I chose to ask Nick to go to Kaya for this confession because almost three years to the month, in the same restaurant, I had made a similar confession to Daniel who rejected me because I was not Christian.

When Nick picked me up, we hugged hello. We walked to his car and headed for Kaya. We chatted, but in my head I was replaying my entire relationship with Daniel.

Driving to the restaurant, my thoughts were interrupted by Nick's question: "How was your Thanksgiving?" My heart quickened, feeling afraid of that question.

"It was low-key." I responded. I had spent Thanksgiving with the international students working on their PhDs, students who stayed in the area for the holidays. "How about you?" I quickly changed the subject, for fear he would judge me for not spending it with my family.

"It was good. Good to see family and friends."

To take my mind off my fear, I looked out of the car window and absorbed Pittsburgh. We drove through Lawrenceville, sometimes called "Little Italy." In this small section of Pittsburgh, on Liberty Avenue, you can often find a chair on the street in front of someone's home. This chair means, "Don't park here; it is my spot for when I return home from work." I often wondered, how do they get away with it? I chuckled as I looked out the window. We glided along Liberty Avenue, and then went over a small bridge, to end up on Smallman Street.

We arrived in Pittsburgh's Strip District. While Nick was parking, we talked about the famous Primanti Brothers pastrami sandwich, with coleslaw and French fries right in the sandwich. We laughed about how I don't eat like that anymore.

When I got out of the car, I thought about Daniel and felt defeated. I also thought about how I needed to get my attraction for Nick off my chest. I slammed the door with purpose.

"Whoa," Nick reacted. "Gentle."

We both smiled.

All through dinner Nick and I talked about different things, both trivial and deep. I remembered him saying how bold it was that YWCA's mission was to empower women and girls by eradicating racism.

Just like with Daniel, during dessert, I mustered up some courage to say what was on my mind. "Umm. Nick...I want to bring up something that might seem a bit strange." I exhaled through my nose purposefully. My throat tightened. I took a sip of water. I started talking again, but my voice was scratchy so I cleared my throat and said, "I realize that we have been hanging out a lot as friends, and...and I'm starting to realize that I have feelings for you. The weird thing is...that by not telling you, I feel dishonest. So I just want to get this off my chest."

Nick looked up and had a big bright smile on his face. It felt overwhelming. "I feel the same way, too. In fact, while I was at home, I was talking to my good friend, Laura, about you. She said, "You sure do talk about your yoga instructor a lot. Why aren't you dating her?" Then I realized that I liked you, too."

I drank a sip of my tea, and thought, "This is not going according to plan." I spoke up and said, "Oh, I thought you were going to say, 'Besides, you're my yoga teacher, and I just don't see you that way.'" We both laughed.

Nick and I finished our dessert with the same kind of conversation that would have taken place when we were "just friends" 30 minutes earlier. We talked for another half hour, and then he drove me home.

I leaned in to give him a hug, like all of the other times we had ended our platonic dates, and said, "I can't kiss you yet. I wasn't prepared for you to say that you like me, too."

I opened the door. Happy. I waved goodbye and said, "Please don't act weird in yoga class on Monday." He smiled happily.

※　　※　　※

Nick and I started dating officially. There was one date I will never forget. We hugged at the door and then started walking down the hill to the movies. Then he reached for my hand. His hand was so soft and gentle, yet strong, just like his demeanor. I had a hard time believing that these were the hands of someone who had been in the Navy, in the Iraq war. I had a hard time believing that these hands competed in gymnastics for more than 20 years. In this relationship, I was the one with the rough hands. I felt a bit insecure about this. I said to Nick, "Some time ago, when I was on this date with another guy before you, that guy picked up my hand and said, 'Wow, Saeeda, your hands look like they work hard.'"

"I told him, 'I have the hands of my ancestors. They were slaves, you know. And I got their hands. These hands are the hands of people who picked a whole lot of cotton.' I held up my hands to the guy, turned them up, and over, so he could get a good look, and then I said, 'These are my hands, and they come from a long line of people who have struggled.'"

Nick never said anything about my hands being rough, but when I told him that story, he was quiet. He just held my hands tighter and rubbed them tenderly.

That night he held my hand in his. We walked slowly, not saying too much. In my head was an affirmed message of certainty. "You will be with him for a long time, but not forever." And then I looked up into the sky and saw my first shooting star.

❋ ❋ ❋

I was taking my time with Nick because I looked at him as a potential long-term boyfriend. Therefore, I felt no need to rush our sexual relationship.

"What? You haven't slept with him yet?" My friends Sarah and Holly both said at dinner one evening. I had made the girls a healthy meal, introducing everyone to brown rice night.

"Saeeda, how can you be with him six months and not have any nookie-nookie?" Sarah asked. Sarah was the first woman I had known who could talk about sex and still make it sound fun, romantic, playful, joyful, innocent, but never dirty. She was probably the one person in my world who was über-comfortable with her sexuality. She was my group's Samantha from Sex in the City, but her innocent way made everything feel delightful and charming. I definitely wanted more of that in my life. "It's not like you don't know him. You have been friends and have known each other for two years?"

"More like, 18 months. And besides…there's still lots of mental and physical intimacy."

"That's riDICKulous," Sarah said. Holly and I cracked up laughing.

"I need to go slow. Nick is letting me take my time. He said that because he was married before there was no need to rush into anything or anyone. Besides, we do some stuff." I paused, and then said, "I just have to make sure that this relationship isn't about being with the black girl, or the yoga teacher, or the time-when-I-was-in-grad-school girl."

"If he has stuck around for this long and hasn't hit it yet, you needn't worry about him using you," Holly said. "He genuinely likes YOU." I refreshed everyone's plates.

Holly went on to inquire if I thought Nick was gay or not. She refreshed my memory by bringing up Frederick, who I had met at the bank years ago. Then I started thinking about Frederick's marriage proposal. I paused and said to Holly that I wasn't sure, but believed he was not gay because I had asked him straight out if he was.

Holly and I reminisced, filling Sarah in on my relationship, or non-relationship, with Frederick.

"Oh, my God! Falling in love with a gay guy is the worst," Sarah said as if she had some experience with this kind of situation.

"Tell me about it," I said, rolling my eyes. "And that is why having sex too early in the relationship doesn't work for me right now, not that I ever had sex with Frederick. Besides, if Nick and I do end up together, we will have our whole lives to have sex. I need to see who I am with him and who he is with me. Nick is like my brown rice. I want to cook it slow and have the energy last longer. I hope."

CHAPTER 37

THE BED'S TOO BIG

IT WAS DECEMBER 2000, three weeks before my 34TH birthday. And for the first time in my life, I was officially dating someone where it felt mutual and had momentum. Maybe I was an old maid. But the strange thing was that I didn't see it that way. I felt like a woman who started out at one place and was taking the necessary steps to end up at a different, and better, place. At this point, my age didn't matter to me; my experience did.

Maybe because I never felt rushed to have a baby, I didn't feel like I needed to rush a relationship. Or maybe because I felt like I didn't know how "to be" in a relationship, I didn't force the issue. Or perhaps I didn't want to be in a relationship at all. Or maybe I took my time in this relationship because I wanted to be more healed and less damaged.

It felt unnatural to be openly invited to parties and functions as the official girl who was dating Nick, but I did take a quick liking to it. It felt even more unnatural to have others refer to us as a couple, since I was so used to being an independent woman, both in my family and in the world.

Nick and I did normal date things together: dinners in and out, movies, parties at friends' places, long chats on the phone about any and everything—especially race, spirituality, food, and business. He found it funny that I was often turned on when we discussed strategic business logic. I might have been turned on, but each date ended in the same way—cuddling, massages, and sometimes a sleepover, but no sex. The anticipation felt amazing, but for him I think it was a lesson in controlling himself mentally and physically, something he learned in the Navy. All this happened naturally, but we did have some conversations that helped us clarify what was really going on between the two of us.

One of the things that made him attractive was his patience with me, especially when I explained to him that I wasn't ready for a sexual relationship. He explained that, because he was newly divorced, he understood that life is complicated and we didn't need to rush anything, especially if I wasn't ready.

He had many attractive qualities. He was a great listener. He could straddle various cultures, political arenas, and socio-economic classes. He was wicked smart, yet he wasn't arrogant. He was very unassuming. And, mostly, he had a kind and tender heart, yet there was something about him that made me feel that he could protect me. Wow!—a man protecting me, instead of hurting me. I know that shouldn't be a rare dynamic, but it was for me, and I liked it.

One night, we were out at Petra and Sebastian's house, at their famous Hat Party. Pittsburgh wasn't as cosmopolitan as my soul desired, but I found a comfortable niche of international people with pizzazz who knew how to party into the night (meaning dancing, without drugs) and were still able to get up the next morning and accomplish the day's activities. No slackers in this group. I called them the CMU (Carnegie Mellon University) International House Party.

As we danced, Nick and I bumped up against the other partygoers.

As the songs transitioned from German punk to Turkish techno to African-American funk, Nick and I moved closer and closer to each other, our noses rubbed together like Eskimos', and then our cheeks gently caressed each other. We whispered into each other's ears. He held my waist from time to time, and I embraced his neck. Petra came by and said, "You two have such great chemistry." We smiled at her and then at each other.

I was in love and starting to lower my guard. But was he? I let myself fall in love over the next few months, especially because one major spiritual teaching stated: *If you have the opportunity to love, meaning loving from the heart unconditionally, you win. Even if that love isn't returned to you, you have opened yourself up enough to love someone, and feeling that feeling alone is a win.*

So when Petra could visibly see the chemistry Nick and I had, I felt like a winner. This public display of connection helped me feel what is sometimes called the Yoga of Love, creating union with another person. It was nice not to be hidden. I felt celebrated. Nick and I were enjoying ourselves, even when we disagreed. The disagreements felt safe, the way I'd imagined normal people disagreed about points of view. In this relationship, I felt like I had grown leaps and bounds from my family's world of chaos, where it was still reported that my dad, then age 67, frequently beat up his longtime girlfriend, once with her ending up in a neck brace. I felt like maybe I would be spared such childhood horrors; but still I was afraid.

My fear of being mistreated came out in strange ways. For instance, in February 2001, Nick went to a job fair in San Francisco. He explained that he might meet up with some old friends. I knew that he had casually dated a girl named Pam, who also attended my yoga classes. I knew that I wanted to have some input into this situation, but wasn't quite sure what to say. Then one night I figured it out.

"Nick, do you think you'll see Pam when you're out in San Francisco?"

"I think so. I asked her if she would be around."

Then I said something that surprised me. I told him that if he slept

with Pam, I'd understand. I said that I was not at all encouraging the behavior, but understood that it could happen. I painted him the picture
of two former lovers seeing each other after a year has passed and, unbeknownst to them, romantic sparks are still flying between them. I said to
him, *Who knows what can happen between two lovers, both under the influence
of a few glasses of wine and…*

Since we had only been dating for about four months and hadn't had
any sex yet, I could understand him wanting to enjoy a hanky-panky night
with someone familiar. I reiterated that I wasn't endorsing that kind of
behavior, but could definitely understand.

"Wow. That's very liberal of you."

"Well, I just know how human beings can be around this sort of
thing. And at this point in our relationship, I would just hope that you
would tell me."

"No need to worry. I'm not going to have sex with Pam."

"I'm just saying, after a few glasses of alcohol anything can happen."

He laughed and said, "You are quite unique."

❋   ❋   ❋

As far as I knew, Nick didn't sleep with Pam. He told me that they did
meet up, but it was completely platonic. I believed him and was relieved.
Internally, I started to realize that my openness about his meeting up with
an old girlfriend was also my way of testing what kind of guy he really was.
It was important for me to put that tricky situation out there in the open
and communicate about it.

Nick and I didn't always see eye-to-eye, but I could tell he was also
enjoying our slow pace. His failed marriage seemed to still hurt him deeply. He and I were both trying to see if we were able to have a longer-term
relationship. Neither of us wanted to fail.

❉   ❉   ❉

Subconsciously, I had a lot of milestones to reach before I felt that I could trust him, or myself, to be in a real relationship. It had been about five years since I'd had a full sexual experience. Spiritually speaking, I didn't want to intertwine my soul with some random person, or someone who wasn't serious about me. I wanted the other person to know that it was special for me and that he was special to me. Besides, with all the STDs out there, I was being especially cautious.

❉   ❉   ❉

Nick and I had been dating for about six months when it finally happened. I heard the knock on the door and he must have seen it in my eyes, because he greeted me with a kiss that immediately turned into a deep, impassioned embrace. All time stopped. I was in the present, and only the present moment. After the kiss, I took his hand and led him to my bedroom. The kissing didn't resume, but we sat on my bed, faces toward each other, doing what I called *breathing each other in*. Noses close, letting the air from one person's nose enter into the other person's nose. We did several rounds of this. Then light caressing. He was being very gentle, yet enthusiastically interested. He was mindful of the fact that I had not had intercourse in five years. His actions were very nurturing. Undressing slowly, we moved into a horizontal position and then he mumbled, "This might hurt, since it has been a while for you."

"Uh huh." I wanted to cry happy tears because he cared about how I would feel.

The caring and pace was perfect. Our bodies intertwined and our physical union was yogic, as our breath, skin, and spirits merged together.

This went on for hours. When we separated, exhausted, I had one thing on my mind.

"I'm hungry," I said.

"Me, too," he smiled.

"Let's shower and keep our plans to eat at Kaya."

❋   ❋   ❋

Soon after that, Nick received a job offer from a high-tech company in Arizona. We casually and safely talked about the future. I said things like, "I always wanted to get my international MBA from Thunderbird. I could go to school there while you are working. I can teach enough yoga to earn a decent income." We both laughed in a knowing way.

It was easy for me to entertain this option because, even though I was working hard at the YWCA, we had just hired a new CEO and I was not so keen on the job anymore. I was tired of the minutiae. The new CEO was rude to many of us and didn't empower the women who worked for her. She felt like an anti-YWCA leader. I was ready to throw in the towel and find another job. I didn't act right away, but I did let these thoughts float around in my mind until it was time to make a more formal decision. I was also reminded of the fact that I never wanted Pittsburgh to be my home. I was a visitor.

❋   ❋   ❋

In May, Nick told me that Honeywell had rescinded the offer due to the bad economy.

"What do you think you'll do?" I asked him.

"I don't know. Live with my parents for a while and try to figure things out."

I stayed quiet. This was sad for both of us. One of my biggest strengths, and weaknesses, was empathizing with others.

Soon after, I attended Nick's graduation. I felt honored to be there cheering for him and all of the MBA friends I had made. I helped Nick

pack up his apartment, as he left for Wisconsin and his parents' house.
When he left, he told me, "It doesn't make sense for us to date long distance."

"Oh," I said.

"I don't have a job. I don't know where I am going to be living."

"I understand. You do know that I want what's best for you even if
it doesn't include me," I said. Of course I wished that it would include
me, but it didn't have to. I also was a bit relieved that I had given this
relationship an honest try, and still it was ending naturally. I didn't fight
it. I accepted that we were broken up. Overall, I felt that I was closer to
having a healthier and more permanent romantic relationship, even if it
wasn't going to be with Nick. I also thought maybe this is what I would
have experienced in high school if I'd had a boyfriend. Instead of being
17, I was 34.

❋   ❋   ❋

June 2001, Nick left Pittsburgh and me. Every night for more than a week
or so, I'd fall asleep in my bed around 9:30 P.M. or 10:00 P.M., and then
in the middle of the night, around 2:00 A.M. or 3:00 A.M. in the morning,
I'd wake up, grab my blanket, and head toward the living room. I wrapped
myself up in the blanket like a caterpillar in a chrysalis, lay my head down
on the sofa pillows, and put my back against the cushions. It was the same
thing I had done on my mother's couch when my business was failing,
but the feelings were much different. I'd softly weep tears of yearning and
heartache. I'd breathe deeply until I could fall back to sleep.

After I couldn't stand this routine anymore, I called Tory, my therapist, for an emergency session.

I described my new sleeping pattern. What I didn't tell her was that
I found myself every day mumbling the lines of a famous song by The
Police, "The Bed's Too Big Without You."

I can't sleep with your memory

Dreaming dreams of what used to be

I explained to her that I agreed with Nick's logic, dating long distance doesn't work. And since July 2001, Nick moved from Wisconsin to San Francisco to live with his cousin. He was even farther away.

Tory knew that my work at the YWCA was no longer the dream job I had hoped it would be. In this session, I was thinking about giving up everything that I had built in Pittsburgh.

"Tory, ever since I was nine years old, Pittsburgh never felt like home." As I said this, a memory surfaced. *I'm only nine years old. I get off the yellow school bus at the bottom of Oak Hill. I lag behind the other students. I turn around and walk up the hill backwards, staring off into the distance at brick houses, the George Washington Bridge, a two-lane highway, green grass, and brown clay hill like a mountain, and I say, aloud, "Pittsburgh is not my home. This is not my home." I turn around with my school books in hand and finish walking forward up the hill. I make a right turn onto Ridge Avenue, walk past four houses, and then go inside my two-story house, covered in red brick colored aluminum siding. I walk into the enclosed porch and put my books down. I start dusting the living room furniture and then vacuuming the floor. I grab my books, turn on the TV, lie down on the floor, and start studying my spelling words during the commercials. I walk up the stairs to get my pencil sharpener and stare out of the hallway window, looking over the pine trees and the wild strawberries growing out back. Then I think again, "This is not my home."*

After my session with Tory, I thought about this memory often. I thought about how I decided to treat Pittsburgh like a visitor. I didn't know how long I was going to be visiting. I thought about my time in Pittsburgh: the new job, the reemergence of my yoga and food business (teaching over 250 people a week), the boyfriend, the great apartment, and the amazing friends who were smart, fun, and funny.

I talked to Tory about the natural end of my relationship with Nick.

"I don't know if it is the end of it," she said. "You said yourself, ever since the YWCA got the new CEO, that you were not so keen on working for her. I usually don't step in with my personal opinion, but let me take my therapist hat off for a minute."

Tory stopped for a moment or two to search for the right words. When she gets excited, her voice goes up to a high octave. "You remind me of one of my other clients. He was really in love with this woman, and he had to decide if he was going to move to be with her. He wanted to keep the relationship going, but was hesitant." Tory paused.

"I told him, you should risk it. If you don't do it, you will always be wondering. My client has never acted this way regarding a woman. I told him, I think you should give it a shot. And now, you are in a similar situation."

I reminded her that we broke up.

"Yeah, but you can still investigate where it might go."

"He does call me every few days," I said, as if I were looking for evidence of his affection toward me. He even called me when he decided to live with his cousin in San Francisco. Then, when he was crossing the border from Nevada into California, he called me to say, "I wanted you to be with me as I crossed into my new state."

I said, "Remember, I want what's best for you even if it doesn't include me."

I guess I was trying to protect my heart.

"Think about it," Tory interjected. "You might always be wondering what if."

❋　　❋　　❋

After my therapy session, I did a meditation about what to do. I talked to Buddy, the when-all-else-fails-what-sustains-me friend, who helped me design a plan of action.

"Just start looking for a job," he said.

"You're right. I don't even know if I can get a job anywhere. Honeywell rescinded Nick's offer to work for them in Arizona. He moved out to California jobless."

Buddy encouraged me and said, "Just see what is out there for you. This will help you make a decision."

"Why don't you just come to NYC and be my neighbor, like Mr. Rogers says?"

"No. NYC is a great place to visit, but too gritty for me to call home."

When I said that, my mind flashed back to an old memory about San Francisco. It was 1989 and I was sleeping in the San Francisco Hyatt, at an INROADS alumni board meeting. I had a lucid dream about being in ocean water. I was able to swim freely in this water, and when I woke up I realized that it was a strange dream to have, particularly because I don't swim very well. I had never swum in the ocean. In the dream, the ocean water made me feel like I could emotionally do anything.

CHAPTER 38

THAT TAO GIRL - TAKE 2

IT WAS JULY 2001 and I had made up my mind to create a new life again, this time in San Francisco. To do this, I had to remember everything I knew about being That Tao Girl. I meditated and recalled the time that I decided to move from Pittsburgh to Atlanta. This was similar to that time because I had to use some "spiritual magic" again. Hopefully, the outcome would be better: a job, a boyfriend, and living in a beautiful city.

I remembered the words from the massage therapist at the Peachtree Center Athletic Club: "Damn, girl, you worked it." Meaning that I had created a job, a live-in chef position, and a yoga career in Atlanta. I asked myself, "Can I...can I do this again, and this time not fail like I did in Atlanta?"

❊   ❊   ❊

A few months before I decided to make this move, I sat in on a Carnegie Mellon University MBA class in social marketing. I was a guest and a social marketing subject; one of my yoga students in the program invited me because every time she was out and about in the city of Pittsburgh she heard my name mentioned. She wanted to study my social networking circles and see how it was possible that so many people were connected to me. She believed that I was some kind of social hub, and I learned that MBA business people found that sort of thing important to study.

For several weeks, four women from Carnegie Mellon's MBA program came to my house to interview me. I loved it. When I was in college studying business and computers, I had always wanted to have a business that students would study to see how and why it was successful. I always wanted to be a bumblebee, the insect that aerodynamically should not be able to fly, but does. That was important to me, since everything in my environment said that I should be low-achieving. I wanted these women to give me some insight as to why I wasn't totally failing at life, and what made me different from my siblings.

While the women were interviewing me on the basics of my social circles, I recalled a conversation I once had with my younger brother, when he told me that his boss wanted to promote him to Assistant Sales Manager.

"That makes sense," I said. "You've been working steadily at the store. You have been top earner for several months. People at the mall love you."

He paused, then said, "Well, when I told a few of my boys about the promotion they…" he paused again. "They said that I was tryin' to act like I was better than they are. Working at the mall."

I was furious. "Omar, if your friends don't want to see you progress, then they really aren't your friends."

Even though I knew that I was giving my brother the right advice, I could tell that he was conflicted. He didn't want to lose his friends. He wanted to belong to the group, and yet he loved his job.

I started to see how different I was from all of my siblings. They just wanted to belong to a group where they felt safe, and I wanted to feel at home within myself as I moved from group to group. I also thought that my many small groups made up a much more important large group—a cosmic, universal group that would define all aspects of my personality.

I attributed a lot of my staying afloat and being true to myself to my food and yoga study. I learned five concrete things: First, set an intention. Second, think positive thoughts. Third, speak those thoughts aloud. Fourth, do the deeds to manifest those thoughts. And fifth, detach from the outcome. These teachings gave me a social and emotional buffer to help me begin the healing process from my multi-generational traumas.

During the interviews with the MBA students, I discovered that I made connections with people because I genuinely wanted to listen to others and see each person's worth. Maybe secretly I also wanted them to discover my worth, too.

I was learning to listen more deeply to myself, That Tao Girl. Daily, I sat down at my altar and did a meditation and ritual to focus my attention on the things I wanted to create in my life. I burned sage to clear out the negative energy. Then I burned incense, Nag Champa, to remind me of life's sweetness. Next, I focused on what goals I wanted to create. I made a vision board, a concrete representation of everything that I wanted to make real in my life.

My routine brought me comfort, and yet I could see the humor in it. For instance, if I had been spying on myself from another building, I would have sworn that I was a witch casting magical spells. Yet I loved this part of my life, the paranormal interpretations. Who doesn't want magical powers? Come to think of it, this definitely would have freaked out Daniel, the one who wanted to be with a Christian woman.

Just like I did back in 1993, I applied for jobs nationwide. It felt good to cast a wide net. I had some good reasons to leave my life in Pittsburgh in exchange for a new life somewhere else.

But I knew that I wasn't moving anywhere until I found a job.

I was interested in seeing if my food and yoga business could take root in another location. If I could go from being a big fish in a small-ish pond to a small fish in a much bigger body of water, then that would really test my growth potential.

Last but not least, I wanted to give the Nick-and-Saeeda relationship a chance, a fresh start.

Nick was clear that I was no longer his girlfriend. But all of his actions said otherwise. For example, he sent me Craigslist job postings, which made me feel that he was encouraging me to live and work in the Bay Area. This was the opposite of my dad, who was all talk and no action. Nick's actions suited me just fine, so I never nagged him about what he wanted to call me.

So I became That Tao Girl–*Take 2*, and, to my surprise, I landed a job within two weeks, at the Marin County Health Club. It was the same position I had at the Pittsburgh YWCA, Director of Health and Wellness. This was particularly interesting because it came at a time when the dot. com world was crumbling. I had one month to get ready.

One Sunday in Pittsburgh, I announced at the end of my yoga class that I had accepted a job in San Francisco, and I would only be teaching for a few more weeks. "Noooo," A few students cried out. One woman, visibly upset, grabbed her things and her mat and walked out quickly. I couldn't run after her, since there were about 40 people in class who were asking me questions.

On my way home, I thought about how yoga had been so magical for so many, and how it changed lives. I vowed that the next time I made this announcement, I would be more careful and let my students know how their future needs can be met.

My last few weeks in Pittsburgh were precious. I tried to make heart-to-heart connections with everyone who needed or wanted an extra special goodbye.

The woman who ran out of my class came up to me the following week and said, "This class is so special to me that when you announced you were leaving, well... I just lost it and had to go home."

Another student, Janet, came up to me and handed me a gray jewelry box. With some hesitation and fear, I opened it. I was confused and pleasantly surprised. Inside was a beautiful gold bracelet, in a woven pattern. I had never received such a fine gift before, from anyone.

"I just wanted to show you what you and your teachings meant to my life," she said. "I've stopped smoking, and I decided to become a yoga teacher. I signed up to go to Sivananda, the school you attended."

I was grinning from ear to ear. I told her she would be an excellent yoga teacher, and we hugged a tight hug for a long time. I still wear the bracelet almost every day.

Later, at my going away party, I gave Janet my Sivananda teacher's training manual. I told her to use it and then pass it along to the next person, one of her students.

At the end of August 2001, I packed up everything and gave my seasonally organized dried goods to Merritt, who was a yoga student and teacher, and a fine cook and pastry chef. Merritt was a wise student who had always said to me, "Saeeda, you need to branch out. Pittsburgh is too small for spirits like us."

With a heavy heart, I left my students and spiritual family on September 3, 2001. They holistically fed me in so many ways, making me feel like I was somebody special. But imagining a new life on the west coast filled my spirit with joy. Nick started sending me Craigslist postings for apartments close to my job. He knew that I didn't like long commutes.

CHAPTER 39

FAILING TO PUT OUT FIRES

ON MY WAY TO SAN FRANCISCO, I flew to Madison, Wisconsin. I was Nick's date to a wedding. Even though he didn't consider me his girlfriend, this was a chance for me to spend more time with him and his family. I was certain that they were all checking me out to see if I was good enough. Meanwhile, I was also trying to decide if I would fit into a Midwestern middle-class family.

Nick's mom came out of her ranch-style suburban brick house to greet me. She was simply adorable—5'2", brown skin, short salt and pepper hair, and open arms. She gave me a big and warm welcome, with a hug that I returned in a way usually reserved for my closest girlfriends. The family and the house felt warm, but I wasn't sure that this kind of life would be for me—not that anyone was asking. But this was my time to observe what kind of life Nick came from, and what he might want or expect from me.

All I knew was that I didn't want to repeat the life my parents had created and destroyed. I wanted a home, but I wasn't sure what that would look like and if it would fit my future partner's vision of home. I knew that I wanted an indescribable feeling of partnership, a feeling of we're-in-it-together-babe. I had images of washing the dishes and my partner drying them. Cooking the meals and my partner taking out the trash. Looking for ways to make and keep each other happy.

I watched his parents closely. They had been married for more than 30 years and seemed to still love each other very much. I remember thinking, This is what a normal marriage looks like. That comforted me. I didn't want exactly what they had, but it was close. His dad and I got along. We had some good philosophical conversations about yoga, and he gave me an old copy of his Raja yoga book. I was pleased. As for his mom, she was kind to me, but I did feel like our value systems didn't quite match up. I felt that my quest for self-discovery might seem a bit odd to her. I didn't quite have the value that family is everything, which I knew was extremely important to her. This made me nervous. I suspect it made her nervous, too.

After the wedding, I flew to San Francisco.

I stayed at Nick's place with his roommate the first few days. My stuff hadn't arrived from Pittsburgh yet.

Mark, Nick's roommate, introduced me as Nick's girlfriend.

"She's not my girlfriend," Nick would say.

"That's right. I'm not his girlfriend," I confirmed, not hurt or anything. This feeling was new for me. His actions didn't match his words.

After a few days, I moved into a condo with a woman named Jenny. It was right across the street from my job at the Marin County Health Club (MCHC). It was a job with the same title in the same industry, but the job's true responsibilities were the polar opposite of my YWCA position in Pittsburgh.

For one, the Marin County Health Club was housed on the top floor of the building, while the Pittsburgh YWCA's health club was housed in the basement.

At the YWCA, I was hired to empower women from all walks of life. At the MCHC, I was hired to be more like a hotel concierge. In fact, my boss actually described it that way. I was basically providing clients with top-of-the-line products and services. Everything at the MCHC was bigger and better. The clientele were men, women, and kids who were already empowered by being from wealthier backgrounds. It was in a bedroom community, a suburb, not in a downtown urban area like the YWCA.

I did walk to work, but there were no sidewalks. This was not the San Francisco that I knew or imagined. I was living in a place called San Rafael, in the suburb of Marin County. I wondered: *How could there not be any sidewalks? Don't people walk or run around here? Is this the job, the place, and the city that I prayed for? Did I really visualize this life?* The first few days, I put on my heels and slacks, then a simple, yet elegant, solid-color cotton T-shirt. I'd walk along the graveled part of the road to the parking lot. The temperature was in the low 90s. The ground was hot. The grass was dry. You visualized this. It might not feel right, but you gotta stick with it. It's just new. I tried to convince myself while starting to feel suffocated.

I met new people each day, but never really clicked with anyone like I had at the YWCA. I thought going from the YWCA to the MCHC would merely be me going from a big fish in a small pond to being a little fish in a big pond. But instead, I was just a fish out of water in a dry, hot climate, flopping around.

One morning, I had arranged to go to a Carnegie Mellon University job-networking event with Nick. He was still looking for work, and I wanted to mingle with a familiar crowd. Nick drove from his house in Oakland's Rockridge at 6:00 A.M. in the morning to pick me up in San Rafael so we could go to the event together.

He rang my bell around 7:15 A.M.

I opened the door, and we got into his car.

"Guess what?" he asked.

"What?" I kissed him good morning.

"A plane crashed into one of the Twin Towers."

"What?!"

His cell phone rang. His dad reported that a second plane crashed into the other building. They talked for a few minutes, and I heard him say something he hadn't said before: "I *love* you, too. Dad." He emphasized the word love.

He reached down and held my hand.

We drove, mostly in silence, to his apartment in Rockridge with the radio on, listening to the details. He and I exchanged a few sentences:

"Peter and Britta work in those towers," he said.

"Buddy's friend John works there, too," I said.

"I hope everyone is okay," I said.

Nick was in the Navy before he attended business school, and he had a good grasp on the gravity of this international situation. Perhaps I, like most Americans, had lived a life with a certain sense of freedom, in an insular bubble that didn't require us to learn or understand others. Our survival hadn't really depended upon it. I remember discussing with Nick that the U.S. military is so effective that we didn't have to worry or care much about events happening outside of the United States. But all that was about to change.

In the weeks that followed September 11, 2001, America's transition would be a difficult one.

Around roughly the same time, I was going through a difficult change in how I saw myself and my new life in Marin, California.

※　　※　　※

During the month of September 2001, I was trying to put out fires at my new job, such as dealing with a MCHC member whose CD player had been stolen.

"Was it out of your locker?" I asked him.

"No, I left it on a machine, and now it's gone."

Long story short, this man busted my balls over something that was his fault. It escalated to my boss and me trying to decide what was fair. The man wanted us to pay him for it. I couldn't help but think that it was his way of telling me who was top dog. The real problem was that I just didn't give a shit about his CD player, or him for that matter. This was not how I wanted to spend my time. During all the time I was cooking for people, doing "domestic work," I had never felt like the help, but at the MCHC, I did.

Then, although they never really came out and said it, my superiors wanted me to fire my assistant. I didn't know her beforehand and had no reason to fire her, but it was clear that she wasn't welcome.

When I told Nick, he asked me if the MCHC was unionized. I told him they weren't. Then he explained that if they weren't unionized before and they were being organized then, it probably meant that some people felt abused there. I told him that my assistant had been trying to organize the MCHC workers into a union.

I had never worked in an environment where the people who worked for me were in a union.

"Well, you better familiarize yourself with the union's guidelines, so you're not caught in a compromising situation," he firmly told me. Nick was quite sharp about organizations, politics, and unions. He cousins were major union leaders and organizers.

I was scared. It made sense, but not the kind of job I wanted to be involved in.

Each day, I was going into work performing responsibilities that I wasn't good at and not doing the tasks that I valued the most. I was a human Atari trying to put out fires that I simply didn't care about. I wasn't developing any wellness programs or teaching yoga. I wasn't empowering anyone to be his or her personal best. Instead, I was trying to figure out whether or not my assistant should be fired, or if she had a point regarding the workers needing a union. It all just felt wrong—or, better said, it all felt wrong for *me*. Too often, I heard an annoying knock at my then often-closed office door.

"Saeeda, this is the second time my kid has been bitten in the daycare."

I exhaled. Did I mention that I was managing the day care center, too? I didn't know how to resolve three-year-olds eating each other alive while I felt like my job was eating me alive.

"Ugggggghhhh," I thought to myself. "I hate this life." I was caught in a trick conundrum. If I changed my job because it's not right for me, was I being ungrateful for getting a job that I had visualized having?

I worried that I couldn't get another job. And what would it look like if I moved out of my house so soon after moving in? What would Nick think? What would his parents think? This was weird, worrying so much about what other people would think.

How can I be so unhappy? I got what I thought I wanted. How could I make another change now? I was afraid of looking ungrateful and perhaps weak. Maybe Nick's parents would think I was a failure and an unstable woman. I wasn't sure what to do, but I did know that I didn't belong in Marin. I needed to be somewhere where I could step outside onto a sidewalk and hail a cab if I needed one. I needed to be in a city, not a suburb. I needed to see more diversity. I needed to be able to take the bus, hop on a train, and go into a coffee shop. Then I needed to be able to go into a bookstore, a novelty card shop, and then a movie theater to see a foreign film. I needed to sit down on a park bench outside a fine-dining restaurant and watch the hustle and bustle of a busy downtown. I needed to be minutes away from the center of life—by foot, by bike, by cab, or by public transportation. I didn't want to have to own a car.

This was not what I had visualized.

In October 2001, my boss, who was Jewish, hosted a Jewish cultural team-building meeting offsite. I was no stranger to Jewish culture. In fact, I had two Jewish friends who I considered family: Paul who was my father figure, and Susan who was like an older sister. I had also been hired by some clients to make kosher macrobiotic meals for Passover and Rosh Hashanah.

During the meeting, my boss started passing around the Shofar, the ram's horn used for the Yom Kippur holiday. She asked each of us to share something about our families or something intimate. When it got to me, I couldn't keep it together.

"Well, I..." I paused and thought about the state of my biological family. Then I thought about my Jewish family and how I missed them terribly.

Out of nowhere, I sobbed loudly and uncontrollably. I felt embarrassed, which made it worse. I kept thinking about Paul and how his friendship was 3,000 miles away. I thought about the devastation from September 11th. I thought about Susan, who lived in Atlanta, and how we were no longer able to cook together. I thought about the stress of my job and how it wasn't right for me. I thought about how every day I experienced something that said, This is not the job for you. *This is not the house for you. This is not the life for you.*

I said nothing and just passed the Shofar to the next person. I tried to listen to the next person's story, while we all tried to politely move on.

❋　　❋　　❋

My life in San Rafael was a nightmare. I felt like I was buried alive. I'd wake up each day and feel dead. And to not feel dead, I'd buy tea at the coffee shop inside the MCHC. Literally, it was called Awake. It was the strongest black caffeinated tea I'd ever had. I usually drank greens and herbals. This was one of the first times that I started to feel what some of my food clients had described to me. "Saeeda, I have to drink so much coffee just to get through the day, and then at night I have to drink alcohol to wind down, and sometimes I'll even pop a sleeping pill just to fall asleep."

At this job, I became one of those people. My work life was so bad that I was using a strong stimulant to start and push me through my day. I'd never really lived like that before. As the weeks progressed, I was in the habit of putting two Awake tea bags in a 20-ounce cup of scalding hot water just to be able to go into work and sit down at my desk. I'd eat fatty croissants instead of fruit and warm whole grain cereals. I was getting first-hand experience on how and why fat, sugar, and caffeine in the morning were such a great combination for people who were not living the life they wanted to live. The caffeine sped me up, while the fat dulled my senses, and the sugar let me pretend for a minute or two that things were sweet. Right before my eyes, I was becoming a weirder version of myself.

I wasn't doing any yoga. I was coming home, vegging-out, and looking for ways to bury my inadequacies. I started watching TV. I hadn't had a TV in quite a few years, but that was all I did when I got home. Not doing my yoga was also a way to not be present or feel what my body was trying to tell me.

I wasn't cooking much, either, but I was getting somewhat decent food from the café at the health club. They had some whole grain products and good veggie side dishes, but it wasn't the same as nurturing myself with the intention of creating better health. I was hanging on by a string. With all the caffeine in my system and doing a job I hated, I was coming more undone every day. The puzzle pieces that had been so carefully put in place from the time I moved from Atlanta to Pittsburgh, up until the time I left the YWCA, were all being pulled apart and scattered far from each other.

"You have been through much worse times," I told myself.

CHAPTER 40

THE DOWNWARD
SPIRAL

IT WAS OCTOBER 2001, a month after I started working at the Marin County Health Club (MCHC). I saw Nick on weekends. I still wasn't considered his girlfriend, but I don't think I was bothered because I wasn't living in the shadows of his life.

One day Nick's roommate, Mark, who didn't have a girlfriend and wanted one, shook his head while we were all having dinner together. Then he said, "I don't get it, Nick. Saeeda's great. Why isn't she your girlfriend, again? She's here every weekend. You seem to get along. Dude, I don't get it."

Nick didn't answer. He was like that. If he didn't want to or couldn't, he didn't answer you. It appeared that he was ignoring you, but I knew that he was thinking. For some reason, this didn't bother me. It was just his way. Besides, I was focused on Nick's actions, not his words.

While Mark was talking, I thought back to the time when I first told Nick that I loved him. It was an April day 2001, at three in the morning. We had only been having sex for about a month, six months after my first date with him in

November 2000. I still wasn't the girlfriend, but we'd had a good lovemaking rendezvous—the kind where each person communicates to the other how they really feel. Just as I couldn't hold back then because I felt dishonest, I couldn't contain these feelings of love. I confidently whispered, "I love you." I didn't need him to say it back, but I did need to say what I was feeling. I was remembering the words from my spiritual teacher: "When you can unconditionally love like that, YOU WIN."

He immediately caressed my skin in response. His thumb gently rubbed the fleshy part of my hand, between my thumb and index finger. This is the part of the hand that an acupuncturist might squeeze to alleviate a stress headache. Nick wasn't squeezing it. He was stroking my flesh. He stayed connected to me. His actions showed me how he felt. I didn't need him to love me back. I just needed to feel safe enough to express my love.

The next weekend after Mark asked Nick those questions, Nick invited me to a San Francisco bar named Basque with some friends. Nick knew the bartender. He grabbed me by the hand and said, "I have someone I want you to meet. We walked up to the bar; and he said to his friend, "This is Saeeda, my girlfriend."

I smiled, but I was also laughing inside to myself. I wondered, "What changed his mind? Was it Mark's comment?" I didn't object, and I didn't care what changed his mind; I was just glad he acknowledged our relationship to himself and to others.

❋   ❋   ❋

By November 2001, we were officially a couple again.

I wanted to be Nick's girlfriend again. But this time being a girlfriend had no end in sight, and that was new to me. I must admit, I was frightened.

Nick started to ask me questions like, "Do we have anything on the calendar for this weekend, because Bob wants to know if we can have dinner?" or "The group is getting together for a barbeque; do you want to go this weekend, or do you want it to be just us? We could stay in."

On the other hand, if he scheduled something without me, I was immediately hurt and felt left out.

This felt strange, but good; a good kind of strange and a strange kind of good. It felt like the kind of relationship I should have had in college, maybe even in my senior year of high school: simple, slow, uncomplicated, and kind. I also felt like a girl, a dumb little girl, because even though I'd had spiritual training in how to love others and myself unconditionally, I had only a few good relationship role models. *How does one bond and grow with a significant other healthfully?*

In San Francisco, Oakland, and Marin, we went to the movies, watched videos, went to museums, had dinner with friends, went on hikes, talked, laughed, and even cried sometimes.

One thing Nick and I shared was napping. Every weekend, usually on a Sunday, we would organically find ourselves locked together, midday, in bed, sound asleep. He would spoon me and I would curl up like a fuzzy caterpillar.

One particularly pretty East Bay fall day, I was taking a nap while he was outside at the neighborhood block party. The neighbors had the street closed off so they could "bond." Nick lived in a place with great sidewalks and shops, a place where upper-middle-class families wanted to play and party together. The street was tree-lined on both sides, and the leaves were bright and bountiful. The music was festive, but it didn't disturb my slumber. In fact, knowing that people were having a good time and bonding made me feel more peaceful. I could sleep much deeper knowing that all was right with the world.

"Hey," Nick said, shaking me to wake up.

"Whaaaat," I replied softly, yet a little bit irritated.

Nick leaned in close. I could feel the warm heat from his body hovering over me like a cozy comforter. He said, "Hey, I have something to tell you. Wake up."

"Yeah."

"I love you," he whispered into my ear while my eyes were still closed.

"Wow," I said. "You're going to make me cry." He softly kissed me on the lips, and then he went back outside to the block party and I fell into an even more restful and peaceful sleep. The live jazz band was playing "All Blues," a popular Miles Davis song from the *Kind of Blue* album.

Later that day, I teased him, saying, "It took you nine months to say that you love me."

"Well, it took you six months to have sex with me," he said.

"Funny, we live in a time where the sex happens before the love."

We both smiled and then continued with a general conversation regarding how men and women date today compared to other time periods.

For the next few months I watched us function like boyfriend and girlfriend. My job still sucked, and I couldn't wait for the weekends. I wasn't sure what I should do. Nick hadn't found a job yet, and it had been seven months since he graduated.

The holidays were approaching.

I was used to spending the holidays doing something spiritual, or alone or with some good friends. I didn't want to be that girl who insisted that I should go to her boyfriend's family's house. I could see Nick struggling to determine if it was the right time to invite me home for Christmas. It had crossed my mind, too. Perhaps it was too soon to share such a holiday with his family.

Although I didn't hear the conversation in its entirety, I knew that Nick was discussing with his mother the possibility that I would come to visit Madison for Christmas.

Later that day, Nick asked me to come home with him, but he was also honest about his mother's concerns. His mom wanted to know why I wasn't going to Pittsburgh to be with my family during the holidays.

I didn't show it right away, because I wasn't sure what my thoughts and feelings were, but I remember being highly pensive about that question.

I thought about it a lot, because I knew Nick's Latin mother believed that family was everything. For the first time in a long time, I felt trepidation.

Nick and I did normal dating things, and we did them a lot. For me, our connections reinforced trust. Mostly every night, we'd talk on the phone. Several times a week we had an outing to local museums, coffee shops, dinners, movies, hikes, friends' functions, and walks through the neighborhood. I found myself thinking, *This is how regular people do it. This is how they fall in love, even more simply than in the movies.* I noticed his guard was dropping, the guard he'd had up to protect his heart from feeling hurt from his divorce. My guard was dropping too, the guard that I had up from always living in the shadow of a man's life.

One night, I sat on the edge of his bed, my back toward him and the window. I had just returned from a late-night trip to the bathroom. It was dark. I had my bare heels resting on the bed's cold metal rod.

Nick woke up as he felt my body crouched over the edge. He sat up.

In a low whisper, I said, "What kind of woman am I? What kind of woman doesn't love her mother?" I started to sob softly, then more heavily, but making very little sound. It was late, and I didn't want to wake up Mark or the neighbors downstairs by wailing.

"Hey, hey, it's all right," he said, feeling my body shake. He held me close and just let me cry. Nick didn't offer much in the way of therapy or resolution; he just let me cry, and that was therapy enough.

I didn't have resolution, either. I just knew that I had worked for a long time to have a relationship with my mother. I tried to love and protect my mother during my childhood, adolescence, and right after college up until the time I had the breakdown on the 71A Negley bus in Pittsburgh. I even pretended to love her afterwards, even when I knew that I loved her less and less every day. So when Nick's mom wanted to know, "Why isn't Saeeda going to Pittsburgh?" I began to feel like a freak.

I once learned that a lot has to happen for a child to stop loving his or her parent, but once he or she does stop, it is nearly impossible for them to love that parent again. That was happening to me. My love for my parents—any love that I had left—was dissolving every day.

I knew that Nick's mother, who valued family above all, wouldn't understand me or my choices. This was going to be trouble, especially since I didn't quite understand everything myself. I definitely couldn't explain in a way that would present me or my choices in the kind of good light that she would want shining in her son's life.

In December 2001, I had never felt more trapped or unprotected. In all my years of growing up in poverty and domestic violence, I had never felt trapped. I'd always thought that I could get out of the drama eventually. But this was different. Nick's life was something that I wanted to be a part of, but it came with his family. Between the MCHC and being Nick's girlfriend, I didn't feel in control of my own destiny anymore. My true self was being buried by expectations and values that I didn't know how to integrate into my own values and expectations. In my family, I was a solo operator.

❋　❋　❋

Madison, Wisconsin, in the wintertime was cold. I mean, you can go ice fishing cold. I had donated my Pittsburgh winter coat to Goodwill the day I knew I was moving to California. "Let someone who is staying in Pittsburgh enjoy this coat," I thought as I put it into the donation bag. So, when I got to Madison, I had only a light jacket. I planned on staying in the house most of the time, next to their toasty fireplace.

It was two days before Christmas, and the Greens were having a holiday dinner party. I'd never had *arroz con pollo*. I didn't really eat much chicken or Latin food for that matter, but in the same spirit of my eating chicken with Linda Fiorentino, I wanted to break bread with Nick's family, and eating his mother's cooking was important to me. I didn't feel pressured, but it was important for me to be flexible.

Before the family holiday party, I took a shower to refresh myself from hanging out with his family all day. I put on black opaque pantyhose, a rust-colored suede miniskirt, a black turtleneck, and black high heels. I didn't care much about clothes or how to put together a look, so I leaned toward a simple and hopefully elegant outfit.

I walked down the stairs from the second floor to the first, and at the bottom of the stairs stood a Turkish woman, Nick's godmother and Mrs. Green's best friend. I looked at her as I held the railing with one hand and smoothed out my skirt with the other. Her eyes gave me a slow, piercing once-over. Then she said, as my high-heeled foot landed on the bottom step, "Let me meet the girl who is good enough to be with our Nick."

I thought to myself, *This doesn't sound like a compliment. This sounds like a dig.*

"Yep. She needs to be a special kind of girl to be with our Nick," she repeated.

I'm sure that I was polite enough, but at that point I tuned her out. Mostly, I observed the family dynamics, played with Nick's two-year-old niece, and enjoyed what it was like to be part of a solid family—a white, Latin middle class family.

Nick, his dad, and I played my favorite board game, Scrabble. Mr. Green was great. He was definitely the kind of father every girl should have: consistent, firm, and loving.

Over the course of the week's visit, I met more of his extended family. I couldn't gauge whether or not I was being accepted, but everyone was kind to me. Nick's mom presented me with a beautiful gift, an Eileen Fisher sweater. She also had one for herself. She said, "Saeeda, this color goes well with our skin tone." The sweater was a honey-mustard yellow, my style and my taste. I was truly grateful. I could tell she put some effort into it, and I felt like she did want to please me.

One night while I was there, Nick and I were talking about the fact that I was four years older than he was. He blurted out, "I'm sure my mother thinks you're too old for me."

This worried me. I had a feeling that I was not measuring up to what she wanted for her son. "Yeah. I'm sure you're right," I said. Then I told him about a conversation his mother had with me the day before.

His mother had been teaching Maria to bless everyone in the family, and when they blessed Tio Nick, Maria would immediately say, "and Sa-dee-da." And then his mother told the little girl, "But Saeeda is not part of the family."

Nick looked me square in the eye and said, "Yeah. My mom is serious about family. Family is everything. She is very protective about our family."

I sat there in his family's home, hurt. I was also philosophically confused because that statement wasn't a Christian teaching, especially to a two-year-old. And then, an even stranger wave came over me. If I was his mom, I would be that protective too. I was hurt, but at the same time I admired Mrs. Green for being an excellent Mama Bear, preserving her family and its future.

I know for certain that if I were in her position, I would want the very best for my son. Quite frankly, if someone had come to me with my background and my family issues, I'd hesitate. I might even say those same words, "Saeeda is not part of the family."

It was sad for me, but at that time Mrs. Green and her friend only reinforced what I thought about myself. I tried to let it roll off my back, but I was in my most vulnerable state. I felt like life was getting a little worse every day. I had brought the MCHC Health and Wellness Department budget with me on vacation, and I couldn't figure it out. My mind wasn't clear. I was failing at work. I was failing this family interview. I was failing myself by doing things that weren't me at all. During my visit, I would sometimes look in the bathroom mirror after my shower and ask myself "Who are you? Why are you here?"

I left the Greens before Nick did. Usually, this would have been great because I like to have some solo time in between gatherings or events, but I was coming back home to shit, pure shit. Nick took me to the airport. I flew back alone, and the moment I got on the plane from Madison to Chicago, I felt very alone in the world. I had a small layover, and then I boarded the plane to San Francisco.

As I buckled my seatbelt and leaned back in my seat, I thought, "If a terrorist blew up this plane, I would be free from all of this. It would be sad for the others who are not ready to end their lives, but I am ready to be blown to bits. … THE END. I am tired, so damn tired."

I was tired of trying to piece together a life. I was tired of trying to be friends with my mother. I was tired of hoping that she would be the mother I needed. I was tired of thinking about how to answer the question, "Do you have brothers and sisters? What do they do? What does your dad do? You live so far away from your family, you must miss them." I was tired of tensing up every time a Pittsburgh number appeared on my phone, since it might be bad news about someone in my family. I was tired of thinking about my sister having been raped and my dad beating her afterwards. I was tired of not feeling good enough for the Greens because of what my family represents. I was tired of thinking about the mental health statement that said, "If two of your major three things (primary relationship, job/career, and family life) are not working in your life, it is just cause for a nervous breakdown. I was tired, tired, tired…. mostly because all three things in my life were fucked.

Then I fell asleep, not waking up until the plane was about to land. I stared out of the window, wondering, "How am I going to do this next part of my life?"

I got home. I went to work, and then I caught a nasty cold. I called in sick. I don't remember what day it was exactly, but the coughing and sneezing got worse. I took a common cold medicine, diphenhydramine, the drowsy kind, to suppress the cold symptoms. It knocked me right out. I slept for a long time. I turned the phone off. When I started to wake up again, I popped another pill. I fell right back to sleep. It seemed to be an easy and innocent way to not face my life.

Eight hours later, I woke up again, groggy. This time there were messages from my boss. "Saeeda, I know you are out sick today, but I could really use your support right now."

I couldn't face her requests, and this time I took two pills at a time. I hazily eyeballed those pink pills, thinking, "I could keep taking these pills, adding one more pill each time I wake up, and then it will be all over."

I stared at the pills and my phone. More messages from my boss and from Nick. I looked up at the stucco ceiling, and then I hazily looked around my room: the desk with the small black lamp, the photos, the old carpet, the bathroom door. I reviewed my life with pills in hand and thought, *This next slumber could be the end of me.*

Then I was mysteriously transported back into that Washington D.C. hotel room, with Buddy standing in the doorway saying, "Hey! Wake up! I wanna know, *what sustains you when all else fails?*"

"What?!"

"I'm serious. … I wanna know, *what sustains you when all else fails?*"

I sat up in my bed and said to myself, *Remember, Saeeda? You said the present moment is what sustains you. How true is that for you now? What do you choose to do? You owe no one anything. So what if you will appear to be a loser in the eyes of your boyfriend, his family, his friends, and the MBA friends that you admire? So what if you look like a failure to your friends, family, previous colleagues, and yoga and food students? So what if they admire you? Remember, they admire you because you practiced being true to yourself. What's most important is that you remain authentic to your journey and earn approval from yourself.*

I pushed the pills away. I got back under the covers and said to myself out loud, "I am not dead. I am not worthless. I am not afraid. I am just tired." Then I started laughing a little bit, "That's funny. Just tired."

I sat up, lotus style, with the covers surrounding me like a Buddha, and started to repeat a chant that Kathy taught me:

I have nothing to need, nor hide from, nor fear
I am whole and complete right now and right here.

I repeated this chant while sitting like a Buddha. I wouldn't lie back down until the stupor of the pink pills wore off. Those words soothed me.

The next day I woke up and realized what I needed to do.

❋   ❋   ❋

I stopped the highly caffeinated black tea. I had rested deeply, undrugged. I started to feel like myself again. I looked into the mirror and mothered myself.

I went into work and said, "Judy, I am sorry that I have not been available for you or this job. It's not working out for me."

"I know. We need to figure out a mutually beneficial exit strategy," Judy said with compassion.

I left her office feeling free again.

I knew that I might look like a failure to just about everybody I knew. I started to understand more of what my siblings might have felt during their personal struggles—the embodiment of pure shame and worthlessness, whether real or imagined. It is a rabbit hole that is hard to climb out of.

Shame, and the projected shame, of what I thought others might be thinking consumed me—from the inside out. There, at that edge, was where I really understood how shame could be an express portal into a downward spiral.

I told myself that I loved me, no matter what. I started going to the yoga mat again, doing sun salutations. I did a version of the sun salute that was most humbling and submissive to a higher power. I went back into the kitchen and started with basic brown rice and steamed veggies. Brown rice is the one food that is the closest to our blood's sodium and potassium ratio, and it felt healing. I did these simple techniques and, just like they had in the past, they cleared my mind and body so I could see my self again. I didn't like what I saw, but underneath the physical appearance I could contemplate my deeper, more genuine self. That self said to me, *I love you, for you. Stay on your path, your authentic path.*

CHAPTER 41

NEW, HUMBLE BEGINNINGS

FROM MID-JANUARY 2002, I walked back into the Marin County Health Club every day for six weeks. I was sure that everyone had his or her version of what went wrong with me. I didn't try to explain or blame anyone. I let people tell the story they needed to tell, but I paid no attention to them. At this point, I couldn't take on one more person's version of who they thought I was.

On the outside, I must've looked my worst—weak and stupid. But to myself I looked like a young woman who had entered into the darkest part of her life, but didn't let her light go out.

In March 2002, I finished up my work at the MCHC and packed up my belongings from my Marin condo. Stacey from Atlanta was then living in Oakland on Lake Merritt, and she agreed to help me move my stuff from my condo to my new one-room sublet in an Oakland house with some college girls.

I moved from the condo—surrounded by the aroma of pine trees, the sight of deer, and the touch of the hot sun beating down on my skin—

to a neighborhood that had a sprinkle of the homeless, granola-crunchy Berkeley types alongside some professional white liberals and some hip black folks.

Stacey and I picked up the first box together, a long and awkward one. I was holding my end a little bit clumsily. I couldn't really get a firm grip. Stacey was strong and focused on her end, like a professional mover. We carried the box to the car. "Slide it to the right, so we can fit the other stuff in more easily. That way we can make fewer trips," she said.

"Like this?"

"Yep," she replied. The hot sun glared down on both of us.

I moved my end in the way she said. Stacey had an eye for how things fit together. We walked back into the house, where it felt remarkably cooler, to get more boxes. Before we picked up anything else, she said, "You know..." She paused. "You know, you need to do better." She paused again. "You need to do better in your life. You can't ... keep..."

I interrupted her and said, "I know. I know, Stacey. I feel the same way you do about me. In January, I ..." then I looked down at the floor, not knowing if I should tell her my secret. Then I blurted out, "... I tried to kill myself over not being able to *do* better."

"Oh Sy ... I'm sorry. I didn't know."

"Nobody knows."

"I feel like a heel." Then she opened up her arms to give me a hug.

I walked into her arms and said, "No need for you to feel like a heel. I understand where you're coming from. You care." We hugged for a while, and then let go.

We continued loading boxes. Stacey made sure the car was packed tightly. She was right. We only had to make two trips.

It must've been painful for those who had watched me live my life, just as it was painful for me to live it. I don't know how others learn to integrate trauma and drama into their daily lives and still find a good way to navigate forward, but I had to learn how to do it for myself. I understood on a human-soul level that no one else could do it for me.

Truly understanding that no one else could do it for me reminded me of the day I was visiting my friend and yoga student, Liz Berlin, a Rusted Root band member. Her son was a few years old and he was sitting on the toilet, trying to poop.

"Mom, help me. Poop for me."

"I wish I could, honey, but you have to poop for yourself."

She and I chuckled.

She was right. He had to poop for himself, just like each person has to live life for him or her self.

Life had become much clearer to me. No one else can live this life for you, even if you are living the life someone else wants you to live. You still have to live it.

So from March 2002, I set up a new daily schedule for myself. Each morning, I set my spiritual intention, then I went to the mat to do yoga. I ate a whole grain breakfast. I planned the day's dinner menu. I ate with Nick four nights a week. I looked for a job. I napped and I wrote.

I worked on writing this book, which I had submitted to my agent as an idea in winter 1999. After several months of intense writing, it was clear that I didn't know how to write a book. But I kept writing down my experiences. I took it all in stride, even though I was sometimes fearful and sad.

I still don't know the exact feeling of shame that pulled my brothers and sister into their drug-addicted and alcoholic lives, but I do understand how they might have felt defeated every time a negative thought entered their minds. I felt it when those thoughts entered my mind. Which was why, during this time, I made sure I ate whole grains at least twice a day. The whole grains kept my brain chemistry balanced—a nice opposite action to the two bags of Awake tea I was drinking just a few months before.

Today science is coming out with new studies showing how yoga and whole foods help to heal various traumas like PTSD. Scientists are starting to identify how traumatic memories are being healthfully managed in the brain by our participation in yoga, eating well, and meditation. These three activities help glands in the brain like the hippocampus, amygdala, pituitary, pineal, and hypothalamus process experiences more healthfully. They help reduce the fight or flight triggers and calm down the nervous system. I didn't know it at the time, but each and every time I ate well, practiced yoga, and meditated, my brain was being rewired. I felt refreshed.

So I made sure that I practiced the basics, wholesome food and a healing yoga practice, when I had thoughts of people saying things like:

Saeeda's nice, but not for our Nick. What kind of woman doesn't go home for the holidays?

What the hell happened to her? She left Pittsburgh, got a job in the Bay Area and is now unemployed? Guess she's not hot stuff after all.

Serves her right, after she tried to steal my clients.

...or

Did you hear about Nick's girlfriend? Her job? What's wrong with her? It didn't work out. What a loser.

I also made sure to call my "home base," Dr. Victoria Butterworth. Tory was the one person who had the time and the historical knowledge about my past to help me create a safe place to put my life's puzzle pieces together all over again. My work with her would help me reconstruct the life that I wanted to live.

Tory also had a background in organizational psychology, which was helpful when she used a personality-testing tool to determine my professional strengths. It was good to see that my personality was more suited for teaching, presenting, creating ideas, and being a part of a team that inspires others. I wasn't suited for implementing day-to-day operations. I am not a Chief Operating Officer; I am more of a Chief Executive Officer. I am a connector who wants to listen well to others. This was important for me to understand. I wanted to learn and grow, but it had to be in the areas where I had skill and interest; otherwise, I would set myself up to fail. Tory and I had phone sessions a few times a month. She helped me see where I add value in my professional life and what bits are not suited for me. I likened it to the fact that you wouldn't ask a hammer to do a screwdriver's job.

For six months, I followed my simple, self-imposed schedule. I finished a very bad draft of my book, but it felt great to just write it out, warts and all.

As I wrote down my experiences, I learned writing was also a teaching and healing tool for me. I could see even more clearly the power food and yoga had in my life. I could see I wanted a job that would empower others to take care of themselves on a basic level. To borrow the old adage, "The teacher teaches what she needs to learn the most." This was the kind of job I wanted, a job that challenged me to live a holistic, healing life.

From April 2002 to August 2002, I sent out countless résumés. I decided to not care much about status, title, or money. Instead, I was looking for proper fit. I went on a lot of interviews and received lots of rejections. I rejected a few jobs, too. I kept up my routine, using yoga and whole foods as my way to stay grounded.

I also didn't follow my grandfather's philosophy. I wanted a job I would like. I knew it was a luxury for me to be able to choose. But I felt that, since I didn't have anyone to support outside of myself, I could choose the right job that matched the path I wanted to travel.

By August 2002, I found a job with the San Francisco Unified School District. I was elated that a public school district thought that my background in holistic nutrition was a good fit for their Nutrition Education Project team. I wasn't a registered dietitian, physical education teacher, farmer, or restaurant chef, but my holistic nutrition and yoga background appealed to them. This was SFUSD's first year in putting together a diverse team of food and physical activity educators. They wanted us to collaborate in new ways toward getting low-income kids involved in eating more fruits and vegetables, and helping to eradicate the growing epidemic of childhood obesity.

❋　❋　❋

I started being invited to speak at meetings called SSTs, or Student Success Teams. These were meetings that the school staff had for at risk students, whether the risk is academically or otherwise, an emphasis on the whole child.

Each student's name was written on the board with columns highlighting his/her strengths, weaknesses, actions for improvement, and a few other descriptive words. A social worker led the meeting, but the room was filled with each child's parent(s) and teacher, the school nurse, the principal, and me—the site nutrition coordinator.

In these meetings, I told the parents why it is important for their children to have breakfast, and how that impacts learning.

A funny thing started to happen in these meetings. I'd hear the team leader say things like, "Dad didn't show up for the meeting," or "We also need to understand that the mother has reported that he beats her," or "The kids seem to be raising themselves. It's hard for [a fifth grader] to listen to us, when at home she is the adult," or "We need a mentor for this kid because her mom is in and out of treatment programs," or "We have our work cut out for us, but we have to help these kids rise above their circumstances."

The list went on. It started to feel like I knew each kid personally, because each one somehow was a reflection of someone in my family—or a reflection of me.

I wish I'd had known about Child Protective Services (CPS) when I was in elementary school. I don't know if I ever would have called them on my parents, but I would have wanted to. I smile a knowing smile when I hear of kids who actually do call CPS on their parents. Kids know when things are not right, and they want it to be right. Kids just want to survive and have an environment where everyone can thrive.

It wasn't easy working with kids and their families from low-income and poverty-stricken areas. Some families were very troubled, and some were just poor, but this work felt like an authentic and genuine part of my path. It felt like a job that kept me on my own journey toward health and healing. At the same time, it was a job that gave me the opportunity to share with other boys and girls who might be growing up in situations similar to my own.

After I secured the job at SFUSD, I moved into another shared condo in San Francisco, at 24th and Guerrero. Nick moved a mile up the street from me with his friends. The day I moved in, I unpacked my things and noticed that I needed some toilet paper, so I walked to my new corner store. I saw a taxi, a bus, bikers, and people walking on the sidewalk. At that moment, I knew I was home. I knew that I wanted to do whatever it took to always be a resident of San Francisco.

❋   ❋   ❋

Once I moved into the city and felt a little more secure, I started to look for additional work teaching yoga in the city where all the masters live and teach: Judith Hanson Lasater, Rodney Yee, Patricia Walden, John Friend, Janet Stone, and Rusty Wells, just to name a few. This city opened my mind to a wider range of yoga disciplines. I wasn't sure where I would fit or if I could fit, but I was willing to try.

I asked myself, *Can I teach in this city where all the masters live and teach? Will anyone hire me?*

My fears included the fact that I was not a hardcore Type A yoga instructor. I was not the most knowledgeable of instructors, either. I couldn't do all the poses perfectly, and I didn't know all of the Sanskrit names for the postures. I also wasn't the master of adjusting students, and my knowledge of anatomy was limited. I feared people would hate what I had to offer.

I recognized my fears, and I put them aside and created a professional yoga résumé with my printed newspaper and magazine clippings. I set up my spiritual intention to attract the classes and the students who could benefit from what I had to give. I knew that I couldn't be all things to all people. However, I knew that there would be a group or groups out there that needed exactly what I was offering. I was That Tao Girl—a teacher in the words of Theodore Roethke:

She lives at the edge of life as a creative act, continuous and evolving, not infrequently terrified of her own godliness; not infrequently enraptured by the joy and fun of it all; always grappling with her own humanity.

I never thought that I would be teaching children nutrition and yoga, especially not in the public schools. But I was willing to start a new, humble beginning, and to be a very small fish swimming—and sometimes flopping—around. I was a becoming a beginning teacher all over again, one who had found a niche in the Bay Area, and one who had grappled with her own humanity.

CHAPTER 42

LOVE AND FORGIVENESS

I FELL IN LOVE with the city of San Francisco more and more each day. Starting in fall 2002, I had a life that I had never experienced before and never thought was possible. I was doing meaningful work, in a functional relationship, and continued to have deep friendships while making new friends. Life was moving along nicely.

I was part of a whole with Nick and his family. After the first Christmas with his family, I spent Christmas with them each year thereafter. I started to experience the expectations of a functioning family; for the most part, I liked it a lot. But I must admit, it was odd. I felt like there were unsaid rules of engagement. Like his family accepted me but perhaps still wanted someone better, more accomplished, and less damaged.

Nick and I, living one mile away from each other, often had our meals together. I would sleep over at his place and in the morning I'd make a quick breakfast, like apples and almonds, that could be eaten in the car during the morning commute. There were some relationship bumps, but they were normal everyday bumps like scheduling conflicts and household chores.

In winter 2003 we decided to move in together, and a profound thought persisted in my head: *Perhaps my family's dysfunctional curse will finally be lifted from my head.* This thought made me breathe more easily.

We set up house, but slowly. Here I was again, not knowing exactly how to do this. I simply didn't know how to function as a live-in couple. While Nick had been married before, it was totally new to me.

We started by buying a washer and dryer and a dining room table. Often, we entertained friends with small dinner parties.

Starting my day in a peaceful way was still important to me. Nick agreed to wake up early every day during the week to have a sit down breakfast by candlelight. This kind of breakfast was significant because it represented the happiest times of my life—not to mention all the studies that say that starting the day with breakfast impacts the rest of the day positively.

On weekends he would go to Destination Bakery on Chenery Street and buy me a black currant scone or fruit Danish and then make me a cup of hot tea, which he served to me in bed. It was nice to eat my wholesome breakfast foods during the week and have a treat on Saturdays. He also cooked one day a week, making his mom's Colombian Spaghetti dish.

The relationship was healing for me. Being around Nick and his other male friends helped me trust men more and more. It gave me hope. I witnessed healthy compromise between couples, especially his parents.

A few months after living together, I started having nightmares, and we started fighting about our future. I don't know which started happening first, but both were becoming increasingly frustrating.

One morning I woke up and said, "Nick, I'm mad at you," while lightly punching his arm.

"What?! You just woke up. What did I do?"

"You were trying to smother me with a pillow. You tried to kill me."

"Sy, it was a dream."

"I don't care. I'm mad. You tried to kill me."

Nick got out of bed, chuckling and shaking his head. "It's only a bad dream. You know that I would never hurt you."

"I know, but I'm still mad," I said, laughing a bit.

Our life routine continued. And then I had the same dream again. I was uneasy. I didn't tell Nick how often I had the dream because I knew he would never hurt me. He was my gentle Oso ("bear" in Spanish), but I'd wake up exhausted and fearful from my dreams, where I was fighting all night for my life.

I hadn't wavered from wanting us to be partners in the relationship. But I also didn't want to be a girlfriend, fiancée, or wife who had to nag her man about taking out the garbage. And every week I was in fact reminding him to take out the trash. I felt like this was symbolic because I knew that, on some level, he didn't think things were fair. I didn't earn as much money as he did. However, we did agree to contribute the same percentage of our salaries toward household expenses. I did more household management to make it more equal between us, but we both sensed that we had an imbalance.

Soon our communication became more and more strained. I couldn't understand why each of us was not treating the other like their customer—my made-up marriage-business model. I wanted to go to counseling. He agreed, but had his doubts and fears. The last time he went to counseling it was in the last stages of his marriage, and he got divorced soon after. But I felt stuck and wanted someone else to intervene, because the normal daily routine of life didn't seem right for me. I needed to go deeper, emotionally and spiritually. I needed to feel like we were on the same page, going in the same direction.

In counseling we discovered that, at the point where Nick was feeling satisfied with us and where we were, I was just starting to feel connected and wanted to go deeper. Nick either didn't or couldn't understand my need to go deeper and become more vulnerable with one another. Or perhaps my request for that kind of intimacy was unreasonable or impossible.

The therapist once described us as a Velcro strip that couldn't quite match up together, making it hard to function properly.

The therapist also said that Nick was afraid to fully express himself with me and he used passive-aggressive ways to handle situations, especially since he knew I was so afraid of having fights that could spin out of control and into violence. He never said this, but perhaps my fears bullied Nick in some way. Perhaps it was my flaw of perfectionism rearing its ugly head, or just two people with two different value systems regarding the quality of life they wanted to live.

Over the next year of living together as mismatched Velcro strips, we made each other sadder and sadder. I think we both thought that we would get married someday. But then one day I realized that *I was being smothered by this life, and that's why I was having those repeated pillow smothering dreams.*

The saddest part of all of this was that, when it comes to men, faults and all, I believed Nick was a gem. One of the best. Even during our many disagreements, I'd tell him, "It's sad, because I believe that you are one of the best in the bunch. I probably can't do better, and still it's suffocating me."

In spring 2005, I woke up and knew it was over. I couldn't breathe normally anymore. This wasn't the life I wanted. I had to make one of the hardest decisions of my life: to break up with Nick, a man who was not only my boyfriend; he was my family. I had no one else. I wanted our relationship to work, and I wanted to be committed to him forever. I trusted him, but I didn't know how to not feel so smothered. Even in therapy I felt more and more smothered. Then I started to feel unprotected. I didn't necessarily want to be alone, but for me to grow I needed to set myself free. I needed to be free so that I could go deeper within myself and learn more about who I was and where I fit. But mostly, I needed to heal. I thought I could do that with him and his family present, but it was too constraining.

※　※　※

That summer, Nick and I moved out of our apartment. I was sad, yet relieved. Then I immediately went to China to make one of my dreams come true—studying Mandarin Chinese.

I lived with a Chinese family and had the uncomfortable pleasures of being a foreigner. I taught yoga classes to my host family and the other overseas students studying Mandarin. Beijing was hot, 104° F, on a regular basis. I didn't mind for a while, but toward the end I was roasting.

One particular day in class, I noticed that I was speaking significantly slower than the other students. Every time I opened my mouth the Korean students who were also studying Mandarin in China would laugh out loud at me. It was unbearable. So I decided to switch to a more appropriate level.

I went to the main student office. I spoke in English, but the secretary didn't understand me. So I explained my case in my best Mandarin, and when I was finished she looked at me for what seemed like a long time. I felt myself shrinking more and more the longer she looked me over. Then she spoke up in Mandarin, "If you can explain in Mandarin why you should be in a different level, then you're not in the wrong level. Go back to class." I left the office, part of me feeling more defeated and the other part of me feeling strangely accomplished.

I went back to class the next day. The more I spoke, the more the other students snickered. I was humiliated day after day. I thought about quitting and going sightseeing for the remainder of the summer, but I wanted—no, needed—that certificate of completion. I needed a success after my breakup with Nick. And I never wanted to have that conversation with friends about how I just couldn't finish the course. During this time, Nick accepted my calls. He allowed me to vent my frustrations.

During the first phone call, I was crying and talking at the same time. He interrupted with his caring words of, "Hey, Hey." Then I cried even louder. He continued, "Sy. Hey! Remember, you are the man in the ring."

I grew silent, thinking about a conversation I once had with him about that. Nick described how he had noticed that it was more important for me to be the person in the ring, fighting, making mistakes, and taking the punches, as Teddy Roosevelt had said. Nick knew that I never wanted to be the person on the sidelines criticizing others. He knew I wanted to have an active life, one where I proved to myself that I have fully participated.

Then Nick said, "Say something in Chinese." And I did. From that simple act, my spirits picked up. Just then I knew that I could continue going to class and succeed according to my standards, whether or not the students laughed at me. For the next few weeks, I studied and practiced each day until I was exhausted.

At the end of the summer, I took an eight-page test all in Chinese characters, answering essay questions and filling in the blanks. I also demonstrated my conversational Mandarin with my instructor. I scored a solid B, better than most, if not all, of the Korean students in class. Everyone was surprised, even the professor. But no one was more surprised than I was.

When I returned home, Nick and I had a few chats to catch up. But by that time, he was seeing someone else. Both of our lives had moved on. During our last chat, we did a very new-agey exercise. We forgave each other for everything, even for things that we may not have known caused hurt to the other. It felt right.

❋   ❋   ❋

Summer 2006, my eldest niece explained to me how she was able to forgive her mother—my sister—for abandoning them all. My niece simply said, with pain in her voice, "I knew that I wanted my mom in my life, so I forgave her."

Here was a great spiritual example of her desire being greater than her pain and anger. I admire my niece's clarity and strength, and her willingness to forgive.

❋ ❋ ❋

My sister Rahima had stayed clean and sober for almost two years. She was living in Braddock near her three adult children, ages 26, 22, and 19, and near her three grandchildren, belonging to my niece. Rahima worked a steady job as a jitney "gypsy" taxi driver. It was all coming together again for her. I had not seen her happier. She was with her grandchildren every weekend, and they loved their Nana so much.

❋ ❋ ❋

Then at 6:00 A.M. one October day in 2006, my mother called to tell me that my nephew had been shot and killed. My mom and I spoke about the details for a few minutes as I silently wept. Soon after I hung up the phone, I remember feeling frozen. Tears frozen. Life frozen. Heart frozen. This is my sister's second child. *What's going to happen now to my family, to my sister?*

For a few days after, I walked the San Francisco streets in a fog. Then, out of the blue, I bumped into Nick. I told him what had happened to my nephew. He hugged me, immediately and tight. His hug gave me strength. I felt strong enough to fly home and face my family's latest tragedy.

Ameer's story was not the typical one. He wasn't a gangbanger. He wasn't a menace to society. In fact, he was an upstanding young citizen. He went to church regularly. He worked two jobs, coached little league, and was trying out to play semi-professional baseball. He had purchased a house in the neighborhood and was building a life for himself. He was a role model for other young black men. The mayor, John Fetterman, had recognized him for his leadership ability with the youth. After the murder, the mayor tattooed the date of Ameer's death on his arm.

My nephew was in the wrong place at the wrong time, shot in the back of the head. Dead; an example too many black boys know all too well. The only image I could picture was a puddle of salty tears and sticky blood mixing on the pavement.

When I boarded the plane to Pittsburgh, I had my sister on my mind. Could she handle another heartbreak?

❋　　❋　　❋

Rahima seemed to do well for a while, but then a final straw caused her to break. My sister couldn't handle the fact that Ameer's dad, who had said over and over for decades that he would not marry any woman, was finally going to marry. After Ameer's death, his dad found Christ, became a deacon in the church, and married the woman he had been with for so many years after my sister went to Atlanta. My sister hasn't been the same since. Rahima became a recluse and might have even started using drugs, but she didn't let any of us get close enough to her to find out. On different occasions, I've heard her mumbling to herself, "He should have married me. He should have married me."

❋　　❋　　❋

When I returned to San Francisco from my nephew's funeral a lot weighed heavy on my mind, especially whether I would follow through with my plans to spend my winter break in Kerala, India. Was this the right time to make a pilgrimage to India for my 40TH birthday?

CHAPTER 43

LIFTED AND ENCOURAGED

IN DECEMBER 2006 I BOARDED THE PLANE TO KERALA with a lot on my mind. The last two years and the last two decades had been quite a whirlwind. The vortex of events spiraled inside my head. When I buckled my seat belt across my lap, I noticed that I had wanted to disappear from life so much that my physical body had receded immensely. I had to pull the belt tight to make sure that my waif-like body did not slip out.

During takeoff I let out a big sigh of relief. I knew that I needed to go halfway around the world to nourish my mind, body, and spirit. It was as if I faintly heard Swami Sivananda whisper to me his enchanted words— *Serve, Love, Give, Purify, Meditate, Realize.* That was what I wanted to give myself for my 40TH birthday, to be in a place with a group of people whose intentions are to serve, love, give, purify, meditate, and then realize.

After a few layovers, I finally landed at Trivandrum airport. The air was hot and sensual, especially at 2:00 A.M. The heat helped my body begin its initial expansion. I hopped into a local taxi, as suggested by the yoga management to be the cheapest and safest way to get to the ashram.

✻ ✻ ✻

On my birthday, I woke up at 5:20 A.M. to the sound of the gong at the Sivananda Yoga Vedanta Ashram. The air was cool in the mountains as I walked toward the meditation hall. I sat down, thinking *Here is where I can practice the five points of yoga.* My body needed to bathe in the asanas of Hatha yoga. My breath needed to reactivate its life force, my prana. My nervous system needed to heal through the deep relaxation of Savasana. My body needed to consume wholesome foods. My mind needed to be still and think positively by meditating and chanting. I was happy that I could do this all day, every day well into the New Year. The first day was my birthday. No one knew me. No one wished me a happy birthday. I was alone, but not lonely. I was surrounded by 250 people who were each there practicing the monastic life for reasons of their own. I felt alive.

The memory of my nephew had been massaged into my heart and although the pain burned it was being lifted each day. I felt his presence each time I chanted his mother's name—Rahima-Ma. In the midst of these tragic thoughts, my soul kept whispering, *Remember him, but don't get stuck in your grief. Love humanity more.*

The days were routine. I met new people, did my yoga, ate simple food, and cleaned bathrooms. Most days I experienced a healing, but at random times, my heart suffered a crushing pain over my nephew's death, my sister's grief, and my breakup with Nick. Some days I wanted to just sleep in and not follow the Sivananda schedule, but that was against the rules. I remembered my first swami saying: "People come to the ashram for many different reasons and something about us attracts them to live this life, so we encourage them to follow the schedule. It usually turns out to be quite beneficial even when they initially resist. No one is held here against his or her will, but sometimes people won't do what is necessary until they are told 'Here are the rules.'"

I understood him completely. It reminded me of my teacher's training experience, I wanted to follow the rules because they might just take me somewhere special.

During my stay, we were instructed to climb Sahyadri Mountain before sunrise on several occasions. The first time, we had to wake up at 5:00 A.M. instead of 5:20 A.M. We dressed warmly, and several of us wore headlights to help illuminate the path. Part of our meditation was to walk there in silence. We passed barking dogs that most likely had rabies. As we continued our silent walk into the woods, we could peer into one-room shacks made of ribbed metal walls, where we could hear a chicken cluck or a goat bleat. Deeper into the woods, we saw sap oozing from trees with wooden cups there to collect the liquid. Later, we learned it was organic latex that would be used for everyday products.

The path was winding, then it became steeper and steeper. While the trees disappeared, the stones and rocks populated more of the landscape. The altitude was rising and a foggy mist surrounded us. We climbed on and on. The day started to break, and we were almost to the top. "Take off your shoes and socks from this point on," our guide said, breaking the silence. I thought, *He must be crazy. It's cold and I can't afford an injured foot, especially on vacation.* I looked up; the remainder of the rock was a smooth dome. The precipice was a vertical quarter of a mile up. A quarter of a mile never seemed so far away before. *I can stop here. I can see the horizon just fine. I don't need to reach the top. What if I scrape my toes or hurt my feet? Why is this the sacred mountain anyway?*

I watched Jade, whom I nicknamed "G.I. Jade." She was fearless. She had a double black belt in karate from a Sensai in Japan and was fluent in Japanese. When we started our walk, I followed her. She had the confidence and the headlight. I watched her take off her shoes and socks. Slowly, I took off my shoes and then my socks. I examined my dainty, bony feet. I rubbed them and said, *This is my destiny. These are the kinds of experiences and risks you want to have and take. You are the man in the ring. I have always said, if something bad is going to happen to me, let it be in another country doing something that I deemed important instead of it happening in my neighborhood because I was afraid to take a risk. I have seen too many tragedies happen to people who haven't had a chance to really live or leave the block where they were raised.*

Taking the first step, my long narrow foot gripped the mountain, which felt like a cool stone of pumice. My head down, breathing hard, afraid of sliding backwards, I watched the red polish on my toenails while my toes dug in and my heels clamped down. In order to not fall back, I had to lean forward and place my hands on the spherical mount. I resembled Spiderman. Exhaling, I crawled upward, feeling both scared and powerful.

Crawling up and up and up, I reached the top. I joined the others who were already seated in meditation. I gazed outward, seeing the clouds and other mountaintops below. The sun's rays permeated the horizon, giving us a wide range of hues from red to yellow. Everyone was quiet. Then one of our leaders started up a call and response chant. While I chanted, I could see the faces of my nephew, his mother (my sister), and Nick in the bright sky. Strangely, I felt lifted and encouraged.

Descending from the top of the mountain was another adventure. I had to sit down on my butt, hands behind me and feet and legs in front of me. I crawled down, in reverse, doing a crab walk. The last quarter mile of this mountain had become a strange metaphor for my life: To reach a peaceful pinnacle, I had to crawl up on all fours; to return to my basic humanity, I had to creep down on all fours, humbly.

After climbing this mountain a few times during my stay, I felt some strength returning to my body. So much strength that I volunteered to be the MC for the Christmas event. The MC is in charge of the show, booking the acts, setting up the lineup, managing time, and doing stage right, stage left kind of stuff.

This job was fun, but hectic. I enjoyed meeting new people. It was business meets pleasure—entertain them, but make sure we were all in bed that night by 11:00 P.M. In between the acts, I had the opportunity to share with the 250 guests some of my personal story. I mentioned that I had started my yoga journey in 1990, became Sivananda certified in 1993, and was celebrating my 40TH birthday and the New Year with a group that has rooted my spirituality. I expressed how grateful I was for this opportunity.

At the end of the night, a woman approached me. She looked familiar, but I couldn't place her exactly. She said, "You might not remember me, but you were my first yoga teacher." She put her hand on her heart and continued, "I'm Liz, Liz McDonald from Carnegie Mellon University."

"I remember you." Then we hugged.

"You gave me my first yoga mat. I am now a yoga teacher because of you," she said. It had been five years since I had seen her. "Funny running into you," she continued. "I wasn't supposed to be here. We changed our plans last minute."

"It was meant to be, just when I needed an affirmation that my earlier life meant something to someone," I told her. While I spoke, I was thinking, *I still trust life, its ups and its downs.*

We smiled, my heart glowed, and then she began to fill me in on her journey since graduating from Carnegie Mellon. I also told her about my life in San Francisco. I remember how her face lit up as I told her about teaching nutrition and yoga in the San Francisco Public Schools.

"Man, what a gift that you get to share this work with little kids," she beamed. Her words warmed my heart and made me feel lifted and encouraged again.

CHAPTER 44

PUBLIC EDUCATION

IT'S AUGUST 2012. Monday mornings, I wake up, usually without an alarm, between 4:30 and 5:00 A.M. I prepare my tea and heat up my steel cut oats or some other whole grain cereal. I put the tea in a drinking thermos and the grains in a different wide-mouth eating thermos. I load up my backpack with my computer and my nutrition lesson plans for the day. I head off to the grocery store at 5:45 A.M. and shop for the food I will need. I grab a cart and fill it up with colorful fresh fruits and vegetables.

Next, I put one or two whole grain products and some organic yogurt in my cart. Then I unload the food onto the conveyor belt. The cashier, Mike, is usually there, with a nice 6:20 A.M. greeting. "Good morning," he says. "Glad you chose my checkout line."

"Morning, Mike," I say, smiling and on the verge of laughter. It has been about 11 years now that he and I have followed this routine. It never seems to get old. He begins to ring up my items, and without fail he says something like, "If people shopped like you, they wouldn't be so overweight. Yep. They would look like you. You're in great shape. Why don't people shop like you?"

I tell him that people do their best, and that it's hard to change habits.
I give him a knowing wink.

"Go'on girl. Teach those kids. I hope they know how lucky they are
to have you do this work. I didn't have a nutrition teacher when I was in
elementary school."

"None of us did."

I pay him and grab my two strategically weighted bags.

I leave the supermarket, cross the street, and stand at the Church and
Market Muni station. I wait for the J Church trolley. It reminds me of
Mr. Rogers' trolley, bell and all, going into the Land of Make Believe.
I am happy, even though it's very early. It feels like I am in the Land of
Make Believe.

I get on the J train and take an open seat. Hardly anyone is aboard, so
I spread out. The ride is about 20 minutes, so I do TM, Transcendental
Meditation. It's a great way to start the day.

I arrive at school and review my lesson plans while having my oats
and tea. I prep the fruits and vegetables for the day. At around 9:00 A.M.,
I teach my first class. It goes something like this:

I enter the classroom and say, "Raise both your hands if you have
washed them."

Hands go up.

"If you want to learn something new today, stand up straight, keeping your clean hands in the air."

Smiles appear on kids' faces, and they all get up with their arms in
the air.

"If you are ready to start the lesson, please have a seat."

They all sit down and are eager to begin the food lesson.

"Last week, we made tomato salsa with blue corn chips. This week
we are going to make pear jicama salsa on a Romaine lettuce leaf. At the

end, we'll do a Venn diagram." For homework, I ask them to use the list of words in the Venn diagram to write a page, three paragraphs, comparing and contrasting two salsas.

Each student gets his or her ingredients, we review knife skills, and then we all start chopping. All the students are engaged.

We make the salsa. Then I explain the extra credit homework, "Let's brainstorm what other fruits or vegetables we could use to make a different kind of salsa. Ask your parents if you can make a fruit salsa as one of the sides for dinner. Tell them it's a homework assignment from Ms. Saeeda. Take pictures, if you can, of you making the dish and your family enjoying it."

At the end of the day, I prep for the next day.

When I leave school I get on another trolley and, like I did on the 71A Negley bus in Pittsburgh, I sometimes cry. I cry about the state of some of my SFUSD low-income families. I cry about the obesity epidemic in this country. I cry because, even though I love my work, it's strange that this work is necessary for the growth and health of an entire nation. Even though I've made peace with my family members, I often cry regarding the struggles they still face. I worry about them all deeply and wonder if they are finding their own unique ways to heal from our multi-generational suffering. A part of me wishes we were all closer and healthier, but I accept that we all must live life in our own way and in our own time, authentically.

But mostly, I cry tears of joy. I live in a city that I love more and more each day. I have work that fulfills me. It's not an easy job, but it's a dream job. Each time I step on the yoga mat or step into a classroom, which I get to do almost every day, I know that I am on my authentic path. I have very little drama in my life. My heart appreciates all the people around me who cheer me on. And the people that I get to cheer for, too.

I still chuckle that I get paid to teach yoga, holistic nutrition, and cooking to kids and adults. I don't make the salary of a banker, but I do make a living, and it's a life that I get to share with others.

For 20 years now, I've been able to share with my students my passion for food and yoga and the healing that has been released within me. And now, when I pull the chord and hear a stop-requested bell I'm no longer primed for a fight against my deep childhood trauma. The Healing has taken place. Now it's time for me to help someone else. "Ding. Ding." Gotta go! Someone needs me.

EPILOGUE

BEFORE COMPLETING THIS BOOK, as a courtesy, I sent many of the chapters to my family members, starting with my mom and dad. When I told my friends of this action, they were surprised. But I felt like I could not finish this work unless they knew what I was about to do. I prepared myself for their anger, denial and accusations. But instead what I heard were things like this:

> My dad getting on the phone stating, "Well, ever since I got into that bar business I became a man that I didn't want to be."

I was shocked and could feel my heart mending. I didn't have high expectations of creating a close father/daughter relationship, but to have my father say that with such rooted sorrow meant the world to me.

> My mother clearing her throat in order to not stutter said, "Well, it all happened. I see this book helping other women who find themselves in similar situations. ...I did my best and I am sorry."

Her words have soothed my soul and fueled by desire to get this book out to others who might benefit from the story. It was comforting to have my mom this time not call me crazy or say that I was the one who needed the help.

My older brother's response was incredibly supportive. I didn't expect that since he often goes in and out of addiction. I thought he might be mad and jealous. But instead he said, "Sy, be as raw as you can be. Tell the story from a real place. Readers want you to be real. Don't hold back." Then he said in a kind and encouraging way, "How did you become the writer? I was supposed to be the writer." He paused. "Do it. Tell the story."

I will never forget my younger brother's response, "Sy, mom and dad need to know what happened to us. What they put us through." Then he went into reminding me of things that I had forgotten. He told me things that happened to him that I didn't know about at all. I listened intently. Then, he asked me, "Do you think that that's why I am an alcoholic today? Do you think a damaged soul like mine can heal?" I told him, "Of course, keep showing up and doing the healing work. We can all heal." Then I reminded him of a quote that we both liked from the *Malcolm X* movie by Spike Lee, "If you take one step towards Allah, He will take two steps towards you."

My niece could not get past the first few chapters. She cried, saying, "Aunt Sy, it is just too depressing." I understand that she might not be ready to absorb the past just yet, but her daughter might want to know when she comes of age.

My auntie said that she was happy that I found a way to heal from the past.

My auntie was right. I have healed from the past and I have found a vibration of happiness that pulsates through my mind, body and spirit like no other feeling I have known before. However, I know that healing is organic and dynamic as I continue to interact fully with the world, thus I consider myself always in the stage of healing something or someone in the present and in the future. Ahimsa!

Elva
- past trauma
- takes time
- feeling of freedom
- Continuous healing to the rest

RECIPES

Basic Winter Vegetable Soup

2 tablespoons safflower oil

1 large onion, diced

1 celery stalk, diced

1 large carrots, sliced half moons medium thin

1 turnip, medium chunks

1 parnips, medium chunks

½ cup dry white or navy beans, soaked over night or canned

4–5 cups filtered water or vegetable broth

1–1½ tablespoons barley miso or ¼ teaspoon sea salt

¼ teaspoon pumpkin oil– finish each bowl when serving (optional)

Scallions, sliced on the diagonal

1. Heat oil in stock/soup pot.

2. Add onion and celery, sauté for 3 minutes or until soft, but not brown.

3. Add carrots, turnips, and parsnips sauté for 3–5 minutes.

4. Add beans, drained.

5. Add water or broth and bring to a boil.

6. Turn down heat, cover pot and simmer for 45 minutes or until beans are soft.

7. Extract ½ cup hot soup broth from pot. Dilute 1 teaspoon miso, per serving bowl, into hot broth. For example, 4 bowls of soup = 4 teaspoons miso.

8. In each bowl, equally pour diluted miso liquid. This technique keeps the miso from boiling, thus saving the digestive cultures.

9. Serve hot, drizzle pumpkin oil on top of each soup bowl as a finishing garnish.

Note – always add freshly diluted miso to soup just before eating it.

Steel Cut Oats

1 cup steel cut oats

5 cups of filtered water

Toppings

1. Rinse oats.

2. Heat pot.

3. Lightly toast oats.

4. Add water.

5. Simmer on low heat for 60–90 minutes or until the oats are the preferred consistency.

6. Add toasted nuts or seeds, fresh fruit slices and dried fruits and or 1 tablespoon of maple syrup.

   Or follow simpler directions on the packet.

Collard Green Ribbons

2 bunches of collard greens, washed and center stems removed

3 garlic cloves minced

2 tablespoons tamari or shoyu

1–3 tablespoons olive oil

Black pepper to taste

1. Stack collards 4 leaves high, roll tight, and cut rounds very thin to make ribbons.

2. Heat skillet medium high and add olive oil.

3. Add garlic, sauté until very fragrant, but not brown.

4. Add collards, gentle separating the strands, stir gently.

5. Add tamari, stir, and cover for 5 minutes or until soft but not too tender.

6. Add pepper and serve hot.

Black Bean Stew

1 small onion, diced

1 carrot, diced

1 cup dry black beans

2 cups filtered water

Sea salt to taste

1. Rinse and soak beans overnight with a 1 inch piece of Kombu (To reduce the cooking time, use canned beans which don't require soaking).

2. Put black beans in a pot with diced onions and carrots and water.

3. Bring to a boil.

4. Then simmer for 1–1½ hours; stir periodically.

   The more you simmer the creamier the beans. (If using canned beans, simmer for 30–60 minutes).

5. At the end, you can add sea salt to taste. Serve over rice or any grain.

   Note – this recipe is intentionally long and slow cooking, this is the kind of energy you want for winter, long and slow so you can endure the bitter cold.

Soft Barley Porridge

½ cup of barley, cooked, per person

½ cup filtered water, per person

¼ cup raisins per person

1 tablespoon toasted nuts or seeds, pumpkin or sunflower.

1. Simmer raisins in equal parts cooked barley and filtered water for 15–20 minutes.

2. Serve hot with toasted seeds.

Baked Sweet Potatoes

2 large sweet potatoes

Oil (olive, unrefined
corn or safflower)

Water

1. Pre-heat oven 350°F.

2. Wash sweet potatoes.

3. Rub oil all over the sweet potatoes.

4. Put in a baking dish with a little water.

5. Bake until soft—about 60 minutes.

Mushroom Barley Soup

1 small onion, diced

1 celery stalk,
diagonally cut

1 cup of button
mushrooms, sliced

6 dried shiitake
mushrooms, soaked
and sliced (remove
bottom stem)

1 tablespoon of olive oil
or unrefined corn oil

½ cup barley

5 cups water

¼ cup shoyu (soy sauce)

scallion garnish
(optional)

barley or alfalfa
sprouts (optional)

1. In stockpot, heat oil, and sauté onion
until translucent.

2. Add water (filtered) and barley.

3. Bring to boil over high heat, and then
reduce to a low heat.

4. Add shiitake mushrooms, and simmer
40 minutes or until barley is soft. Stir
occasionally. If the soup becomes too
thick or sticks, lower flame and add ¼
cup water.

5. Add button mushrooms, celery and
shoyu; cover pot, and simmer for 10–15
minutes more.

6. Serve hot, and garnish with small amount
of sprouts or scallions.

Hiziki - Caviar Style

½ cup hiziki, soaked,
then drained

1 tablespoon sesame oil

Filtered water

1 tablespoon tamari
(soy sauce)

Shallot topping

1 shallot, minced

2 tablespoons capers

1 tablespoon lemon juice

1. Soak hiziki until soft, about 15 minutes.

2. Drain and discard soaking water.

3. Mince hiziki.

4. Heat oil and sauté hiziki for 3–5 minutes.

5. Add filtered water to cover, bring to a boil, add soy sauce, and simmer until liquid evaporates.

6. In bowl, mix shallot, capers and lemon juice.

7. Serve hiziki on bread, pita chips, cocktail toast or endive, then top off with shallot mixture.

Steamed Kale

1 bunch of kale (curly or
dino), chopped finely

½ lemon, juiced

Toasted sesame seeds

1. Wash kale, while looking for sand between the leaves.

2. Bring pot of water to a boil with metal steamer at the bottom.

3. Put in the kale.

4. Steam until kale turns bright green, not brown.

5. Squeeze juice from ½ a lemon on top.

6. Then sprinkle with toasted sesame seeds.

7. Serve hot.

Raw Veggie Press Salad

This makes the salad veggies more digestible while keeping the live enzymes ready to be a natural probiotic.

½ cup green cabbage, shredded

½ cup red cabbage, shredded

1 medium carrot, julienne

1 celery stalk, sliced thinly on the diagonal

½ small red onion, minced

½ teaspoon of sea salt

1 tablespoon of brown rice vinegar

1. Prepare each vegetable.

2. Place in a glass bowl, then toss.

3. Sprinkle salt and vinegar over veggies.

4. Press in a pickle press for an hour or do the following:

   Put a plate that fits directly on top of the veggies in the bowl, then put a heavy weight on top of the plate so the veggies can begin to process as a natural probiotic.

Gourmet Baked Apples

4–6 apples cored

2 tablespoons tahini or sunflower butter or peanut butter (optional)

¼ cup raisins or currants

Cinnamon

Maple Syrup (optional)

Water

1. Preheat over at 375°F.

2. In a small bowl, mix together tahini, dried fruit, cinnamon, maple syrup.

3. Core apples, and then pack each apple with mixture.

4. Add water to the bottom of an 8x8-inch baking dish.

5. Place apples in dish.

6. Bake for 35 minutes until apples are tender.

Sweet Veggie Drink

1 cup butternut
squash, cubed

1 cup carrots,
diagonally, sliced

1 cup green cabbage,
shredded

1 cup onion, diced

8–9 cups filtered water

1. In a large pot, layer squash, carrots,
   cabbage, onion, and water.

2. Bring to a boil. Simmer for 30 minutes.

3. Drain liquid into a glass carafe or pitcher.

4. Drink cold or hot, ½ cup – 1 cup daily or
   several times a day.

Carob Cake with Raspberry Jam Sauce

¾ cup whole wheat
pastry flour

¾ cup unbleached
white flour

3 tablespoons carob
flour sifted

½ teaspoon sea salt

2 teaspoons baking
powder (non-aluminum)

¼ cup plus 2 tablespoons
vegetable oil (any flavor
neutral oil)

⅔ cup Maple Syrup
(real, organic)

1 teaspoon vanilla

¾ cup soymilk (carob,
vanilla or original flavor)

1. Preheat oven 350°F. Oil the bottom of
   9-inch pan.

2. Combine dry ingredients in a bowl.

3. Add oil and Maple Syrup in second bowl
   and emulsify.

4. Mix in vanilla and soymilk.

5. Bake approximately 40 minutes or until an
   inserted toothpick comes out clean.

6. In a saucepan, dilute 1 tablespoon organic
   raspberry jam with 2 tablespoons water
   and simmer until thinner. Drizzle jam on
   the plate around carob cake slice.

   Adapted from – Melanie Ferreira,
   Chef at The Natural Gourmet

Veggie Bowtie Pasta Dish

2 cups Bowtie pasta (use whole grain pasta)

Water

1–2 tablespoons of olive oil

Crushed garlic clove

½ cup onion, diced

¼ teaspoon of sea salt

½ cup carrots, julienne

½ cup yellow squash, thin rounds

½ cup broccoli florets

¼ teaspoon juice from fresh lemon

Pinch of sea salt as a finishing salt (optional)

1. Bring water for pasta to a boil.

2. Prepare vegetables, check on water.

3. In a wok or skillet, heat oil. Add garlic sauté for 2–3 minutes.

4. Add onions, sauté until translucent.

5. Add carrots and yellow squash, sauté 5 minutes.

6. Put pasta in boiling water, follow directions on the package.

7. Add broccoli to skillet.

8. When pasta is ready, drain and add to skillet.

9. Serve on plate. Squeeze juice of lemon wedge onto dish, optional sprinkle finishing salt onto dish.

Short Grain Brown Rice

1 cup short grain brown rice

2 cup filtered water

Pinch of salt

1. Rinse rice.

2. Drain then put rice and salt into pot with filtered water.

3. Bring to a boil.

4. Reduce heat and then cover with a tight lid.

5. Simmer for 20–25 minutes.

6. Turn off heat and let the steam cook the rice for another 20 minutes. Don't lift the lid.

Creamy Black Beans with Garlic

1 cup dry black beans

3 cloves of garlic

2 cups filtered water

Sea salt to taste

1. Rinse and Soak beans overnight with a 1 inch piece of Kombu (Use canned beans to reduce the cooking time).

2. Put black beans in a pot with 3 cloves garlic and water

3. Bring to a boil.

4. Simmer for 1½–2 hours the more you simmer the creamier the beans. (if using canned beans simmer for 30–60 minutes).

5. The beans will be nice and soft with a garlicky flavor.

6. At the end, you can add sea salt to taste. Serve over rice or any grain.

Note – this recipe is intentionally long and slow cooking. This is the kind of energy you want for winter, long and slow so you can endure the bitter cold.

YOGA POSES

Savasana (Corpse Pose)

Deep Relaxation Posture

1. Lie flat on your back.

2. Legs are mat width apart.

3. Hands are about a foot away from the body.

4. Breathe deeply. Inhaling, feeling the stomach rise towards the ceiling and exhaling as the stomach flattens towards the floor.

5. Gently, imagine each part of the body releasing any and all tension

6. You can hold this position for as short as 5 minutes. The recommendation is between 15–25 minutes for deep relaxation.

Child's Pose

Massages internal organs and stimulates heart meridian

1. Gently sit down on your heels, legs folded underneath the body.

2. Fold the body over the thighs. Make a pillow with the arms. Rest head on the folded arms

3. Focus on your breathing. Inhale, expanding the stomach and the chest; exhale, emptying the lungs.

4. Do the chair pose to counter the child's pose.

Chair Pose

Stimulates the acupressure points located in the toes, especially eyes and sinus.

1. Stand up straight with your legs slightly apart.

2. Inhale while extending arms forward, shoulder height.

3. Exhale while lowering down, balancing on to the tips of your toes.

4. Make sure the knees are parallel to the floor.

5. Engage your core, while letting the low back anchor towards the floor. Hold for 30 to 60 seconds.

6. Repeat and hold as often as you like. This is a great posture to use when transitioning from standing to sitting and vice versa.

The Forward Bend

Helps to eliminate toxins from the body through the kidneys.

1. Sit up straight on the floor, legs together and stretched out in front of you.

2. Inhale, lifting the arms above the head; the back is straight.

3. Exhale, bending forward and leaning the chest and arms towards the toes.

4. Rest the arms and hands wherever they fall along the legs. You can rest the hands along the thighs, knees, shins, ankles or toes.

5. Hold for at least 30 seconds and no more than 60 seconds.

6. Inhale, lifting the arms, head, and chest back to an upright position.

7. Exhale, lowering the arms out to the side and down.

8. Repeat 3–5 times. Do at least 3 times a week.

Single–leg Raises

Helps to lengthen muscles in the back of the legs and low back, while warming up the body for more static postures.

1. Lie flat on your back, in the corpse posture.

2. Bring your legs together and your arms close to the body, for lower back support, place arms and hands underneath the body.

3. Inhale, pointing the toes while lifting the leg up towards the ceiling.

4. Alternate right and left leg for three times each.

5. On the third lift, interlace the fingers behind the lifted leg and gently move the leg closer to the body. Hold for 1 minute or so.

6. Do at least 3 times a week.

Knee to Chest Pose

Helps to strengthen and massage the large intestines.

1. Lie flat on your back, in the corpse posture.

2. Bring your legs together and your arms close to the body.

3. Inhale, bending the right knee in towards your chest.

4. Exhale, giving your leg a gentle but firm hug.

5. Inhale, lifting your head towards your knee.

6. Hold the posture for 30–45 seconds, while breathing deeply into the abdomen.

7. Release and relax, returning to the corpse posture.

8. Do at least 3 times a week.

The Basic Spinal Twist

Strengthens the digestive organs by helping to eliminate toxins from the stomach, pancreas, and spleen.

1. From the Knee to Chest pose, using the right leg. Take the left hand and place it the right knee.

2. Gently move the knee across the body towards the floor while turning the head in the opposite direction. Go to the point of a gentle stretch, feeling it from the left shoulder, which is resting on the floor, to the right knee.

3. Focus on the breath. Inhale as you twist the torso.

4. Exhale completely, flattening the stomach. Hold for a minute or so, while breathing deeply.

5. Repeat, using the left leg.

6. Gently release the posture. End with knee to chest to posture counter the basic spinal twist posture. Do at least 3 times a week.

Headstand

Strengthens the heart and brain.

CAUTION – Headstand really should be achieved initially with the guidance of a skilled instructor. So, for that reason, I have not included instructions.

The Shoulder Stand

Gently massages the heart and strengthens the immune system toxins from the stomach, pancreas, and spleen.

CAUTION – Shoulder stand, like headstand, really should be achieved initially with the guidance of a skilled instructor. So, for that reason, I have not included instructions.

GLOSSARY

AHIMSA - To do no harm.

ASANAS - a static body position used in the practice of Hatha yoga.

KOMBU - a dark green or brown seaweed used in Japanese cooking, especially as a base for stock, cooking beans and grains.

MILLET - a cereal plant (grain) that is widely grown in warm countries and regions with poor soils, a staple food in Africa and Asia, a small yellow seed that is nutty and fluffy when cooked.

PRANA – Breath or vital force of air.

QUINOA – an Andes grain (grass) seed used to make salads, porridges and side dishes.

SATSANG - an assembly of persons who listen to, talk about, and assimilate the scriptures and readings after meditating and chanting.

SEA VEGETABLES – marine plants that are used for food.

SORGHUM – an African cereal plant (grain) that is widely grown as a staple food in Africa.

SWEET RICE – a glutinous brown rice use to make mochi, a thick rice cake.

TEFF – an Ethiopian grain (grass) often used to make flour for the staple bread crepe called Injera. It is also a very small seed that mixes well with other grains, such as millet, quinoa and rye.

UMEBOSHI PLUM – a salty, pickled plum.

BIBLIOGRAPHY

Baldwin, James. *Nobody Knows My Name.* Vintage Books, 1961

Connelly, Dianne M. *All Sickness is Home Sickness* Traditional Acupuncture Institute, 1993

Covey, Stephen. *The Seven Habits of Highly Effective People.* Free Press, 1990

Haas, Elson M. *Staying Healthy with the Seasons,* Celestial Arts, 1981

Hay, Louise. *You Can Heal Your Life.* Hay House, Incorporated, 1994

Kushi, Michio, Stephen Blauer, The Macrobiotic Way. Avery Publishing Group Inc., 1985

Levin, Cecile Tovah, *Cooking for Regeneration,* Japan Publications, Inc., 1988

Mandino, Og. *The Greatest Salesman in the World.* Bantam Book, 1968

Oriah Mountain Dreamer, "The Invitation" HarperONE, 1999

Peck, Scott M. *The Road Less Traveled.* Simon and Schuster, 1985

Roethke, Theodore. *Straw for the Fire Ed.* David Wagoner. Seattle, WA: University of Washington Press, 1980

Turner, Kristina. *The Self-Healing Cook Book.* Earthtones Press, 1988

ACKNOWLEDGMENTS

No one goes it alone. Many writers say that writing is a solitary endeavor. Well, I have found it to be the opposite, and I believe that no one goes it alone. So many people have been involved in the writing of this book from the very beginning. I hope to thank everyone here, but I know that is impossible. So, if I don't mention someone by name, please understand it is not because I have forgotten them; it is because if I thanked every single person who held my hand, cheered me on, or whispered *I believe in you*, the list of names would be as long as this whole book.

This book would not be possible without the hard work of Linda Huff-Paul. Linda was with me at the very beginning, in the late 1990s, and there with me again at the tail end, in 2014. Her coaching work with me in the beginning helped me understand that I had a story to tell and that I owed it to myself to tell it in my own voice. And her copy editing throughout was invaluable.

I also want to thank every writers' group that I've ever been in, and the amazing friends that I have made along the way. My *spiritual writing group* in Pittsburgh planted the seed of how important it is for me to share my gifts with the world and become the best person I can. The *Writing Salon* in San Francisco is a place unto itself. Jane has made a space for every type of writer and non-writer to dig deep and participate in the story they want to tell. The *Writer's Grotto* in San Francisco rocks the house with all of its celebrity authors. The teachers there make a writer feel as if they belong, regardless of what stage of the writing process they are in. Janis Cooke Newman is a teacher/author who gets results. And

Constance Hale's passion for writing, grammar, and structure enabled me to embrace language and appreciate its potential power.

My editors have been phenomenal. If it weren't for Rachel Howard, I would not have a book at all. She gave me tough love when I needed it, and she validated my experiences. She encouraged me to be more honest, even when I thought I was already being my most honest self. She helped me dig a deep well inside myself. Nora Isaacs has a powerful way of guiding me toward trimming the fat while still telling a full and robust story. David Gleeson, who has felt like my own private cheerleader, has extended himself far beyond what anyone can expect from an editor—and a friend. David is my Harriet Tubman, leading me along my own personal underground railroad.

Deep appreciation goes to Victoria Butterworth, Ph.D. To call her a "therapist" is too limiting. Tory has been an amazing home base for me. She has held up the mirror of sanity for me when I thought I was going to go absolutely mad. Thank you, Tory, for acknowledging my journey every step of the way, even when we didn't agree.

A special thank you to Josh Michels, who put clothes on my naked story by designing the book's cover, and its overall look and feel. His efforts have made my story tangible for me, and for those who will read it.

A most sincere thanks to Petra Dierkes-Thrun who, when I was at the point of deep frustration with this book, literally convinced me to not burn or erase all of my living copies. We agreed that I could have a bonfire at Ocean Beach with just a few copies.

Thanks also to Frances Von Wong Photography for a fun, productive yoga postures photo session.

Many, many thanks to those friends who read drafts of this book along the way, and enthusiastically cheered me on while being kind with their constructive criticism. Hugs to Maria Acosta, Diane Akshak Alexander, Zed Armstrong, Jessica Barros Barreto, Angela Chen, Heather Donnell,

Stacie Dooreck, Josh Eisenberg, Joe Gross, Rachelle Henry, J. Quincy Jones, Karen Kane, Heather Easley-Kasinsky, Kim Klausner, Geeta Kothari, Ken Lang, Pam Lewis, Kevin Madzia, TerriAnn McDonald, Leilani Mears, Eliza Menzel, Aife Murray, Volker Pasternak, Lynne Piade, Henry Phong, Meru Rattehalli, Siri Schubert, David St. Martin, Caroline Sterling, Susan Stryker, Besty Reiling, Tracey Scott, Susan Beallor-Snyder, Melissa Hurley, Jim Van Buskirk, Edwige Riou, Ozgur Sahin, Kandy Smith, Penfan Sun, Francina Temple, Sebastian Thrun, Karen Topakian and Daniel Vocke.

ABOUT THE AUTHOR

Since January 1990, Saeeda has been experiencing the power of her yoga practice and the benefits of eating a whole foods diet. Her initial encounter with this holistic lifestyle led to a personal transformation that ultimately led her to become a certified yoga instructor and holistic nutrition educator for the last 20 years.

Saeeda currently holds a position at San Francisco Unified School District as a site nutrition coordinator, where she has been teaching basic holistic nutrition and yoga to kids and adults for the past 12 years. She also teaches yoga to adults at various San Francisco health clubs and studios, including the YMCA, Fitness SF Fillmore, and several corporate clients. She has appeared on various radio and television programs and has been featured in several national and regional publications. Her public speaking engagements have educated the public in yoga, holistic nutrition, and healthy living from coast to coast.

Saeeda is a graduate of Temple University in Philadelphia, with a degree in Business and Management Information Systems. She has studied at the Sivananda Yoga Vedanta Centers and Ashrams, and the Natural Gourmet in New York City.

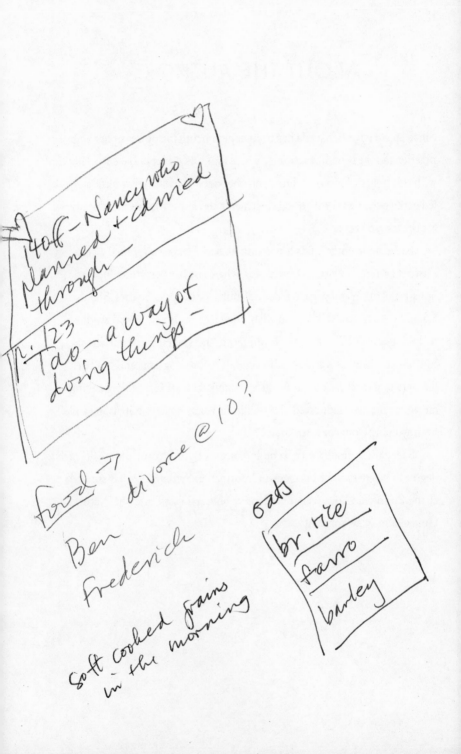

140f — Nancy who
Nanned + carried
through —

P. 123
Tao — a way of
doing things —

food → divorce @ 10?

Ben
Frederick

Soft cooked grains
in the morning

oats
br. rice
farro
barley